Anatomy of an Explosion

MISSOURI IN LUTHERAN PERSPECTIVE

Kurt E. Marquart

Associate Professor of Systematic Theology

With an Introduction by Robert D. Preus

Anatomy of an Explosion
Missouri in Lutheran Perspective

Edited by
David P. Scaer and Douglas Judisch

Copyright (c) 2022 Lutheran News, Inc. All Rights Reserved. No portion of this book may be reproduced in any form, except for quotations in reviews, articles, and speeches, without permisison from the publisher.

Fourth Printing © 2022
Library of Congress Card
Lutheran News, Inc.
684 Luther Lane
New Haven, MO 63068
Published 2022
Printed in the United States of America
IngramSpark, TN
ISBN #978-1-7366844-6-7

TABLE OF CONTENTS

FOREWORD i
I. NEEDED: A REALISTIC "MODEL" OF THE
   MISSOURI SYNOD CONFLICT 1

BACKGROUND

II. THE BASIC PRINCIPLES 9
   A. THE CONFESSESSIONAL PRINCIPLE
      1. The Lutheran Confessions 9
      2. Background: Europe-Prussian Union 12
      3. Background: America 15
      4. The Church in the Confessions 17
      5. "More" than the Confessions? 22
      6. A Fatal Fallacy: Doctrines or Documents? 31

   B. THE BIBLICAL PRINCIPLE 37
      1. The Bible in the Confessions 37
      2. Rationalism, Historical. Criticism, and Missouri 39
      3. Luther in Fact and Fiction 45

FOREGROUND

III. THE COUNTER-CONFESSIONAL (ECUMENICAL)
    ATTACK 52
    1. Sclerosis: Prelude to Hemorrhage 52
    2. The Collapse of Confessional Concepts of Church and
       Fellowship 55
    3. The Use of the Confessions As a Rabbit's Foot 71
    4. The Question of Church Politics 82

CENTER STAGE

IV. THE COUNTER-BIBLICAL (CRITICAL) ATTACK 109
    1. The Critical Contagion in Stages:
       ULC-ALC-LCMS 109
    2. Historical Criticism: Definitions and Distinctions . . . 121
    3. Gospel and Incarnation 127
    4. Lutheran "Controls": Law/Gospel or
       Sola Scriptura? 134
    5. Theology of the Cross-or Secular Crinire? 146

V. EPILOGUE 152
APPENDIX A
  Church Fellowship 154

APPENDIX B
  Fellowship In Its Necessary Context of
    The Doctrine Of The Church 156

FOREWORD

The story had to be told, the story of a large, confessional church body gradually, almost imperceptibly but seemingly irrevocably, losing its evangelical and confessional character and identity. But then, contrary to all expectations and historical precedent, a reversal of a trend which has dominated modern church history! The lay people and rank and file clergy of the Missouri Synod take a stand. They elect new leaders with a mandate to turn the direction of their synod back to the old ways, to the evangelical orthodoxy they had learned and known so well. They support an investigation of the doctrine of the largest and at the time most prestigious seminary of their synod. They study the issues confronting their church, they review their doctrinal position; and in convention assembled they take the bold unprecedented step of condemning the doctrine taught at that very seminary which was founded by and flourished under the greatest theological leaders the synod had ever known. The majority of the faculty members denounce the action of their church, and at what seems like a propitious time they refuse *en masse* to carry out their call to teach in the church. Students by the hundreds follow their professors into what was called an exile, but was really more a sort of captivity, led by the prestige and persuasions of their teachers and by the incredibly great pressure of their peers. And for the most part both faculty and students are still lost to the church, lost not because their friends and former brethren have not tried to retrieve them, but because they reject their synod, not merely its leaders and some of its actions, but also its theology. The scars inflicted on their church by their departure are deep, and they will last beyond the lives of any of us.

Yes, this story, so bizarre, so ironic, so tragic, had to be told. But who was to tell it? Some bright graduate student at Seminex (the rump institution founded by the dissident faculty of Concordia Seminary, St. Louis) with a horizon no higher than the confines of the classrooms of St. Louis University, the Jesuit institution that offered Seminex shelter, no broader than the explanations and excuses of Seminex professors for their untoward actions? Or should some historical theologian of Seminex tell the story? But the involvement and the guilt in a decision to leave one's call and attempt to destroy a seminary of one's church hardly lends credibility to any serious and unbiased writing of one's own history. But perhaps some secular or theological pundit-writing for money, of course—and these people seem to be everywhere, pontificating on what has befallen Missouri—could do the job honestly and objectively. I would merely ask, has it been done thus far in the scenarios and the often wild improvisations of the events which have thus far distorted history and discredited our church body?

For a time some of us who were in the minority at Concordia Seminary, St. Louis, thought of pooling our resources, which were vast in terms of experience and hard evidence, to write an account of what really happened. But God kept us all too busy for that, thankfully. For we too would have revealed our prejudices and biases concerning all the events that had occurred throughout the controversy in St. Louis. For a time we looked for an older, perceptive soldier of the cross who might tell the story with sufficient wisdom and perspective not merely to relate, but analyze the events in the light of God's economy and thus teach the reader. But no such person appeared.

Then Prof. Marquart returned to our country, after a long pastorate in Australia, to accept a call at Concordia Theological Seminary in Fort Wayne. He was the ideal person to tell the story. He was uninvolved in the events and so had had little occasion to form prejudices or animosity toward any of the principal actors in the drama. And he was far enough from all that happened to be unhurt and unaffected personally by others' "hurts." At the same time, like the late Hermann Sasse, the astute German-Australian observer, who as a historian took a consuming interest in our synod and said on several occasions that the future of historic, confessional Lutheranism lay, if anywhere, with the Missouri Synod, Prof. Marquart knew throughout the years exactly what was happening in our church and at his *alma mater*. Like Sasse he knew us better than we knew ourselves, and saw before most in our country what was happening. Moreover, and most important, Prof. Marquart is able to rise above personal biases and single dramatic events to the real issues that underlie the whole struggle and brought about the explosion which took place in Missouri—to the doctrinal issues. These are what he speaks of and explains and analyzes in this book. And only when we carefully follow him as he leads us through our past will we understand what really happened. And perhaps, as an adjunct to this learning experience in church history, the history of our own synod, we will by grace become more understanding and forgiving and loving. And again by God's grace some healing and reconciliation can take place.

Because what Prof. Marquart says is true, his judgments (which are not directed against people) are factual and correct. Although always challenging and instructive, Prof. Marquart's book is not at all times easy to read. After all, it is not a novel written for relaxing enjoyment. Prof. Marquart is compelled by the very purpose of his book to mention many men and events of the past which are not always of direct interest to the reader. Moreover, he must delineate and clarify the doctrinal issues which directly effected the explosion in Missouri, issues which have been dreadfully obfuscated by liberal and confused theologians inside and outside the Missouri Synod. But, most important of all, Prof. Marquart perceives as his burden also to evaluate according to Scripture and our Lutheran Confessions what has happened and the new doctrines which split the Synod and caused so much turmoil. In everything he is eminently successful.

It is my great hope that many good things might be accomplished by Prof. Marquart's book. First and foremost, I hope that every reader will be led to a deeper appreciation of the almighty and unbounded grace of God by which our synod is even now being restored to its confessional and evangelical position. For it was not the fumbling power or wisdom of men which did this marvelous thing. And I hope that the reader will be led to a greater appreciation for purity of doctrine as a living power in the life of the church; for when the doctrine of the Gospel is denied or ignored or compromised, or when false doctrine is tolerated, terrible things happen in the church: people are deceived, lives are hurt, friendships and relationships destroyed. And I hope lastly that this telling of the story will set the record straight once and for all. And then by God's grace our church will more than ever be united in its evangelical mission and ministry.

Robert D. Preus
President
(1974-1989; 1992-1993)
Concordia Theological Seminary
Fort Wayne, Indiana

I. NEEDED: A REALISTIC "MODEL" OF THE MISSOURI SYNOD CONFLICT

"If you join at eleven o'clock a conversation which began at eight you will often not see the real bearing of what is said. Remarks which seem to you very ordinary will produce laughter or irritation and you will not see why—the reason of course being that the earlier stages of the conversation have given them a special point."[1]

The lively "conversation" in and around the Missouri Synod today also cannot be understood without knowing something of what has gone before. And not only pastors, as the divinely appointed teachers of the church, but also the people of the Synod have a right, if not a duty, to follow the conversation and to take part in it—for their own spiritual fate and that of their children is at stake. This little book is intended as a modest aid towards such understanding.

History, to be sure, and especially a recital of obscure old controversies, is not everybody's cup of tea. Yet a certain amount of this cannot be avoided if the necessary background is to be filled in, however sketchily. What have the Bible and the Lutheran Confessions meant to the Missouri Synod in the past and why? Without some such inquiry the current dispute must needs seem baffling if not pointless. And, of course, the present essay, although it seeks to serve historical understanding, cannot claim to be a "history" in the usual sense. It is far too condensed for that. The aim is simply to highlight what has always been considered basic and decisive among confessing Lutherans, in order to have at hand a frame of reference within which to make sense of our present debates. Unless we do make an effort to understand our situation in a churchly way, we shall fall prey to the myth-makers of this world, who deal seductively in "images" not realities.

What is the reason for the phenomenal public interest in the recent doings of The Lutheran Church-Missouri Synod? That church's internal controversy was for several years among the top ten religious news stories of the country. Indeed for Christmas, 1974, President J. A. O. Preus even made *Time's* cover-story—a feat unmatched by all the huffings and puffings of conventional "public relations"! Part of the hubbub is no doubt to be explained by the well-known media connections of Dr. John

Tietjen, former president of Concordia Seminary, St. Louis, and also former executive secretary of the Division of Public Relations of the Lutheran Council in the USA (LCUSA). But there is a deeper reason for the public interest. The fact is that our modern society is simply not accustomed to the sight of a confessional church. While there are conservative remnants and resistance pockets among the grass-roots of most main-line churches, the official inter-denominational machinery is finely attuned to secular, and that means liberal sensibilities. The public therefore tolerantly expect to be bored by ecclesiastical grotesqueries about "Human Concerns"—directed with predictable selectivity against South Africa, not Soviet Russia; Chile but not China; Indochina before, but not after "liberation." But a moderately large church doing more than purring perfunctorily about Christian truth is a distinct novelty. The spectacle of the Missouri Synod cleaning house doctrinally, and even reclaiming its own prestigious seminary, has about it the sensation-impact of a dinosaur gnawing disagreeably at the St. Louis Arch!

Taking full advantage of the prevailing secular mindset, Missouri's "moderate" publicists have created a plausible *scenario* of the controversy with a view to winning sympathy and support among the rank and file:

SCENE I

As the curtain rises, we see a post-World War II Concordia Seminary, St. Louis, emerging from a long winter of dogmatic hibernation. Spring has arrived at last, and at the seminary earnest evangelical scholars are plying their trade conscientiously. Conservative, confessional Lutherans all, these men nevertheless are not narrow. They see that the old truths must be restated in fresh, contemporary ways, and made vital for the church today. And so they open windows, letting in fresh air and Gospel-sunshine, dispelling legalistic fogs and sectarian smells. Hidebound traditions, in the guise of dogmatics, yield like a receding ice-age, before the advance of Biblical Theology. Soon past mistakes are overcome, Concordia is steadily gaining the respect of scholarly circles, and there is a new openness towards other Lutherans and Christians. At last there is in sight the realization of Walther's grand dream of one united confessional Lutheran church in America. Concordia's architectural coronation, the completion of Luther Tower, signals that theologically she is now in full bloom, rich in promise of renewal, through "a more excellent ministry", for a tired church in a jaded world.

SCENE II

For years professors at Concordia Seminary had been hounded with charges of heresy by rigid traditionalists who simply could not and would not comprehend what was going on. At first the *Confessional Lutheran* and later *Lutheran/Christian News* raised such a smoke of accusations and innuendo that many in Synod began to think that there must be some truth at the bottom of it all. The seminary tried with noble silence to remain above the fray, but its motives and actual position continued to be misunderstood. At this point conservative power-brokers behind the scenes decided to exploit the climate of fear which had been created. They chose an "interloper" of Norwegian background to head their forces, and succeeded in capturing Synod's presidency from incumbent Oliver Harms in 1969. These "reactionary" forces have been consolidating their strangle-hold ever since.

SCENE III

As the fountain-head of Synod's evangelical renewal, Concordia Seminary naturally became the prime target of the Preus forces. Under cover of a Fact Finding Committee, a thorough "inquisition" was now launched to purge the seminary. Since the faculty could obviously not be convicted under the old doctrinal criteria enshrined in Synod's constitution, namely the Scriptures and the Confessions, new criteria had to be created. And so a quick new confession was forced through the New Orleans Convention (1973) by majority vote, together with a ready-made condemnation of the St. Louis faculty. This effectively, if unconstitutionally, narrowed the church's doctrine to but one thin strand of its former rich heritage. As biblical, evangelical Lutherans, Tietjen and his men naturally could not submit to such a distorted, impoverished theology, and to such dictatorial measures. Hence, when Tietjen was deposed, faculty and students went into exile, to continue genuine, pre-Preus Missouri Synod theology at "Seminex". The moral is: choose between the real Missouri and its official counterfeit!

This version of the conflict has a number of obvious propaganda advantages. For one thing it is simple, straight forward, easily grasped, requiring no effort at theological or historical understanding. It is a case of unfair management, and every good union member must go out on strike. Secondly, there is just enough painful truth in the diagnosis of theological arthritis in the aging synodical bones, to make the new post World War II direction seem like a wholly legitimate, indeed a much needed renewal. A host of individual facts can then be pieced quite convincingly into the frame of reference thus created. One or two authentic touches often suffice to create a devastating caricature. Thirdly, the Preus-as-Grand-Inquisitor theme can count on being carried, free of charge, by powerful media-fomented currents of popular feeling and prejudice—for example, "academic freedom," the identification of authority with dictatorship, the naive belief in change and novelty, the confusion of goodness and sentimentality, the pragmatic hatred of absolutes, and so on. Add to this explosive mixture a few sinister allusions to Watergate, and the whole thing is ready to go into orbit.

Nevertheless, as a serious explanation that scheme simply will not do, even if fleshed out with footnoted particulars. Nor can any other secular explanation cope with the reality.[2] The conflict is, after all, theological, as both sides have insisted. Any account of it, therefore, which is content to skim photogenically across the surface, penetrating into the substance "as deeply as the water-spider into the water" (Luther), cannot lay claim to being truthful or adequate. A responsible treatment of the dispute must come to grips with the central questions of truth on which it turns. And these questions are not, as some imagine, so complicated that they cannot be made plain to the satisfaction of any interested person. Like all great issues of life and death, they are at bottom simple. And they have a certain context or setting which needs to be seen in order to make sense of them.

Pastor Herbert Lindemann, one of the original "Forty-Four" signers of the controversial "A Statement" of 1945, reflecting a quarter of a century later on this turning point in the history of the Missouri Synod, wrote that it was the doctrine about the Church which had been "basic to the issues which were agitating the Missouri Synod at that time, *and it is this same doctrine which still lies at the heart of the present controversy*"[3] (my emphases). This judgment is, if anything, even truer than the writer intended. For it can be shown that after 1945 there came into prominence in the Missouri Synod a new way of thinking about the church. At first it was simply a reaction, perfectly understandable, to legalism and theological stagnation. In time, however, the cure became worse than the disease, because the inadequate new doctrine of the church could not register, much less resist, the relentless corrosion of Christian substance taking place under the banner of the modern Ecumenical Movement.

The long lists of doctrinal differences sometimes compiled to show what finally brought the Synod's tensions to a seething climax at New Orleans in 1973 can all be boiled down to two root issues: Scripture and the church. All else—Job, Jonah, JEDP, joining-fever, and JAOP's jurisdiction—are simply symptoms of the underlying divisions as to Scripture and the church.

Now as it happens the doctrines about church and Scripture were never considered during the first century of the Missouri Synod's existence to be foggy, "open-ended" entities or side issues. They were at the very heart and core of the Synod's well-defined doctrinal stand. The reason is not hard to find. These were, after all, the very issues which had shaped the nineteenth-century confessional Lutheran Awakening in Europe, out of which the Missouri Synod and the other confessional synods of the American Midwest were born. Confessional Lutheranism was fighting for its very life against two related forces: Rationalism, the dictatorship of human reason over Scripture and faith, and the so-called "Prussian Union", which surrendered the Sacrament and thus the Lutheran Confessions and Church to a government-enforced church union with the Calvinists. We would, therefore, expect to find Bible, Church, and Confessions as focal points of theological attention among the founders of the Missouri Synod. And so they were.

To get hold of the issues in an orderly and intelligible way, this study sums up Missouri's traditional stand on these matters under the headings "The Confessional Principle" and "The Biblical Principle" respectively. The latter is, of course, logically prior. But since the doctrine of the church is most conveniently treated in connection with the "Confessional Principle," and since historically Missouri's doctrinal collapse began there, we shall deal with this matter first. Another reason for giving more than passing attention to the Confessional Principle is the attempt of today's "moderates" to present themselves as champions of the Lutheran Confessions.

Having expounded both Principles by way of "Background,"

and explained the collapse of the Confessional Principle as "Foreground," we can get into proper view, "Centre Stage," the fate of the Bible. It is clear that the Biblical Principle in the Missouri Synod crumbled under pressure from the historical critical approach, which was naively mistaken simply for objective scholarship. While the predecessor-bodies of the present ALC, and the General Council component of the ULC (now LCA), had on the whole stood for the strict, traditional doctrine of inspiration, after World War I the historical-critical principle began to conquer the leading Lutheran seminaries, first in the ULC and later in the ALC. Denial of the old doctrine of inspiration and inerrancy came to be tolerated in the Missouri Synod largely because Lutheran union received top priority. Any doctrinal obstacles were perceived as dead weight to be cast overboard if Missouri's ecumenical balloon was to rise towards ALC-ULC-LCA fellowship, LWF membership, and beyond. But since it was not so easy to deny traditional doctrines in the Missouri Synod, ways and means were found to "re-interpret" them.

The author cannot close this introductory chapter without expressing his deep gratitude to the many friends and colleagues who gave help, advice, and encouragement. He must confess however that for his understanding of the biblical, Lutheran doctrine of the church he is indebted well-nigh totally to those two "patriarchs" of contemporary orthodox Lutheranism, the late Professor Hermann Sasse, D. Theol., D. D.,[4] and Professor emeritus William Oesch, D. D.[5] Any blunders in interpretation or application are, of course, the fault of the author.

II. BACKGROUND

For over a century the name "Missouri Synod" has stood, with friend and foe alike, for a theological stability which seemed rock-like at a time when marshmallow was the fashion. To understand this doctrinal solidity we need to look at the quarry whence it was hewn. And that quarry was the nineteenth-century Lutheran Awakening in Europe. The late Doctor H. Sasse has put it thus:

> It dare never be forgotten that everything still left today of Lutheran theology and Lutheran church in the world, is derived from that Awakening. Whatever may have been the limits of the Lutheran theology of the 19th century, we all live of the heirloom which the fathers of the Lutheran Awak-

ening have transmitted to us. Also the great Lutheran synods and churches of America's Middle West like the Missouri Synod, or the Lutheran Church of Australia, are a fruit of this Awakening. . .[6]

There were essentially two forces against which the Lutheran Awakening reacted. One was the policy of church-union, pursued with notable vigour by the Prussian government. This meant that the Lutheran and the Calvinist or "Reformed" churches were merged by government decree into a hybrid organism whose lack of spiritual virility may well have played a part in paving the way for modern Germany's tragedies. The other force, looming behind the Union-movement, was the spectre of Rationalism, which sacrificed all the holy mysteries of Christianity to a shallow but arrogant "reasonableness." As a result, the differences between Lutherans and Reformed—above all, whether we receive in the Holy Supper the true and life-giving body and blood of Christ, or only pictures and reminders—came to be regarded as unimportant.

Those who treasured the full Gospel riches of the Reformation heritage knew that they could surrender neither the Christ of the Bible to the Rationalists, nor His Sacrament to the Reformed Union. Against this background it becomes perfectly clear why the strict Lutherans, including the founders of the Missouri Synod, gave pride of place to two great principles, the Biblical and the Confessional. And like their opposites, Rationalism and Unionism, the Scriptures and the Lutheran Confessions are not separate, unrelated entities. The Confessional principle presupposes the Biblical, since Reformation doctrine rests squarely on Scripture alone; but on the other hand the Confessions spell out the real thrust and content of Scripture against denials and distortions. Mere assertions of the Bible's authority mean little unless the Bible's actual substance is confessed.

II. THE BASIC PRINCIPLES

A. THE CONFESSIONAL PRINCIPLE

1. The Lutheran Confessions

The official Confessions (also called Symbols or Symbolical Books) of the Lutheran Church are contained in the *Book of Concord* of the year 1580. The real centre, heart, and core of this volume is the Augsburg Confession, presented by the "Lutheran" princes and estates to the Emperor Charles V at the imperial diet or parliament at Augsburg on June 25, 1530. This is *the* Lutheran Confession *par excellence*. It shows in clear, simple language that the Reformation stood not for some strange new teachings but for plain, historic Christianity, centred in Justification by the merits of Christ alone (Article IV). The stunning effect of the public reading of this document was such that the papalist bishop of Augsburg, Christopher von Stadion, said in a private meeting of pro-Roman dignitaries: "What has been read to us is the pure, unvarnished, and undeniable truth."

In the *Book of Concord* the Augsburg Confession is fittingly preceded by the three Ecumenical Creeds. The earliest and simplest Christian creed was "JESUS IS LORD" (Romans 10:9; I Corinthians 12:3; Philippians 2:11). When a man confessed this he was ready for Baptism (Acts 2:38; 16:31-33). In the course of time this basic Christian confession was expanded into our Trinitarian Creeds. These creeds add nothing new but merely spell out, in the face of denials and distortions, what is meant in the New Testament by this confession-in-a-nutshell.

The earliest of these creeds is the Apostles' Creed, a baptismal creed the origins of which may be traced back to second century Rome. The Nicene Creed was named after the Council of Nicaea (325), which had to confess the full Godhead of Jesus Christ against the Arians, whose errors have been revived in our time by the Jehovah's Witnesses. The Council of Constantinople (381) added most of the third article, on the Holy Spirit. The third great creed of antiquity is the Athanasian, named in honour of St. Athanasius, the great champion of the Nicene Creed. This longest of the three creeds confesses in detail the mysteries of the Blessed Trinity and of the Person of Jesus, the God-Man. The Augsburg Confession, in its very first and third articles, takes its stand squarely on these Trinitarian and Christological confessions of the ancient church.

Immediately following the Augsburg Confession we have its Apology (meaning defence), a much longer document also written by Philip Melanchthon, Luther's friend and co-worker, and published in 1531. There is an interesting story behind it. The Roman theologians who had been ordered at Augsburg to prepare an answer to the confession of the "Lutherans" had done such a poor job of it that the Emperor had personally struck out most of it and sent it back to committee. It was short on arguments but long on insults. Finally, after several revisions, the Emperor accepted the document and had it read to the Diet on August 3, as the "Roman Imperial Confutation" of the Augsburg Confession. So silly was the Confutation's reasoning in parts that people sniggered openly. Although the Emperor demanded that the Lutheran party accept the Confutation as the imperial settlement of the issues, he refused their request for a copy. Finally he offered to let them have a copy if they promised not to publish it or to quote from it publicly! This they, of course, refused. By September 22 Melanchthon had the first version of the Apology ready, in which the Augsburg Confession is thoroughly defended against the argumentation of the Confutation. The Emperor however declined to receive the new document and simply demanded submission. As a masterful explanation and defence of the Augsburg Confession the Apology has an important place in the *Book of Concord*.

The Smalcald Articles were written by Luther himself for a consultation of Lutheran leaders at Smalcald in 1537. The intention was to submit these articles to the council which the Pope, after years of foot-dragging, had finally agreed to call together. It was to begin its sessions in Mantua later that year. As it happened, however, neither did the council convene (it began only in 1545 at Trent) nor did the Smalcald meeting adopt Luther's statement. Instead, the meeting adopted Melanchthon's Treatise on the Power and Primacy of the Pope, a valuable tract on church and ministry, which has always been a thorn in the flesh for Romanising Lutherans. The *Book of Concord* included both documents as classic definitions of genuine Reformation doctrine.

The two Catechisms of Luther were intended to help fathers and pastors to teach their households and parishioners the ABC's of Christianity.

Finally, the Formula of Concord settled a number of conflicts which had torn the Lutheran Church apart since the death of Luther. Melanchthon, Luther's scholarly friend and right-hand man, lacked Luther's depth and decisiveness. After the great Reformer's death Melanchthon himself vacillated on some important issues. Some of his followers went further, and actually formed a conspiracy in the very University of Wittenberg, to replace Lutheran with Calvinistic doctrine. They regarded Luther's belief in the Real Presence of Christ's body and blood in the Sacrament as a piece of extremism which needlessly divided the church. They themselves agreed with Zwingli and Calvin that Christ's body could only be in one place at a time and therefore could *not* be in the Sacrament, since it was now somewhere in heaven! These university professors taught their Calvinistic doctrine in their classes, but publicly assured everyone, even to the point of perjury, that they were sticking faithfully to Luther's doctrine and to the Augsburg Confession. They were not open and honest but rather were "Crypto-Calvinists"—Calvinists in secret. Had their trickery not come out into the open, so that the pious but gullible Saxon prince could finally see it, they might well have succeeded, humanly speaking, in destroying the Lutheran Church from within. Articles VII (Lord's Supper) and VIII (Person of Christ) of the Formula are directed specifically against these Calvinists deceptively masquerading as champions of the Augsburg Confession. The Formula of Concord was meant not as a new or stricter doctrinal position, but simply, in the words of its title, as "a thorough, pure, correct, and final restatement and explanation of a number of articles of the Augsburg Confession" which had been in dispute.

These three Ecumenical Creeds and seven Reformation Confessions make up the *Book of Concord* published in 1580. Scripture, of course, remains the only final authority. Because the Bible is the Word of God, "no human being's writings dare be put on a par with it."[7] In relation to the supreme and final authority of Scripture, creeds and confessions are "merely witnesses and expositions of the faith, setting forth how at various times the Holy Scriptures were understood in the church of God by contemporaries."[8] But *because* its doctrine is "drawn from the Word of

God," the *Book of Concord* is our church's commonly accepted "pattern of doctrine . . . according to which . . . all other writings are to be judged and regulated as to the extent to which they are to be approved and accepted."[9] The *Book of Concord* therefore sees itself not merely as an historical example of sixteenth-century faith, but as "a public, certain witness not only among our contemporaries, but also among our posterity, as to what our churches' unanimous position and judgment regarding the controversial articles has been and *shall* [the Latin adds *"perpetually"*] *remain.*"[10] Contrary teachings the confessors "do not by any means intend to tolerate in our lands, churches, and schools, inasmuch as such teachings are contrary to the expressed Word of God and cannot coexist with it."[11]

2. Background: Europe

During the next hundred years the doctrinal heritage of the Reformation was elaborated and defended by the giants of the so called Age of Orthodoxy, men like Chemnitz, John Gerhard, Dannhauer, Quenstedt ("book-keeper of Orthodoxy"), and Calov ("watchdog of Orthodoxy"). Few today appreciate the monumental work of these men, and even fewer know it.[12] Yet the Swedish scholar Bengt Haegglund has paid them this high tribute: "With respect to its versatile comprehension of theological material and the breadth of its knowledge of the Bible, Lutheran orthodoxy marks the high point in the entire history of theology."[13]

Lesser lights regrettably fell into a hair-splitting disputatiousness with little evidence of spiritual life and warmth. A reaction came in the form of Pietism, a movement which stressed life rather than doctrine, sanctification rather than justification, experience rather than sacraments. At first the pietists intended to hold on to the fulness of Lutheran doctrine, meaning only to stress the necessary spiritual fruit in the lives of Christians. However, a one-sided concentration on private piety, feelings, small prayer groups and Bible study circles, and the like soon led to an unhealthy subjectivism. The church's public liturgical and sacramental life and public preaching were disdained. Thorough theological work beyond the immediate needs of "practical" piety seemed wearisome, even unspiritual. Unconditional subscription to the Lutheran Confessions *because* they agreed with Scripture, was now felt to be inappropriate.

Its doctrinal substance having been softened up in this way, the church was virtually defenceless before the onslaughts of the rationalistic Enlightenment. This movement believed with a vengeance in the supremacy of human reason. Mankind had come of age, it was thought, and no longer needed primitive superstitions and religious authorities. Enlightened human intelligence itself could establish everything necessary to religion, namely the existence of God, the immortality of the soul, and morality or virtue as the way to heaven. All the mysteries beyond the grasp of human reason, such as the Trinity, the Incarnation, the Redemption, the Sacraments, and the like, were discarded as so much ancient nonsense and mumbo-jumbo. The French Revolution even enthroned a prostitute on the altar of Notre Dame to represent the goddess of reason!

In the pulpits rationalistic lecturers droned on about common sense trivia. Everything had to be very "practical." One Good Friday sermon, for instance, on the text "what I have written I have written," occupied itself with the importance of making one's last will and testament in writing![14] It is not difficult to imagine how this sort of drivel simply drove the people out of their churches *en masse*. The Lutheran territorial churches of Europe have never recovered from the devastation of those years. The dead hand of rationalistic unbelief ruled the theological faculties of the state universities where the clergy were trained, and through them the parishes and church administrations.

Religious turmoil was accompanied and followed by the political upheavals associated with the rise and fall of Napoleon. These crises had their chastening effects. A humbled Prussian king, Frederick William III (1797-1840), ruler of the largest and most powerful of the German states, set about to renew and restore a crumbling Christendom. To this end he deemed it essential to unite the two Protestant churches in his realm, the Lutheran, to which most of the population belonged, and his own Reformed or Calvinistic church, comprising a small minority. Only by combining the spiritual resources of both churches into one united front against unbelief, so it was thought, could the Christian cause be preserved.

Accordingly, the king had already in 1808 merged the Lutheran and Reformed church administrations into one single government department. After 1817 the Minister for Spiritual Affairs was, oddly enough, the unbeliever Baron von Altenstein, at whose dinner-table the subject was sometimes discussed of whether Christianity would endure another twenty or thirty years! For the three-hundredth anniversary of the Reformation (October 31, 1817) the king arranged a combined Lutheran-Reformed communion service in his court-chapel; but it was not widely imitated. Then in 1821 the king issued his infamous *Agende*, or liturgy-book, with its compromise form of service. Finally, impatient and irritated by the opposition to his plans, the king simply ordered the introduction of the new union liturgy, including the Reformed custom of breaking the bread, for the three-hundredth anniversary celebration of the Augsburg Confession in 1830.

Distinctively Lutheran services were now simply forbidden and conscientious Lutherans, like Professor Dr. J. G. Scheibel of Breslau, removed from office and persecuted in various incredibly ferocious ways—despite Prussia's claims that it followed an enlightened policy of freedom of religion! Noblemen and merchants were fined heavily for allowing Lutheran services on their properties. Lutherans had to meet secretly in forests, cellars, and barns. Judas-money was paid for the betrayal of faithful pastors. Midwives had to report the birth of all Lutheran children. Lutheran baptisms were declared invalid, and babies were sometimes forcibly rebaptized in the official union-church under police compulsion. Faithful pastors were imprisoned. In one village the faithful Lutherans were attacked on Christmas Eve by a military force of five hundred men, who drove the weeping women away from the church with swords and bayonets, forced open the church-doors, and "installed" the union pastor with his union liturgy. The army refused to end the occupation till the protesting parishioners would start attending the union services.[15]

Already in the jubilee year of 1817 a Lutheran pastor in Kiel, Claus Harms, had vigorously attacked both rationalism and the royally promoted church union. Harms had re-issued Luther's original ninety-five Theses, along with ninety-five of his own, the seventy-fifth of which read:

> The Lutheran church is to be treated like a poor maiden who is to be made rich through marriage. Be sure you do not perform the ceremony over Luther's bones. This will restore them to life, and then woe to you![16]

The prophecy was richly fulfilled in the Confessional Awakening, which finally led thousands of Lutherans, from many walks of life, to emigrate to the New World, so that they and their children might be free to confess and practice their Biblical, Reformation faith without compromise. This mass migration to Australia[17] and to America laid the foundations of the Lutheran church on the former continent, and of the Confessional, Midwestern synods on the latter. Several boat loads of emigrants bound for the seaport of Hamburg sailed right past the royal palace in Potsdam, singing the old chorales of the church. The king's spiritual advisor, Bishop Eylert, reports his own and the king's reactions:

> My heart became soft and sorrowful, and I sighed: Father, forgive them, for they know not what they do. The other day I heard that the King said about the emigrants at the royal table: Don't like hearing about it; is unpleasant for Me. Unheard of in a country in which freedom of religion and conscience rules. But freedom is not unbridled licence, which cancels all order and refuses all obedience. The misguided people call themselves Lutherans. What would Luther say if he were still alive. Pity! May they fare well.[18]

Only after the death of Frederick William III (1840) was the hitherto underground Lutheran church allowed to exist in Prussia as an independent body (1845).

3. Background: America

By the time of the Confessional Lutheran invasion of the American Midwest, Lutheranism had already been in this country for over two centuries. But this older, Eastern Lutheranism had lost its Confessional consciousness and decisiveness. The large Pennsylvania Synod, for instance, already in 1823 withdrew from the General Synod (a rather mild federation of synods formed in 1820) "partly because it feared that such membership would interfere with the proposed Lutheran-Reformed union."[19] In 1845 the General Synod itself went so far as to state in a formal letter to the Prussion Union Church in Germany:

> In most of our church principles we stand on common ground with the Union Church of Germany. The distinctive doctrines which separate the Lutheran and the Reformed Churches we do not consider essential. The tendency of the

so-called Lutheran part seems to us to be behind the time. Luther's peculiar views concerning the presence of the Lord's Body in the Communion have long been abandoned by the majority of our ministers.[20]

In 1855 the General Synod's leading theologian, Dr. S. S. Schmucker, published, anonymously at first, T*he American Recension of the Augsburg Confession*, which purported to "correct" the Augsburg Confession by deleting five alleged "remnants of Romish error," including baptismal regeneration and the Real Presence of Christ's body and blood in the Holy Supper. This mutilated "confession," designed for union with the Reformed, was suggested unsuccessfully as a "Definite Synodical Platform" for the entire General Synod. This approach was quite consistent with Schmucker's earlier (1838) *Fraternal Appeal* to all Protestant churches in America to unite on the basis of (1) the Apostles' Creed and (2) the "United Protestant Confession" concocted from various sources.[21] Among the General Synod Lutheran pulpit and altar fellowship with the Reformed denominations was taken for granted.

It is not surprising, then, that the newly formed, so-called "Old Lutheran" synods of the Midwest simply could not recognise the General Synod as Lutheran. C. F. W. Walther in St. Louis had started his publication, the *Lutheraner*, already in 1844, precisely to raise a public banner for genuine Confessional Lutherans.

Nor was it simply a matter of doctrines on paper. The differences found expression also in the forms of church life and practice. Benjamin Kurtz's *Lutheran Observer* crusaded for the emotional, revivalistic ways of the American Reformed churches. The "Old Lutherans" found these ways repulsive, and rejected them as unchurchly "new measures,"[22] just as they opposed the bare ways of Puritanism generally.[23] In opposition to revivalistic emotionalism Lutheran doctrine insisted that not personal feelings, experiences, "testimonies," and the like, but only the objective means of grace, the Gospel and sacraments of Christ, should be central to the church's worship and shape its practical life. Attention must be focused on God and His gifts, not on man and his moods. We catch an illuminating glimpse of this conflict in the Missouri Synod's *Lutheraner* of September 23, 1856. Here Walther reprints, under the amused heading "Peter in der Fremde" ("Peter in a Strange Country"), a letter by a J. B. McAfee, which had recently appeared in the pro-revivalist *Lutheran Observer*:

> I left Leavenworth City, Kansas Territory, on July 17, and arrived in St. Louis on Saturday night, July 19. Sunday morning at 5 o'clock I left the boat in order to seek out a Lutheran church. First I went to Concordia College, but finding no church there, returned to the city, and wandered from place to place till nearly 11 o'clock, when I found the long-sought object. Upon entering I found all seats occupied, with the exception of one, which I took. Here I saw, for the first time in a Lutheran church, image and crucifix. I crune to the conclusion that I had come to the wrong place and was in a Roman church. The preacher was attired in priestly vestments, the sacrament was to be distributed, wax candles burnt on the east side of the altar, wafers were used, etc. People bowed towards the images, and as I supposed, before them.*) Thus the ceremony ended. Rarely have I seen a preacher seemingly more solemn, serious, and zealous. But do not believe that because I admire the zeal of the man (Brother Schaller) I also admire the ceremony. This is something to which I am totally opposed. ... .

Besides inserting Schaller's name, Walther added only the following note at the place marked: "*) That is untrue. We bow before no image, but we do begin the altar service bowing with a silent sigh to God."

4. The Church in the Confessions

How does the Lutheran church understand herself in relation to the one holy universal church of Christ, and also in relation to other Christian churches? The classic Lutheran understanding of the church is stated in Article VII of the Augsburg Confession:

> It is also taught among us that there must be and remain at all times one holy Christian Church, which is the assembly of all believers, among whom the Gospel is purely preached and the holy Sacraments are given according to the Gospel. For this is sufficient—for the true unity of the Christian Church, that the Gospel be preached unanimously according to a pure understanding of it, and that the Sacraments are given in accordance with the divine Word. And it

is not necessary for the true unity of the Christian Church that uniform ceremonies, instituted by men, be everywhere observed; as Paul says to the Ephesians, chapter four: "One body, one Spirit, as you have been called to the one hope of your calling, One Lord, One Faith, One Baptism."

The remarkable thing is that the *whole* church is here tied up with the *whole* saving Gospel ("*purely* preached"). Common sense would suggest that one must choose between the whole church and the whole truth but that one cannot have them both together. For if one embraces the whole church, all Christians, one must, it would seem, reduce the Gospel-truth to some bare minimum or common denominator. Or else, if one wishes to hold on to the complete Gospel, including the Sacraments, one will have to let go of large parts of Christendom, and end up with but a small orthodox fraction or segment of the whole. How then does the Augsburg Confession resolve this "truth or unity" conundrum?[24]

Following the divine admonition to walk by faith, not by sight (2 Cor. 5:7); Luther realised that the mystery of the church (Eph. 5:32, cf. Luke 17:20ff.) is an article of faith, to be believed, not seen. He wrote:

The church is a high, deep, hidden thing which one may neither perceive nor see, but must grasp only by faith, through baptism, sacrament, and word.[25]

> All Christians in the world pray, "I believe in the Holy Spirit, one holy Christian church, the community of saints." If this article is true, it follows that no one can either see or feel the holy Christian church, nor can anyone say, "See, here or there it is!" For what one believes one can neither see nor feel, as St. Paul teaches in Hebrews 11 . . . The holy church of Christ says, "I believe one holy Christian church." The insane church of the pope says, "I see a holy Christian church."[26]

> The church is concealed, the saints hidden.[27]

> This part, "I believe one holy Christian church," is just as much an article of faith as all the rest. Therefore no reason, even if it puts on all its spectacles, can recognise her. The devil can indeed cover her up with offences and divisions, so that you have to take offence at it. So also God can hide her with weaknesses and all sorts of defects, so that you have to become a fool over it, and form a false judgment concerning

her. She wants to be not seen but believed; but faith is of that which one does not see, Heb. 1.[28]

As the Bride of Christ, the church is just as much a mystery, just as inaccessible to natural human reason, as her divine Bridegroom Himself. How then can we find her? As the first Eve was taken out of Adam's side (Gen. 2), so the New Testament Eve receives her being from the Second Adam (Rom. 5:12-21), out of whose side flowed water and blood (John 19:34)—the very elements which together with His life-giving Spirit create His church (I John 5:6-12). Those means by which the one church is created therefore—the pure Gospel and sacraments of Christ—are also the outward marks of recognition by which faith finds, identifies, and grasps His church locally. In this way full truth and unity are perfectly joined together.

In the past we have been accustomed to the terms "visible" and "invisible" in this connection. This is not wrong, if we do not imagine that there are two separate churches. The *Apology* in Article VII-VIII shows the way by distinguishing between the church as "an association of outward ties and rites," on the one hand, and as "an association of faith and of the Holy Spirit in men's hearts," on the other. The latter is the church "in the proper sense" (par. 28) of the word, the former is the church "in the wider sense" (par. 10). The church is only one, but as Christ's kingdom it is "hidden under the cross" (par. 18). It is the "outward appearance of the church" which is described in the parables of the net and of the ten virgins (Matt. 13:47, 25:1ff.), where Christ

> ... teaches us that the church is hidden under a crowd of wicked men so that this stumbling block may not offend the faithful and so that we may know that the Word and the sacraments are efficacious even when wicked men administer them. Meanwhile he teaches that though these wicked men participate in the outward marks, still they are not the true kingdom of Christ and members of Christ, for they are members of the kingdom of the devil (par. 19).

So then the real "inner" church, the invisible Temple of God (Eph. 2:21), consisting of all Christians or children of God, rests on the outward foundation of the pure apostolic Gospel (Eph. 2:20). In this life we can deal with the church only in faith, through the appointed outward marks, never directly, as if the church were a part of this world. We find the one flock not by counting sheep but by following the voice of the Shepherd (John 10:4, 5). The "outward" church, the "association of outward ties and rites" exists simply to build and serve the church in the proper sense. It must, therefore, be judged quite objectively, externally, by its faithfulness or unfaithfulness to the Gospel of the one Christ and His one church.

It is a travesty, therefore, to reduce the Gospel, the foundation of the church's unity, to some short slogan about justification or about the Lordship of Christ! Neither Scripture nor the Confessions offer such a cut-rate, mini-gospel. The Formula of Concord makes it quite plain what it means to agree in the Gospel. It means to agree "in doctrine and in all its articles" and also "concerning the right use of the holy sacraments."[29] Not only the Roman attack on *grace alone*, but also the Reformed attacks on the *means of grace* are grave subversions of Christ's pure Gospel and sacraments. The Formula of Concord explicitly cites Luther, "as the chief teacher of the Augsburg Confession," to the effect that whoever denies the Real Presence of Christ's body and blood in the Sacrament "will please let me alone and expect no fellowship from me. This is final."[30] Of all these falsifications of the Gospel the confessors insist that they "cannot be tolerated in the church of God, much less be excused and defended."[31] Such errors "are contrary to the expressed Word of God and cannot coexist with it."[32]

What then is the Lutheran church? It is simply the "Evangelical Christian" or "true Evangelical" churches, or the "churches of the pure Christian religion," holding to the Augsburg Confession "as the Symbol of our time" which "distinguishes our reformed churches from the papacy and from other condemned sects and heresies," and which is "a genuinely Christian symbol which all true Christians ought to accept next to the Word of God."[33] And the Preface to the *Book of Concord* makes it clear that the blunt doctrinal condemnations are not directed against individual Christian believers, who err from simplicity and sincere ignorance, "and who do not blaspheme the truth of the divine Word, and far less do we mean entire churches inside or outside the Holy Empire of the German Nation. On the contrary, we mean specifically to condemn only false and seductive doctrines and their stiff-necked proponents and blasphemers."[34] In other words, one must distinguish between false doctrines and systems, and individual Christians caught in such systems. To take a political example, it would be foolish to blame the captive nations of our time for all their murderous dictators. It is equally foolish to pretend that hobnobbing with the tormentors somehow expresses friendship for their victims.

The Lutheran church, then, is humbly conscious, on the one hand, of representing, not some sectarian little specialities, but "the pure doctrine of the holy Gospel"[35] and therefore "the ancient consensus" of "the universal and orthodox church of Christ."[36] On the other hand, the Lutheran church is not and has never claimed to be organizationally the sum total of all Christians, the "only saving church." No visible church body can truthfully make such claims, as even Rome today admits. On the contrary, the Lutheran church is deeply aware of that tragic and terrible "Babylonian Captivity" which still torments Christendom in various forms until the Last Day. Indeed, the spiritual oppression of Christ's church and Christians by falsehood and evil is such that at times it even seems "as though there were no church, and it often appears as if she had quite perished."[37]

Luther illustrates this biblical realism about the church with a famous story about two brothers walking through the forest. One was grabbed by a bear, and the other, intending to help his brother, aimed at the bear, but missed and tragically stabbed his brother. That, says Luther, is how the fanatical Anabaptists go about fighting the Antichrist—who, after all, sits not in the devil's stable but in God's temple, the church (2 Thess. 2:4), and therefore has Christians under him whom he torments. Now, the fanatics imagine that by attacking *everything* under the papacy, including the sacraments, they are really injuring the Antichrist. In actual fact, they are injuring captive Christendom under him. "For if they would permit baptism and the sacrament of the altar to stand as they are, Christians under the pope might yet escape with their souls and be saved, as has been the case hitherto. But now when the sacraments are taken from them, they will most likely be lost, since even Christ himself is thereby taken away."[38] The point is to attack the wrong, the abuse, the anti-christian addition, while taking great care not to do damage to the temple of God, which is also there!

The Lutheran doctrine of the church then rests altogether on faith, not on sight. It is broad enough to include all Christians and the whole, full, rich Gospel of Christ, yet narrow enough to exclude all teachings, systems, and institutions which attack or distort this Gospel in any way. And this very narrowness is—sinful human failings apart—a service and duty of love not only to God and to His Word and church, but also and especially to the victims themselves, actual and potential, of the seductive pseudo-, semi-, quasi-, and mini-gospels of our last times.

5. "More" Than The Confessions?

According to popular stereotype, the Missouri Synod began by taking its stand strictly on the Lutheran Confessions, but then "advanced steadily toward doctrinal elaboration and exclusiveness through vigorous theological controversies . . . on doctrines of the church and the ministerial office, chiliasm and the Antichrist, 'open questions,' and predestination and conversion . . ."[39] In other words, the synod changed from being broadly Lutheran to narrowly "Missourian." John Tietjen, in his book on Lutheran unity, charges the Missouri Synod with having "gone beyond the classic confessional documents of the Lutheran Church in order to determine what is Lutheran" by drafting "doctrinal statements in addition to the Lutheran Confessions," thus setting up "new confessional criteria to determine what it means to be Lutheran."[40] But is this a fair interpretation of the facts? To answer this question—so crucial for an understanding not only of the Missouri Synod itself but of the whole "moderate" standpoint as well—we need to see how the Confessional Principle worked itself out in particular cases.

The first great controversy was forced on the hapless Saxons soon after their arrival in Missouri. Their leader, "Bishop" Martin Stephan, had shamelessly exploited their religious zeal to make himself their absolute ruler by means of the emigration to America. And he ruled like a kind of Saxon Mohammed, in pursuit of power, wealth, and harem. Upon his inevitable unmasking the poor victims, pastors and people alike, found themselves utterly swamped by confusion, regret, and guilt. Were there among them even a valid church and public ministry? Must they return to Saxony to make amends for their folly? This deep crisis and humiliation forced the leadership to wrestle with the basic theological questions. The turning point came with the famous debates at Altenburg, Perry County, in 1841.[41] Steeped in Luther's writings,[42] the young Pastor C. F. W. Walther was able to convince the colonists of the rudiments of the biblical, Lutheran doctrine of the church: the church embraces all Christian believers and is therefore invisible; outward separation from an outward organisation does not necessarily separate a person from the one church of Christ; the important thing is to hold on to the pure Gospel and sacraments, which are valid and powerful no matter who administers them, be it "the devil or his grandmother" (Luther). In other words, church and public ministry were still among them, and there was no need to despair, disband, or return to Germany.

These hard-won insights, however, were soon challenged. Nearly a year after the Saxons had landed in New Orleans, a large party of Lutherans fleeing from Prussian persecution arrived in New York in five ships. Their spiritual leader was Pastor J. A. A. Grabau, who had himself been imprisoned for his faith. The group settled in and around Buffalo, New York, and formed the Buffalo Synod. Grabau, however, had extreme and quite un-Lutheran notions about the church and its ministry. For example, he held that the Lutheran church was the one church outside of which there was no salvation! In an early "pastoral letter"[43]— he claimed that the proper pastoral office was necessary for the means of grace to be effective. Apart from properly ordained clergy, he held, the bread and wine in the Sacrament could not be Christ's body and blood, nor could holy absolution be valid. Moreover, pastors could make binding rules even beyond the Word of God, which the laity were conscience-bound to obey. Nor had the laity any right to judge their pastors' doctrine.

There was no reasoning with Grabau. He responded irrationally with bitter and vehement denunciations. The Saxons were accused of fomenting an unchurchly, democratic mob-rule. The 1848 session of the Buffalo Synod denounced the one-year old Missouri Synod as an "Ahab's Synod" and an "Abomination Synod," and its pastors as false teachers and notorious sinners. In 1859 Grabau pronounced a formal "ex communication" on the whole Missouri Synod (over two hundred congregations)![44] The most significant single fruit of this controversy was that great classic by C. F. W. Walther, *The Voice of Our Church in the Question of Church and Ministry,* published in 1852 as the doctrinal stand of the whole Missouri Synod and regrettably not available in English to this day.[45] A master of precise formulation, cutting through side issues to the heart of the matter, Walther set out clearly what the Lutheran church taught about church and ministry, on the basis of Scripture—first of all in her public, official Confessions, and then also in the private writings of her most distinguished theologians, above all the great Reformer himself.

Walther's book was a masterpiece of balanced theological learning and judgment. Avoiding extremist hobby-horses, it did justice both to the spiritual oneness of all Christians and to the decisive role of the pure Gospel and sacraments; to the priestly dignity of all Christians as well as to the divinely instituted office of the public ministry. So impressive was this scholarly, work, published in Germany, where these very matters were hotly debated among conservative Lutherans, that the University of Goettingen offered the author the honorary degree of doctor of theology. The humble and faithful Walther declined politely—because of the Goettingen Faculty's compromising attitude towards the orthodox Lutheran church.[46]

In America the controversy went on for decades, and then came to a dramatic climax in 1866. Grabau, discredited in his own parish and synod, left the Buffalo Synod, together with a handful of his faithful followers. Thereupon the synod accepted Missouri's long-standing offer of a doctrinal consultation. The intense discussions lasted eleven days, beginning on November 20, 1866. The result was that all except one of the Buffalo Synod representatives abandoned their previous stand and declared themselves in doctrinal unity with the Missouri Synod. While a small number went with Pastor von Rohr into a new splinter group and a number of pastors joined the Ohio Synod, twelve pastors and five lay-delegates met on February 26, 1867, for the tenth and last convention of the original Buffalo Synod; they unanimously and publicly repudiated that synod's false doctrinal position and on March 1 adjourned the synod indefinitely. All but one of the pastors joined the Missouri Synod, among them Christian Hochstetter, who later (1885) wrote the standard reference work, *The History of the Evangelical Lutheran Missouri Synod in North America and Her Doctrinal Controversies*, which reports the above details.

Another alleged "narrowing" of Missouri Synod theology took place in connection with chiliasm, the idea that Christ would, prior to His return on Judgment Day, come to earth to establish a thousand-year reign (the so-called "millenium"), in which the church would publicly triumph over all her enemies, the Jewish nation as such would be converted and re-established, and an individual Antichrist would be overthrown. All this was taught on the basis of Revelation 20 and similar texts. Pastor Schieferdecker, then president of the Western District, stirred up such excitement and division over these matters in his parish and elsewhere that the 1857 Fort Wayne Convention of the Missouri Synod, after some ten days of fruitless discussion with him, was compelled to exclude him. Schieferdecker joined the Iowa Synod, but later recanted and returned to Missouri.

It must not be imagined, however, that the Synod simply excluded Schieferdecker after a brief argument over moot points of prophetic interpretation. Walther and others had spared no efforts in dealing personally with Schieferdecker the year before, with seeming success. Nor was it simply a matter of personal opinions, privately held. What the Synod objected to was the public defence and promotion of chiliasm. For one thing, such teaching was clearly contrary to Article XVII of the Augsburg Confession: "Rejected, too, are certain Jewish opinions... which teach that, before the "resurrection of the dead, saints and godly men will possess a worldly kingdom and annihilate all the godless." For another thing, such notions distorted the Christian hope into something earthly, thus creating utopian illusions about the real nature of Christ's kingdom. The scheme also denied the clear biblical teachings that the church would remain under the cross to the end, and that Christ's return to Judgment was to be expected at any time, and not only after a thousand-year warning period (the millenium) which lay still in the future. Nor should it be overlooked that chiliastic fanaticism was then rife both in Europe and in America. The weird fantasies of Seventh Day Adventism's Ellen G. White and of Charles Taze Russell, founder of the "Jehovah's Witnesses," arose out of the chiliastic ferment of those times. Russell taught that Christ had begun his "invisible return" in 1874. Modern "Witnesses" have changed that to 1914. The great spiritual peril of such delusions, which have seduced millions, is a matter of record.

The dispute about "open questions" was not really a separate issue, but arose out of the previous points. Grabau had managed to create friction between his Missouri Synod opponents and the great Pastor Wilhelm Loehe of Bavaria, who had trained many Missouri Synod pastors and had founded the Fort Wayne Seminary (which, after a century in Springfield, returned to Fort

Wayne in 1976). The threatening rift with Loehe, their valued friend and benefactor, was of such importance to the Missourians, that their 1851 Convention deputised Walther and the newly elected synodical president, F. K. D. Wyneken, to go to Germany in person to try to avert the break. The mission succeeded, and Missouri was deeply grateful that harmonious relations with the staunch Bavarian confessor had been restored. But the peace was short-lived. Less than two years after the Walther-Wyneken mission, Pastors Grabau and von Rohr of Buffalo toured Germany, distributing printed attacks on the Missouri Synod. On the basis of their highly misleading reports, the entire Leipzig Conference, an annual gathering of prestigious theologians from all over Germany, was manipulated into issuing at its 1853 meeting an opinion which favoured Buffalo against Missouri. The opinion included the remark that the dispute between the synods was, after all, about matters which were clearly decided neither in the Scriptures nor in the Lutheran Confessions.

The Missouri Synod later answered this ill-advised Leipzig pronouncement so thoroughly that the Saxon *Kirchen und Schulblatt* publicly conceded that the theological objections had been refuted.[47] The Missouri Synod reply took issue especially with the assertion that the doctrines of church and ministry were not clearly settled in Scripture and the Confessions. The damage, however, was done. Grabau and von Rohr published in the Buffalo Synod organ the announcement that all differences with Loehe had been settled, and that full reconciliation be tween him and the Buffalo Synod had taken place. From then on Loehe tried to follow a mediating policy between Missouri and Buffalo. Whereas his pastor-trainees had formerly been directed to Missouri, Loehe now founded the Iowa Synod, which was to seek to avoid the "extremes" of both Buffalo and Missouri. Iowa also took a permissive attitude towards chiliasm, which had during an illness infected Loehe himself.[48]

Iowa maintained with Loehe that certain doctrines of the Lutheran Confessions, notably those on church and ministry, were not yet quite "ready" or settled, but had still to be brought to completion. Till then, various views should be allowed. Since Luther's position on the subject was well-known, and had recently been fully documented in Walther's book, Loehe distinguished between Luther's personal views and the official doctrine of the Confessions. He granted that Walther, indeed, held Luther's own position, and that the Confessions themselves in at least one place (*Tractate*, 59-72) taught the Luther-Walther view.[49] But Loehe maintained that other places in the Confessions, notably Augsburg Confession XXVIII, could be understood differently. Hence the Confessional doctrine was unclear and unfinished.

Whatever the personal faults on both sides, theologically Walther at this point was clearly defending not some peculiar "Missourian" eccentricity, but one of the very chief pillars of the Reformation itself. The Formula of Concord certainly regards Luther as "the chief teacher of the Augsburg Confession," who therefore "understood the true intention of the Augsburg Confession better than anyone else." Therefore "the true meaning and intention of the Augsburg Confession cannot be derived more correctly or better from any other source than from Dr. Luther's doctrinal and polemical writings."[50] Yet such was Grabau's dislike of Luther's doctrine that, when he was reminded of these statements in the Formula, Grabau exclaimed publicly before the whole Buffalo Synod that, if this were true, he would rather be released at once from his subscription to the Formula of Concord![51] So much for the innocent-sounding claim that the differences between Missouri and Buffalo on church and ministry were mere "open questions" to be accomodated under an umbrella of general loyalty to the Confessions. Later the arguments shifted to other levels. But the Missouri Synod never denied that there were such things as genuine "open questions" or theological problems. What it objected to was the practice of stamping everything on which disagreement developed among Lutherans as an "open question"; for this implied that not Scripture alone, but the church, through her Confessions, established doctrine.[52]

Highly significant is the fact that Walther in the end was compelled to distinguish between Biblical teachings which were articles of faith, and therefore church-divisive, and those (like the prohibition of usury) which were not.[53] It is at least misleading, therefore, to suggest without further ado, as Tietjen does, that Missouri and the Synodical Conference insisted on "a resolution of all theological disagreements" and on "complete conformity" as conditions for church fellowship.[54]

The main test of Confessional commitment, however, was still to come. All previous controversies were overshadowed by the great conflict over divine Election or Predestination, which split the newly formed (1872) Synodical Conference itself. Although the full force of that explosion was not felt till a decade later, the fuse was lit already in 1870, when the Iowa Synod's Professor Gottfried Fritschel accused Walther of blindly following Luther on predestination.[55]

What was at stake? The Bible and the Lutheran Confessions teach two great truths which our reason cannot quite fit together: on the one hand, God sincerely offers salvation in Christ, through the means of grace, to all men (*universal grace*); on the other hand, this salvation is also entirely God's gift (*grace alone*). The problem starts at the point where we try to answer the question: Why, then, are some saved and others not? We can try to solve this riddle in one of two ways. Either we say that God does not really want everybody to be saved. This denies "universal grace" and is the error of Calvinism. Or we answer that it all depends on man's own conduct, some accepting and others rejecting grace. But this denies "grace alone" and adds to the only two causes of our election—God's mercy and Christ's most holy merit[56]—yet a third one, namely "something in us," be it foreseen faith, better behaviour, free choice, etc.

But if these two types of solutions are wrong, because they attack either "universal grace" or "grace alone," how does the Formula of Concord itself solve the mystery? It does not try. That is the point. We are to stick faithfully to God's revealed will and Word, and not to pry into His secrets nor seek to answer the unanswerable: "Paul sets a definite limit for us as to how far we should go in these and similar questions (Rom. 9:14 ff.; 11:22ff.).. .. But whenever something in the discussion of this subject soars too high and goes beyond these limits, we must with Paul place our finger on our lips and say, 'Who are you, a man, to answer back to God?' "[57]

Walther's opponents, however, insisted on solving the mystery. Their answer was very simply that God foresaw who would believe and who not, and then chose or rejected people on that basis. That, of course, explains everything very neatly, but at the expense of "grace alone." For faith is then no longer a result of God's election; but, on the contrary, God's election has turned into a result of foreseen faith, in other words, of "something in man"!

Just as in the dispute about church and ministry, the attack was on Luther's doctrine, not simply on Walther's. Fritschel argued that Luther had, in his 1525 book against Erasmus, *On the Bondage of the Will*, taken a false and extreme stand on predestination, which he himself had later quietly abandoned. The fact, however, is that Luther regarded his book against Erasmus as about the best and most important he had ever written.[58] The Formula of Concord also cites it.[59] To what, then, in Luther's book did Fritschel object? To the mystery of predestination. Actually, said Fritschel, there was no mystery at all about why some were saved and others lost: a clear explanation was to be found in man's own free choice! This he put in the crassest terms:

> Whether man is saved or lost depends in the final analysis on man's own free decision for or against grace . . .
>
> . . . of two people to whom the Gospel is preached, one comes to faith, the other not. The reason for this according to God's Word lies solely and alone in the decision of man.
>
> . . . the eternal fate of man is rooted in his personal free decision for or against the grace offered him in Christ.
>
> . . . [God] lets it depend on man's decision on whom He will have mercy and whom He will harden . . . Everything here is referred back to the self-determination of man (not to the dark, secret will of God).
>
> . . . Scripture places the reason for this, that while one man is saved the other is lost, into the will of man, into man's own self-determination.
>
> . . . there is a different conduct of man towards grace, and on this depends his eternal fate.[60]

This doctrine of conversion and salvation by man's own free choice and self-determination flies in the face of the Lutheran Confessions,[61] not to mention Scripture itself. To make his offensive language seem acceptable, however, Fritschel invented a kind of "conversion before conversion": hearing the Gospel liberates man's enslaved will enough to enable him by the use of these new powers to convert himself! So man is somewhat alive while he is still spiritually dead! Fritschel tried to help himself also with other subtleties, such as the distinctions between "natural" and "wilful" resistance to grace, and between broader and narrower meanings of the word "election."

Could such patent falsifications be allowed to stand as valid "interpretations" of Articles II and XI of the Formula of Concord? Such an attitude would render all confessions meaningless. Undeterred by muddles and evasions, Walther set out clearly and uncompromisingly, in the *Thirteen Theses of 1881*, the Pauline-

Lutheran stand of the Formula of Concord. These well-balanced *Theses* refuse, with the Formula, to solve the mystery of predestination by sacrificing either "universal grace" to the Calvinists or "grace alone" to the synergists (people who teach that man is converted and saved partly by his own doing or co-operation). John Tietjen's judgment that these *Thirteen Theses* are a prime example of demanding "more than the Lutheran Confessions,[62] is shallow, for it blandly mistakes every new document for a new doctrine. Also strange was Prof. M. Loy's (Ohio Synod) argument that Walther's stand actually threatened justification by faith![63] The point seems all the more inept for having been urged by a man who at the same time held to a "consideration of man's conduct" as a basis of God's election of the believers![64] Even a highly unsympathetic observer is forced to pay this tribute to Walther on justification:

> At the centre of Walter's theology was the doctrine of justification by the grace of God through faith in Christ Jesus. Walther believed that all other doctrines served the doctrine of justification by grace through faith as presuppositions, or flowed from it as conclusions.[65]

Gottfried Fritschel was a man of considerable knowledge and scholarship, but also of a warm, churchly piety.[66] In some ways his personal reactions to the strains and pains of the fray appear more noble than those of Walther. And he had won a notable victory over Walther when, with prodigious erudition, he had demolished Walther's position on usury.[67] Nevertheless he was out of his depth in the predestination controversy. Here Walther stood, with Luther,[68] rock-like for the theology of the Cross, with all its offensiveness to human reason, while Fritschel and those who followed him skipped along the shallow paths of common sense, like Erasmus. Walther's theology had been shaped and refined in the fires of fierce afflictions and adversities. He knew precisely what Luther meant when he said that God's ways must be understood through suffering and the cross. As a result he saw and could trace with rare Reformation clarity the radical links between "grace alone" and every last fibre of Christian doctrine. That is what made him not merely a great scholar or writer, but a great theologian. Perhaps others, though equally intelligent, lacked similar depths because they had been spared the corresponding agonies of soul.

Since Fritschel had fired the first shot of this war, it seems particularly fitting that a sort of peace was brought about half a century later by his son George. The younger Fritschel had at first written against Missouri's position. By the time of the 1925 "Chicago Theses," however, agreed to by the representatives of the Buffalo, Iowa, Missouri, Ohio, and Wisconsin Synods, Prof. George Fritschel found that position acceptable, on the basis of the Biblical argumentation of Walther's great colleague, George Stoeckhardt. Neve's history notes: "The agreement on the article of Predestination was brought about by Dr. George Fritschel, who, accepting Dr. Stoeckhardt's exegesis of the Epistle to the Romans, succeeded in convincing others that Stoeckhardt had the correct Biblical doctrine."[69]

6. A Fatal Fallacy: Doctrines or Documents?

We are now ready to consider the main thrust of Tietjen's far-reaching thesis in *Which Way To Lutheran Unity?* In its effort to promote union among all major U.S. Lutheran groups today, the book turns its attention, quite rightly, to the nineteenth-century sources of the divisions. The three main groupings of synods, the General Synod (1820), the General Council (1867), and the Synodical Conference (1872) are found to have stood for very different versions of the Confessional principle. In Tietjen's opinion the General Synod favored a broad union on the basis of a loose allegiance to the Confessions; the General Council stood for Lutheran unity by means of "subscription to the Lutheran Confessions"; the Synodical Conference, going beyond the Lutheran Confessions, insisted on complete agreement in doctrine and practice.[70] Clearly, it is a matter of too little, too much, and just about right. The grand conclusion, despite perfunctory reservations,[71] is that the General Council's way of Confessional subscription was essentially the right one, and is represented today by the ULCA-LCA approach.[72] Today, says Tietjen, "All Lutheran church bodies confess allegiance to the doctrinal content of the Lutheran Confessions."[73] Hence "it is simply intolerable for Christians who confess the same faith to refuse to live in fellowship with one another."[74] This book was published in 1966, the same year in which Tietjen became executive secretary of the Division of Public Relations of the Lutheran Council in the U.S.A. The book's advice to U.S. Lutheranism is unmistakable. But how correct is its historical perspective?

For one thing, it is quite wrong to attribute to the General Council a principle of "Confessional subscription" in anything like the ULCA-LCA sense which Tietjen evidently intends. In the first place, the General Council at its formation adopted a detailed document of a "confessional character," entitled "The Fundamental Principles of Faith and Church Polity." This confessional document was embodied in the Constitution as "fundamental and unchangeable," hence was regarded as a condition of membership in the Council.[75] Why does not Tietjen treat this as a case of going "beyond" the Confessions to establish "additional" criteria like the Synodical Conference? Secondly, the General Council formally adopted Dr. Jacobs' theses about the basic differences between it and the General Synod. The theses stated that a mere look at the wordings of the "Confessional declarations" was not enough. "To be understood, they must be considered in their historical relations, and in the light of the prevailing life and practice of churches, synods, and leaders."[76] Is not this a clear reference to "doctrine and practice" in addition to "Confessional subscription"? Thirdly, Jacobs, and with him the whole General Council, added:

> While an entire Church Body cannot be held responsible for the inconsistencies of a few individuals, never-the-less, when a violation of principles declared in our Confessions becomes widespread, and, in spite of repeated protests, continues, no professed endorsement of the most explicit Confession of Faith is adequate to give standing as Lutheran pastors and teachers to those indifferent to such departures from the faith. It is not subscription to any particular Confession of Faith, but it is the holding of the faith of that Confession that renders one a Lutheran, and worthy of recognition and co-operation.[77]

In other words, not "Confessional subscription," but actual adherence to the Confessions in doctrine and practice was demanded. This had really been said already in the "Fundamental Principles of Faith" (IV): Those who subscribe the Confessions "must not only agree to use the same words, but must use and understand those words in one and the same sense."[78] The distinguished General Council theologian and president, Dr. Theodore Schmauk, co-authored a justly celebrated classic, *The Confessional Principle and the Confessions*, the orientation of which is shown in this sample: "The real question is not what do you subscribe, but what do you believe and publicly teach, and what are you transmitting to those who come after?"[79] And Professor H. E. Jacobs wrote on behalf of the General Council:

> The unity of the Church does not consist in subscription to the same Confessions, but in the acceptance and teaching of the same doctrines . . . .
>
> It is well to notice that it is not the acceptance of the unaltered Augsburg Confession, but the acceptance of its *doctrines*, which determines the Lutheran character of a teacher or Church body. A man who has never subscribed the Augsburg Confession, or even never seen it, is a Lutheran if he teach the doctrines which it maintains. A man who makes his subscription to the Confession an object of especial boast, is no Lutheran, if "by equivocation or mental reservation," or even by excusable misunderstanding, he depart from any of the doctrines therein clearly and professedly taught.[80]

So much for the notion that the General Council was satisfied with "Confessional subscription."

It is to the General Synod that we must turn to find that modern ULCA-LCA notion of "Confessional subscription" which Tietjen mistakenly credits to the General Council. Granted, the General Synod limited its subscription to the Augsburg Confession and then only to "the fundamental doctrines." Yet Professor Milton Valentine, while dismissing "the doctrinal definitions and developments in the other writings, especially in the Formula Concordiae, so far as they are not contained in the Augsburg Confession" as "not essential to the Lutheran doctrinal system," was able to claim on behalf of the General Synod: "The General Synod's basis is thus wisely and lovingly adapted to unite *all real Lutherans*."[81] Likewise, "On the common Confession of Augsburg all Lutherans agree." But what about substance, actual points of doctrine? Valentine replied:

> It is manifestly not necessary, therefore, nor even consistent, in this connection, to attempt to specify and set forth the precise Lutheran teaching of the General Synod, on the various topics in controversy in our Church; since it is of the very essence of its confessional position and claim that the Augsburg Confession is itself the statement of what it holds, and that in the differences of understanding and explana-

tion that have always marked, the interpretation of some of its statements, undisturbed liberty shall be enjoyed.[82]

Here we have the whole essence of the modern confessions-as-rabbit's-foot approach. If only one holds on to the Confessions outwardly, one is free to interpret them, like the Masonic "landmarks," more or less as one pleases. The similarity between Valentine's General Synod and the modern ULCA-LCA is striking: "The ULCA declared in 1934 that in its common subscription to the historic Lutheran confessions 'we already possess a firm basis on which to unite in one Lutheran Church in America,' i.e. no further doctrinal tests need be demanded of one another."[83] Here "Confessional subscription" has become a ceremonial formality which need not disturb the actual doctrine and practice in churches, publications, and seminaries.

The distance, in principle, between the Synodical Conference and the General Council was small compared to the distance which separated both from the General Synod. In principle both conservative bodies stood on the same Confessional ground, but the Missouri camp was more rigorous in the area of practical application. Tietjen admits that Sihler's Synodical Conference theses on fellowship made "the Augsburg Confession the essential requirement for Lutheran union."[84] In fact, Sihler had put it even more strongly: The Augsburg Confession is *"the sole external bond of fellowship"* among Lutherans.[85] But because Sihler insisted also on everything which must necessarily follow from an acceptance of the Augsburg Confession in good faith, Tietjen concludes that Sihler "requires something more for church union than acceptance of the Augsburg Confession"![86] Why, then, are not the General Council's "Fundamental Principles of Faith and Church Polity" considered "something more"? These very "Principles," moreover, had explicitly acknowledged also whatever is "derived by just and necessary inference" from the *whole written Word of God*, so that the church's liberty "concerns those things only which are left free by the letter and spirit of God's Word."[87]

Present-day reference works produced by Lutheran World Federation circles are, therefore, basically correct when they describe the General Council's position as "rigorous," though administered "flexibly,"[88] or state that "the Council's tests of Lutheranism were similar to those of the immigrant synods . . . Unanimous interpretation of doctrine was the standard of fellowship. In practice, however, the Council seldom challenged the doctrinal position of synods that applied for membership. Willingness to accept the *Fundamental Principles* was regarded as adequate proof of correct doctrine."[89]

With the benefit of a century's worth of hindsight, it seems indeed a great pity that those two Lutheran stalwarts, C. F. W. Walther and Charles Porterfield Krauth, the great theological leader of the General Council, were unable to join forces. Walther and F. Pieper both paid high tribute to Krauth,[90] especially since he had come to his Confessional convictions after having originally been a defender of the loose "American Lutheranism." It pained Krauth deeply to see himself misunderstood in the Missouri Synod. He wrote to a friend:

> One of the most serious obstacles in the way of the advance of the truth, is the harshness of the men of the Synodical Conference, towards those who have not been able to see entirely with them.. .. While you are doing good by standing up in the General Council for the truth, do good for the General Council by helping the Missouri Synod to look with justice and kindness upon it, for they cruely misunderstand its real spirit.[91]

Did Missouri's attitude finally drive the General Council back into the arms of the General Synod in 1918? Or had Missouri simply been more realistic than Krauth was willing to admit? At any rate, this noble and generous man did not hesitate to defend the much maligned Missouri Synod:

> I have been saddened beyond expression by the bitterness displayed towards the Missourians. So far as they have helped us to see the great principles involved in this discussion, they have been our benefactors, and although I know they have misunderstood some of us, that was perhaps inevitable. They are men of God, and their work has been of inestimable value.[92]

Of course, Missourians made their share of mistakes. But the driving force was the passionate zeal to safeguard the life-giving treasure of Scriptures and Confessions against erosion by the trickery or fickleness of men. Mundinger, despite an occasional flair for iconoclasm,[93] says of the founders of the Missouri Synod: "Not since the sixteenth century, and never on American soil, had a body of men so completely and so sincerely subscribed to the Unaltered Augsburg Confession and its Apology, the Smalcald Articles, the Catechisms of Luther, and the Formula of Concord."[94] They were determined "that the Confessional Writings of the Lutheran Church should not merely be mentioned incidentally and then forgotten, but that they should be a power that would effectively give shape to the constitution and direction to all ways of doing things."

To describe such an attitude as going "beyond the Lutheran Confessions" is more than historically fallacious. It is also theologically mischievous; for it sacrifices, under the spell of grandiose ecumenical visions of pan-Lutheran union, the very gift which can alone create and sustain genuine Lutheran and Christian unity.

B. THE BIBLICAL PRINCIPLE

1. The Bible in the Confessions

Nothing could be more fatuous than the widespread illusion that Lutherans need not worry about the historical-critical at tacks on the Bible's authority because, after all, there are always the Confessions with which to keep the critical wolves at bay. The Confessions rest absolutely on the authority of the Scriptures, and once the foundation is gone nothing can save the superstructure. The great German theologian Werner Elert, was badly mistaken when he imagined that the doctrine of the Holy Trinity needed not only Scripture but "also the ancient church as source"![100] Luther insisted that "the Christian church has no power to establish any articles of faith, has never established one, and will nevermore do so."[101] Again, "Let them scream themselves into a frenzy, crying 'Church, Church!'—without God's Word it is nothing!"[102] The Lutheran Church has solemnly and officially taken her stand with the great Reformer: "the Word of God shall establish articles of faith and no one else, not even an angel."[103] Creeds and Confessions have authority for only one reason: "not because this confession was prepared by our theologians but because it is taken from the Word of God and solidly and well grounded therein."[104]

The Heidelberg theologian, Peter Brunner, has put it well: "Whenever Scriptural authority is lost, the *Confessio* of the church is replaced by the heresies of the schools."[105] He continues:

> In the last 250 years, the Lutheran Church has not been able to overcome the theological crises through which it has had to pass. It is still largely unaware of the depth of its plight. All talk of confessional allegiance is meaningless, if Holy Scripture is lost as the concrete judge over all proclamation and teaching. The confession presupposes Scripture, and Scripture not as an historically given phenomenon, but as a speaking authority! This presupposition has become problematic for many pastors, theologians, and non-theologians. For this reason, confessional loyalty has also be-

come problematic.

"If there was one point of universal agreement" among all parties in Reformation times, wrote A. C. Piepkorn, "it was the authority, the inspiration, and the inerrancy of the Sacred Scriptures. It is not surprising therefore that we do not have an explicit article on the Sacred Scriptures in the Lutheran Symbols."[106] The *Apology*, for instance, refers as a matter of course to "the clear Scripture of the Holy Spirit."[107]

It has been pointed out repeatedly that the terms "Scripture" and "Word of God" are used interchangeably in the Lutheran Confessions.[108] Yet Missouri "moderates" have followed Heidelberg Professor Edmund Schlink's fallacy "that the Gospel is the norm in Scripture and Scripture is the norm for the sake of the Gospel."[109] On this basis Paul Bretscher attempts a bold piece of logical gymnastics. He admits, on the one hand, that the term "Word of God" is used in the sense of "Bible" in the Lutheran Confessions. This is the "inspiration meaning" of the term and is "quite evident as a heritage of medieval piety" in the Confessions.[110] But, on the other hand, he claims that in the Small Catechism "God's Word means essentially the Gospel," not Holy Scripture as such.[111] Yet Luther would hardly have meant something else by "Word of God" in the Catechism than in the Smalcald Articles, where it clearly means the Bible. In the Small Catechism itself, moreover, the questions "which is that word of God?" "which are these words and promises of God?" and "where is that written?" obviously amount to the same thing. Says Fagerberg: "The conclusive thing for Luther was not that the Word possessed a certain quality—e.g., that it could be described as Gospel—but that it is found to be a clear, divine statement in the Bible."[112]

While it is true that the word "inerrancy" is not used in the Confessions,[113] the thing itself is clearly taken for granted, for example, in the Large Catechism: "My neighbour and I—in short, all men—may err and deceive, but God's Word cannot err." The Latin is even more emphatic: "*nec errare nec fallere potest*—can neither err nor deceive."[114] God's Word here can only mean the Bible, not selected snatches from it, such as whatever deals with baptism or other "chief parts"!

The fundamental premise of the Confessions is the *absolute distinction* "between divine and human writings," which requires that the Word of God is and should remain the sole rule and norm of all doctrine, and that no human being's writings dare be put on a par with it, but that everything must be subjected to it."[115] The Latin text makes it quite clear what is meant by "Word of God": the "sacred letters," in other words, Scripture. To wipe out this absolute difference between the divine Scriptures and all other writings, and to demote the Bible from sole and sovereign judge to a mere witness or, worse yet, a defendant subject to human criticism, is to attack the Reformation's *sola scriptura* (Scripture alone) principle. Such an approach cannot truthfully claim to be grounded in the Lutheran Confessions. There is more intellectual honesty in outright denial than in flattering cant and humbug. The noted liberal Lutheran Encyclopaedist Vergilius Ferm, for instance, felt quite free to depart from the Lutheran Confessions, but at least did not pretend otherwise:

> A literally infallible Bible, an assumption implied throughout the Lutheran symbols, verbally inspired, is a view that has passed by the board for good. The authority of the Sacred Writings is no longer found in "the letter" and sustained by some artifical theory of divine in spiration, but in the appeal of its spiritual content.[116]

2. Rationalism, Historical Criticism, and Missouri

Whereas in Prussia the main problem for the Lutherans was the Union, in Saxony it was Rationalism. Unlike the popular Prussian ruler, the king of Saxony, being a Roman Catholic, had to cope with the distrust of his subjects and was anxious to avoid anything that might look like a violation of the established (Lutheran) church's independence. But from the universities, where the clergy were trained, there spread upon the church a fearful mania of self-destruction—rationalistic unbelief. Since man had now "come of age," the external authority of divine revelation seemed embarrassing, if not insulting to his new dignity. Emancipated common sense was considered a fitting and sufficient guide also in matters of religion. The European intelligentsia, their heads turned by flattering visions of human grandeur and progress, were chafing to break free[117] from the hated authority of the Lord and of His Anointed: "Let us free ourselves from Their rule, let us throw off Their control" (Psalm 2:3)! In an age of liberty, equality, and fraternity, it was unthinkable that one ancient

Book, the Bible, should retain any special privileges. Henceforth it was to be treated exactly like all other ancient documents. Stripped of its special, infallible status, the Bible was now treated as just another ordinary citizen in the great republic of letters, all subject to the same laws and to the supreme court of critical scholarship. This and nothing else is the inner essence of the historical-critical method[118] which originated at that time and was perfected in the nineteenth century.

These secular-rationalistic origins of historical criticism are not really in dispute. Edgar Krentz, probably the chief theoretician of historical criticism at "Seminex," admits: "Historical method is the child of the Enlightenment."[119] Again, "The Scriptures were, so to speak, secularised. The biblical books became historical documents to be studied and questioned like any other ancient sources. The Bible was no longer the criterion for the writing of history; rather history had become the criterion for understanding the Bible. . . . The history it reported was no longer assumed to be everywhere correct. The Bible stood before criticism as defendant before judge."[120] George Eldon Ladd puts it even more plainly: "It has also become clear that the historical-critical method itself did not emerge as the result of open-minded, neutral, objective study of the Bible, but was motivated by rationalistic presuppositions which had no room for the biblical claim to revelation and inspiration."[121] Interesting is the observation of the Roman Catholic scholar Norbert Lohfink that the religious background of the rising historical criticism involved a "cultural field of (Roman) Catholics, Calvinists, and Jews, whilst the Lutherans at that time stood aside almost totally, being encased in the rigid theory of verbal inspiration"![122]

It goes without saying that the founders of the Missouri Synod rejected Rationalism and its Bible-criticism, root and branches. This, moreover, was the attitude not only of the Missouri Synod, but of all the Confessional Lutheran bodies. President Schmauk of the General Council said in his official report on the occasion of the Council's fortieth anniversary:

> Since it has been asserted that the General Council is weakening in the doctrine of the Scriptures, under the influence of the Higher Criticism, and since these principles are doing so much in the American churches to disintegrate faith in the letter and the spirit of the Scriptures, I recommend that we reaffirm our position and declare that the

> General Council holds now as ever to the old teaching of the fathers, that the Holy Scriptures are inerrant in *letter, fact, and doctrine*...

We affirm that we have not given way by a hair's breadth to the rationalism, or the rationalising spirit, of the Higher Criticism; nor will we allow errant human reason to be the judge of what is and what is not God's Word in the Scriptures. Not only the revelation and its record, but the history and its record, the whole Scripture, in spirit and letter, is inspired.[123]

American Lutheranism incidentally had been infected with "brazen rationalism" already in the early 1800's, in the person of Dr. F. H. Quitman and other leading spirits of the New York Ministerium.[124] Quitman was a disciple of J. S. Semler himself, "the father of historical-critical theology."[125]

Since, however, it is often argued or implied[126] that historical criticism was more wild-eyed and "extreme" in the last century than now, and that therefore early Missouri's condemnations of critical scholarship do not apply to today's "milder" variety, we need to look at the situation more closely.

Most of the European theologians involved in the Confessional Awakening did not return completely to the old Lutheran doctrine of the Bible's absolute authority and inerrancy. They tried to compromise or "mediate" between the old doctrine, and the prevailing historical-critical approach. "Verbal inspiration was given up in the delusion that in this way one could gain the upper hand over the newer criticism."[127] So wrote the great Wisconsin Synod theologian, A. Hoenecke, whose magnificent dogmatics is in important respects superior to F. Pieper's.

What is so significant is that the main targets of Missouri's opposition to historical criticism were not the outright liberals but those would-be conservatives with their divided, half-believing and half-critical, attitude to Holy Scripture. Pieper in his dogmatics pillories the "conservative" Erlangen theologian, J. C. K. von Hofmann, the "father" of modern ego-theology among Lutherans, even more often than the "grandfather," Schleiermacher! It is no accident that von Hofmann, who replaced both inspiration and the atonement with a curious "Law/Gospel" brew of his own, is today being rediscovered by anti-traditional Lutherans in America.[128] But, of course, Hofmann was not the only one. To appreciate the real flavor of that whole discussion, so bafflingly similar to that of our own time, let us sample some judgments from Walther's old *Lehre und Wehre*, Synod's theological journal at the time. The German theologian Kahnis had written: "Protestantism stands and falls with the principle of the sole authority of Scripture. But this principle is independent of the doctrine of inspiration of the old dogmatics. To embrace it again as it was can be done only with a hardening against the truth." To this Walther replied in 1855, in the very first volume of *Lehre und Wehre*:

> We must confess, when we read these words, we were right heartily frightened by them. Who can go along with a new theology which introduces itself as the further development of the old Lutheran theology, and then deviates from the doctrinal model of our old theology precisely in the doctrine of the principle of theology, of Holy Scripture, viz., of the *ratio formalis scripturae*, of that which makes Holy Scripture what it is?[129]

In 1858 Walther wrote:

> For if the Bible is God's Word, then all affirmations contained in it are decisions of the high divine Majesty itself. But is it not frightful to declare undecided what the great God has decided? When the great God has spoken, to grant liberty to man to contradict him? . . .
>
> He who imagines that he finds in the Holy Scripture even only one error, believes not in Scripture, but in himself; for even if he accepted everything else as truth, he would believe it not because Scripture says so, but because it agrees with his reason or with his heart. "Dear fellow," writes Luther, "God's Word is God's Word, and won't tolerate much doctoring . . . Look, the circumcision of Abraham is now an old, dead thing, and is now neither necessary nor useful; still, if I were to say: God did not command it at that time, then nothing would help me, even if I believed the Gospel."[130]

In 1885 Luthardt had reported, with approval, the even more conservative Theodosius Harnack's attempt to mediate in a battle about inspiration. Walther quoted Luthardt at length, and then called the whole enterprise a *"ghastly fraud"*:

> "Th. Harnack now takes up the false, un-Lutheran*[!]* attitude to Holy Scripture, according to which it, rather than above all Christ, is made the foundation and cornerstone of faith, and revelation itself. [Scripture] is the witness and the

> crowning conclusion of the history of the mighty acts of God, and as such the norm of the church's proclamation . . . Hence also the inerrancy of Holy Scripture is taken as one which must be understood and measured according to the real purpose of Scripture.'scripture, I say with Volek, simply is something better than a book without errors'; so that apart from the revelation of salvation, the possibility of erroneous notions of those times and the like must be assumed from the outset . . ."So far Luthardt.
>
> Until recently the modern-believing theologians treated their doctrine of Holy Scripture, which overturns the foundation of the whole Christian religion, like a secret doctrine for theologians . . . Only last year did it please members of the theol. faculty at Dorpat to step before common Christians with this their new wisdom . . . No doubt the gentlemen thought that by now even non-theologians might have progressed far enough to be able to endure an admittedly somewhat glaring light like the idea that Scripture is full of errors . . .
>
> The most horrifying aspect of the matter, by the way, is the fact that the new prophets want to make the Lutheran Christian people believe that the doctrine that the Scriptures of the prophets, apostles, and evangelists are really inspired by the Holy Spirit according to content and form, and therefore free from all erroneous material—is not the Lutheran but the "pietistic-Reformed" doctrine! That is a perfectly ghastly fraud which is being perpetrated on the Lutheran Christian people.[131]

A year before his death Walther paraphrased Luther's warning against Zwingli's clever device for manipulating Scripture, and applied this warning to the new "conservative" view of the Bible:

> We must apply this to the so-called "divine human character of Scripture" as that term is used by the modern-conservative theology: Beware, beware, I say, of this "divine-human Scripture"! It is a devil's mask; for at last it manufactures such a Bible after which I certainly would not care to be a Bible Christian, namely, that the Bible should henceforth be no more than any other good book, a book which I would have to read with constant sharp discrimination in order not to be led into error. For if I believe this,

> that the Bible contains also errors, it is to me no longer a touchstone but itself stands in need of one. In a word, it is unspeakable what the devil seeks by this "divine-human Scripture."[132]

Elsewhere Walther had written:

> It is absolutely necessary that we maintain the doctrine of inspiration as taught by our orthodox dogmaticians. If the possibility that Scripture contained the least error were admitted, it would become the business of *man* to sift the truth from the error. That places man *over Scripture*, and Scripture is *no longer* the source and norm of doctrine. Human reason is made the *norma* of truth, and Scripture is degraded to the position of a *norma normata*. The least deviation from the old inspiration doctrine introduces a rationalistic germ into theology and infects the whole body of doctrine.[133]

In the light of such statements it is perfectly clear why it had to seem to the latter-day "moderates" of Missouri that Walther's doctrine of the Word "was not wholly Christocentric but tended toward biblicism"![134] At the time, however, Walther's doctrine was the common stand not only of Missouri Synod, but of the whole Synodical Conference.[135] Zoeckler's *Handbook of Theological Sciences* lists as lonely defenders of the old inspiration doctrine Kohlbruegge, Gaussen, Kuyper, and "among the Lutherans, Walther in St. Louis, and with him the Missouri Synod."[136] Nor was there any deviation from this position under Walther's successor, Francis Pieper. Most illuminating in view of today's situation, is Pieper's treatment in *Lehre und Wehre*, four years after Walther's death, of an incident in Kiel, Germany. The general superintendent for Holstein, Dr. Ruperti, had co-signed an invitation to a pastoral conference at which, without Ruperti's previous knowledge, a certain Dean Kier submitted for discussion some controversial theses about Scripture. The title is most revealing: "Holy Scripture remains God's Word for the Christian even when he has had to give up the doctrine of inspiration." While paying lip-service to "the Word," "revelation," and "the Lord Jesus Christ (Who) is our refuge," Kier argued that the Bible was a human book, "marked also by the defects and mistakes which attach to all human works." This, moreover, he claimed, had been "proved, not by the attacks of unbelief against God's Word, but by the historical-critical science about the Bible, which has been produced by Protestantism and is totally indispensable to it." Horrified, Dr. Ruperti resigned his position and membership in the conference, because, as he put it, "the basis on which my Christian conviction and my official position rest is totally different from the basis of a conference at which such theses are debatable." Pieper thoroughly approved this confession of word as well as deed, underscoring particularly Ruperti's stand that "theses like Kier's are simply not 'debatable' at a Lutheran conference, and among Lutherans generally."[137]

This, then, was the Missouri Synod's unanimous understanding of the Biblical Principle from the beginning. Here lies the secret of the Missouri Synod's spiritual strength, despite the sins and frailties which attach to all historical institutions. This became very clear during the Missouri-Buffalo Colloquy (doctrinal conference) in 1866 to a leader of the Buffalo Synod, who was destined to become Missouri's first major historian. Recalling years later the impact of that meeting, which had become such a blessing to him personally, Pastor Hochstetter wrote: "Only there it became quite clear to me that the strength of the Missouri teachers rests not simply in their attachment to the Symbols, but rather in the *fear of God's Word!* Is. 66:2."[138] This utter awe before the written Word of the Almighty can and must confound mere sociological predictions and historical trends. The remnants and memories of this deeply ingrained attitude were still strong enough a century later to surprise historians with a "rather unique event in American church life."[139] Whilst in other denominations liberal takeovers have succeeded and conservatives have been compelled to found new institutions, in Missouri's case the reverse took place. Old Dr. Walther would not have been surprised. At the foundation-stone laying in 1882 for the "new" Concordia Seminary, named after the *Book of Concord*, he had pronounced this solemn imprecation: "Let that teacher's mouth which would ever dare to speak in our new Concordia against Christ's free grace and against His alone-true Word, at once be silenced forever, stricken by God!"[140]

3. Luther In Fact And Fiction

In Walther's day it was already becoming the fashion to hold that the strict view of absolute biblical authority and inerrancy goes back not to Luther, but to the "scholastic dogmaticians" of the seventeenth century, who borrowed the idea from Calvin and hardened it into a rigid system. As we have seen, Walther called this a "ghastly fraud" being perpetrated on Lutheran Christians. Today's "moderate" literature seems quite under the spell of this "ghastly fraud." A cautious but unmistakable case in point is Edgar Krentz' treatment in his apology for the historical-critical method.[141] He states rightly that Calvin "did not follow Luther's christological approach," but suggests wrongly that Luther did not, like Calvin, "derive the Bible's authority from the theologoumenon that God himself is the speaker in the Bible." This is quite false. It was precisely Luther's doctrine, not a mere theologoumenon (private opinion) that God is the author of Scripture, which is authoritative for that very reason. Luther wrote: "I beg and faithfully warn every pious Christian not to take offence at the simplicity of the language and the stories that will often meet him there. He should not doubt that, however simple they may seem, *these are the very words, works, judgments, and narrations* of the high divine Majesty, Might, and Wisdom for this is Scripture, which makes all wise men fools . . ."[142] And again, "When you hear people of this stamp, who are so blinded and hardened as to deny that what Christ and the Apostles spoke is God's Word, or doubt it, then be silent, speak no more with them, and let them go."[143] If anything, it was Calvin, not Luther, who took a looser view of the authority of the sacred text. In his commentary on St. John's Gospel, for instance, Calvin did not hesitate to say that the Evangelists "neglect" a figure of speech in Psalm 22, and therefore "depart from the native sense!"[144]

Walther and Pieper already were thoroughly familiar with the kind of Luther-scholarship which, following von Hofmann's lead, tried to pit Luther against the Lutheran Church on doctrines like inspiration, the atonement, and others. They also understood, as many today do not, that the new, re-interpreted Luther was being opposed not only to "later Orthodoxy," but to the Formula of Concord,[145] and thus to the Lutheran Confessions themselves. Pieper devotes a whole chapter of his dogmatics to "Luther and the Inspiration of Holy Scripture." Having refuted a number of scholarly fallacies, Pieper concludes that for some modern Luther-reinterpreters "their wish to have Luther as their protector was stronger than their sense of historical truth."

What was the basic point at issue? Then as now the question

was whether Luther accepted Scripture as inspired and inerrant totally, or only in some limited sense, which would allow for historical, geographical, and other mistakes and contradictions in the inspired text. Then as now people snatched up some vivid phrases, like "what urges Christ," or "hay and stubble," or "urging Christ against Scripture," tore these phrases out of their context, and then used them to "prove" Luther's liberal attitude to Scripture.

Eugene Klug has recently, in his valuable doctoral study, *From Luther to Chemnitz*, gone over this ground very carefully. He shows that Luther regularly says of Scripture that it "never errs," "has never erred," is "alone inerrant," is the "absolutely infallible truth," "cannot err," "cannot lie," and that "it is impossible for Scripture to contradict itself."[146] Nor are these statements limited to "theological" or "Gospel" themes in Scripture. They apply to Scripture as such, so that Luther regards himself duty-bound to submit his mind, whatever the intellectual difficulties, to what the Bible teaches about waters above the firmament, Eve's creation from Adam's rib, the chronology of the world, and the like. Interesting is Paul Althaus' admission that Luther basically accepted the Bible as an essentially infallible book, inspired in its entire content by the Holy Spirit. It is therefore "the word of God", not only when it speaks to us in law and gospel and thereby convicts our heart and conscience but also—and this is a matter of principle—in everything else that it says . . . Here is the point at which the clarity of Luther's own Reformation insight reached its limit. For it was at this point that Luther himself, in spite of everything, prepared the way for seventeenth century orthodoxy . . . Theology has had plenty of trouble in the past—and in many places still has—trying to repair this damage by distinguishing between the "Word of God" in the true sense and a false biblicism.[147]

Another splendid study is A. Skevington Wood's *Captive To The Word* (published by Paternoster Press in 1969). Wood shows that Luther's view of the Bible is shaped not by abstract notions of inspiration but by the great "model" of the Incarnation: "And just as it is with Christ in the world, as He is viewed and dealt with, so it is also with the written Word of God. It is a worm and no book, compared with other books."[148] But if the Incarnation is the model for inspiration, then the full humanity of the Bible implies error no more than Christ's humanity implies sin or error. On the contrary, Luther's incarnational-sacramental understanding of Scriptures honours God's Word precisely in its humblest outward details. The mystery of the Bible is holy ground; criticism is sacrilege. This approach is the very opposite of the modern Zwinglian-Barthian flight from the concrete text to a "Word" or "meaning" above, beyond, and behind it![149]

It is just at this point that Jaroslav Pelikan's companion volume to the great new American edition of *Luther's Works* fails, despite illuminating insights, to do justice to Luther's actual position. Chapter three of this work spares no effort to create the impression that one must carefully distinguish in Luther between "Scripture" and "word of God,"[150] when the opposite is, in fact, the case. Dr. H. Hamann, Sr., concluded, in a detailed review of this book:

> Dr. Pelikan is, to say it roundly, too greatly influenced by certain modern Luther scholars to be entirely reliable. For he has adopted the literary vice of some *Lutherforscher* who manage to walk, with eyes tightly closed, past dozens and hundreds of the clearest possible pronouncements of Luther in order to pitch and pounce upon some doubtful passage, on the strength of which they attempt to foist upon the Reformer teachings quite different from, and perhaps utterly opposed to, those, which he actually professed and defended.[151]

Pelikan does not,[152] however, hold to the persistent fallacy that Luther's critical comments about books like James prove that Luther had a loose and liberal attitude to Biblical inspiration and authority. Although refuted long ago by Walther, Hoenecke, Pieper and others,[153] this old error continues to be served up anew either quite crassly[154] or more subtly.[155] The fact is that Luther simply renewed the old distinction, never forgotten in the church, between those books which had always been "unanimously confessed" (*homologoumena*) as genuine New Testament writings, and others, whose apostolic genuineness and therefore authority had been "spoken against" (*antilegomena*). Among these "spoken against" books were especially the four which Luther placed at the very end of his Bible-translation: Hebrews, James, Jude, and Revelation. On the other hand, there is no doubt whatever about the four Gospels, Acts, all the Letters of St. Paul, First Peter, and First John. All Christian doctrine rests on these undoubted books. The others must not be interpreted in a sense contrary to the genuine and certain Scripture.

Since the doubts about the genuine apostolic authorship of books like James and Revelation go back to the earliest witnesses, this historical fact cannot be changed by anybody's decrees later on. From the Roman Catholic point of view, of course, it is quite logical for the church, located essentially *above* Scripture, to make decrees about what is and what is not Scripture, regardless of historical facts. It is not surprising, therefore, that the Council of Trent issued an official list of Biblical books, including the "apocrypha," like Maccabees, of which the *Jerusalem Bible* says: "The two books of Maccabees were not in the Jewish Canon of scripture, but their inspiration has been recognised by the Church (they are 'deutero-canonical' books)." More surprising is the fact that Calvinistic confessions, like the Westminster Confession, contain official lists of inspired, Biblical books. The Lutheran Church has no such official list. This means not that there is any doubt about the unquestioned books recognised by all, but that no one today can undo or reverse the mixed, inconclusive testimony of Christian antiquity to the doubted, "secondary" books. The important point is that no Christian doctrine depends on the latter writings. If the Lutheran Church, convinced of the full, Biblical Gospel of Christ, leaves undecided, not the canon as such, but a small margin of it on which no doctrine depends, this is due not to indifference or oversight but to profound respect for the Word of God. As the humble handmaid of Christ, the church cannot presume to tyrannize free Christian consciences by wiping out the distinction between what certainly is God's Word and what might not be, and then decreeing and demanding (on whose authority?) equal submission to the certain and to the doubtful alike.

One thing ought to be abundantly clear: what Luther says about books which he does not consider genuine and inspired may not be construed as if he were speaking about books which he regarded as inspired. To soften or discount Luther's oft repeated strict inspiration doctrine, because of his opinions about books which he regarded as uninspired, is neither logical nor honest. It is like arguing that a person has a low opinion of money because he once burnt a ten-dollar bill which he considered counterfeit. The nature of inspiration is one thing; the question of whether a particular book is inspired is another. The problem which Luther raised about James was not "Is this part of the inspired Bible false?" but rather "Is this a part of the inspired Bible?"

It is a mark of the theological greatness of Missouri's founding fathers that they did not deny or ignore this Lutheran insight even though the obsession of the nineteenth century with historical criticism compelled them to defend the Bible's authority in the strongest terms. Luther's prefaces to the various books of the Bible, today naively treated as shocking discoveries disproving the Missouri Synod's strict doctrine of inspiration,[156] were, in fact, officially printed by the Missouri Synod in its old German days at least three times: first as part of the "Altenburg Bible" (starting in 1888), then in volume 14 of the great St. Louis edition of *Luther's Works* (1898), and thirdly as a separate reprint in 1908. Indeed, Synod's official organ, the *Lutheraner*, had already in 1856 published a series of articles by Pastor Roebbelen about the book of Revelation. Roebbelen, following Luther's judgment, did not regard Revelation as apostolic or equal to the letters of St. Paul and other canonical books. This infuriated millennialists like Pastor Schieferdecker, who stirred up a great uproar in his parish, claiming that Synod's official organ had rejected a book of the Bible.[157] Walther, while disagreeing with Roebbelen's judgment, strongly defended Roebbelen's position against the charge of heresy.[158] On this point too Missouri followed Luther, not the later theologians.

It goes without saying that Luther must, now as then, be rescued from the clutches of his liberal or "trendy" misinterpreters. What may not be so obvious to conservative Lutherans is that they cannot simply be satisfied with Reformed-fundamentalistic "cover-to-cover" slogans, which ignore the organic structure and content of Scripture so clearly recognized by Luther. "Is it possible for a Bible-believing person to deny that Holy Baptism is the washing of regeneration and the bread which we bless in the Lord's Supper the Body of Christ? What kind of faith in the Bible is it that can deny these things?" So asked Sasse in 1951, alarmed at the influence of the Reformed environment on American Lutheranism, particularly the Missouri Synod. Among other things he added: "Even the theologians scarcely have any longer a conception of a Luther Bible with the Apocrypha—something incomprehensible for fundamentalists—with the prefaces of Luther and with a text which was not yet cut up into verses as is the text in our Bibles, in which the letter to the Hebrews no longer appears to be a unified composition but a collection of three hundred Bible passages."[159]

FOREGROUND

III. THE COUNTER-CONFESSIONAL (ECUMENICAL) ATTACK

1. Sclerosis: Prelude to Hemorrhage

Movements solidify into institutions, and institutional arteries harden. Church history shows that the historical forms which hide the mystery of the church in this world are not exempt from this process. Yet Christianity rises miraculously, like the fabled phoenix, from its ashes. In the long term, if the world lasts, Missouri is as doomed as Jerusalem, Constantinople, Rome, Moscow, or Wittenberg; but wherever men celebrate the gift of eternal life in the Divine Son (I John 5:11), there even ashes are but a prelude to resurrection.

It was not to be expected that in the course of a century of embattled orthodoxy nothing but exquisite flowers would grow in Missouri's garden. Truth is the most dangerous as well as the most blessed commodity on earth. To whom much is given from him shall much be required. And where God sows His good wheat there the devil spitefully sows all the more weeds. A brief look at a few such unlovely plants will suffice to show why evangelical churchmen felt that the atmosphere had become unbearably oppressive. Concerned pastors, professors, and synodical officials met for so-called "Round Table" discussions in Chicago in 1926, 1937, 1940, and 1941 to consider the problems of an ingrown legalism and traditionalism.[160] Theodore Graebner, seminary professor, *Lutheran Witness* editor, and one of the guiding lights of the movement, reports:'since the meetings of 1926, '37, '40 and '41 had been utterly ineffective, the 1945 round table presented its findings to our clergy."[161] This was the famous "A Statement," consisting of twelve theses with corresponding rejections, and known as the "Chicago Statement" or the "Statement of the Forty-Four," the latter because of the number of the original signers.

Graebner himself, in one of the supporting essays, gives a

number of examples to illustrate the concerns behind "A Statement":[162]

> ... a brother remarked: "It is absurd to speak about the doctrinal unity of the Missouri Synod: we have two contradictory attitudes on the question of church fairs and bazaars!" This brother believes that a division is made in the body of Christ, when its members are not agreed on the question whether bazaars should be made a source of income to the congregation. I call this separatism.
>
> Titus 3:10 (A man that is an heretic after the first and second admonition reject) was urged as a "stern command" of God against our meeting in committee with the American Lutheran Church. The warning was added: "God is not mocked."
>
> These long years we have had with us the judging of brethren because they depart from *official exegesis*. I could recite examples from the first year of my ministry (when I was listed as unsound because I held that John had some doubts of his own when he sent his disciples to Christ) until this month, when in public conference it is stated without rebuke that the interpretation of Romans 16:17 ff. is a matter on which the unity of the Church depends. (Depart from Stoeckhardt and you have departed from orthodoxy.)
>
> The late Dr. A. L. Graebner was held to be "not quite safe," indeed "dangerously liberal," because he promoted our English work.
>
> ... when those publicly attacked plead to be given the opportunity to settle the matter in private conference, they have been turned down with a curt, "I will not meet you"—for which we have much documentary evidence.
>
> Grossly insulting language is regarded as an overwrought expression of an attitude rather to be commended—a high regard for the truth. It is rare to hear such offenses reproved as violations of the law of love and as expressions of legalistic arrogance. We should do public penance for the spirit which has during the past thirty years invaded our discussions. We have not had theological controversies but caricatures of such.

Foreign missionaries had, if anything, even more occasion to complain of impossible rigidities. E. L. Arndt, Missouri's remarkable missionary in China, shared with his colleagues at a 1926 conference his deep concerns about unevangelical practices. Among many other points, Arndt protested against the assumption "that every missionary not a Missourian is an arch deceiver, hardened in heresy," so that even in staying overnight with such people one must "refuse to join with them even in the hearing of the Word of God and in prayer, even though it is distinctly understood that this means no church-communion and even though any wrong word or deed can easily be corrected."[163] It was on this same issue that another gifted Missouri missionary, Brux of India, became the victim of official over-reactions.[164]

One incident which, no doubt, helped to confirm ill feelings between Missouri's Eastern and Midwestern elements occurred in connection with the 1938 funeral of Pastor Paul Lindemann, editor of the *American Lutheran*. Top synodical and district leaders were present and were to give short addresses after the funeral service itself. But then the prominent ALC theologian Dr. M. Reu arrived, a friend of the family, and was asked to speak also. The Missouri dignitaries opposed this as "unionism," debating the issue in the family home for two hours before the funeral. The result was that no one gave a special address![165]

Another danger-signal was a certain theological stagnation despite the valiant efforts of the "Theological Observer" section of the *Concordia Theological Monthly* to keep readers abreast of European theology. Professor Martin Scharlemann has written in connection with the recent death of Dr. Hermann Sasse:

> We came across this volume [Sasse's *Here We Stand*] rather accidentally just beyond the middle of the thirties while doing graduate work at Washington University. This was during the barren period in our own synodical history when the seminary library in Saint Louis had cut itself off from purchasing European books-a time that lasted from 1917 until 1948, when our Synod's Committee for Scholarly Research sent Dr. Theodore Graebner to Europe with eight thousand dollars to start buying some books for our library with a view of filling up as much of this gap as possible! At the time when we came across this volume, it should be added, no professor at Concordia Seminary had ever heard of Hermann Sasse![166]

Graebner said long ago that a short-sighted legalism would "breed radicalism, liberalism, strife, and division."[167] He was right.

2. The Collapse of Confessional Concepts of Church and Fellowship

Commenting on Missouri's developing crisis already in 1951, Sasse honoured the intention "to repent for the mistakes of the past," but noted that the whole approach of the "44" was purely *ethical*, not *dogmatical*.[168] What was needed was a thorough re-appropriation of the Biblical and Confessional *doctrine* of the church, not merely practical guidelines for this or that situation. Perhaps a kind of Biblicistic isolation of Romans 16:17-18 and of the question of "prayer fellowship" in the "Statement of the 44"[169] was partly to blame for the long and furious but quite hopeless battle which now ensued on those issues, and finally resulted in the break-up of the Synodical Conference. The impossible choice seemed to be: either total fellowship with all Lutherans and perhaps beyond, or else no joint prayer with anybody outside the Synodical Conference! By the time affiliated overseas theologians were asked for help—their first formal gathering or "conclave" took place in Oakland, California, in 1959—it was really too late. Yet their thirteen theses on "Fellowship In Its Necessary Context of the Doctrine of the Church"[170] are probably the best formulation of the issues to arise out of this controversy, and are therefore presented in their entirety in an appendix of the present work.

While the issue at first *appeared* to be merely a difference over the interpretation and application of this or that Bible-text, it is now clear that what was really going on was a radical, revolutionary overturning of the Lutheran doctrine of the church—even though no one at the time intended that! The false development moved in two somewhat contradictory directions at once: on the one hand, the church came to be seen as essentially visible; but, on the other, church-bodies, synods, federations, indeed any formations beyond local congregations, were no longer regarded as being "church" in any legitimate sense at all. Hence the doors were open to the modern Ecumenical Movement with all its pomp and all its works.

The Ecumenical Movement, of course, treats the church as essentially visible. Archbishop Temple of Canterbury had put it like this: "I believe in the holy catholic church—and sincerely regret that it does not at present exist!" Here the oneness of the church is no longer an article of faith—part and parcel of the very existence of the church, Ephesians 4—but an ideal to be realised by patient negotiation, ecclesiastical diplomacy, and compromise! Such a view has no use for the old distinction between the church visible and the church invisible. It was this very distinction—and not merely the Calvinist version of it—which now came to be attacked and rejected in the Missouri Synod.

A recent highly sympathetic study of the "Statement of the 44" reveals some of the background thinking. Valparaiso University president, O. P. Kretzmann, had given an important preparatory paper on the doctrine of the church. The gist of one of his criticisms was that the invisible church had been used "as a dump heap"[171] to avoid outward, visible union. Strangely enough, the man reporting this event does not see that his term "triumphalism," which he has borrowed from Roman Catholic discussions of Vatican II, applies much better to the utopian pipe dream of one visible, united Christendom, than to the humble Lutheran confession of the church as an article of faith. The Ecumenical approach is not content to walk by faith—it must see the Body of Christ. John Tietjen also attacks the visible-invisible distinction discreetly in his published book,[172] more plainly in his unpublished Union Seminary thesis.[173] Lueking is quite right when he makes belief in "the visibility of the church" and rejection of the visible-invisible distinction the characteristic feature of the new, liberal Missouri theology.[174] Only he should not have called that view "evangelical"—for the doctrine of the Gospel, the "evangel," is perceived by the Ecumenical—visible notion of the church as a mean, scholastic impediment to all the desired unity. Lueking's dream "of a day when distressing divisions in Christendom may be healed," with the Missouri Synod "dying as a denomination"[175] —leads instead to the nightmare of an Ecumenical Babylon lacking even the much advertised missionary appeal. Malcolm Muggeridge saw the whole thing much more realistically:

> The Church of Christ has to stagger on under the guidance of those who increasingly sympathize with, when they do not actually countenance, every attack on its doctrines, integrity and traditional practices. By one of our time's larger ironies, ecumenicalism is triumphant just when there is nothing to be ecumenical about; the various religious bodies are likely to find it easy to join together only because, believing little, they correspondingly differ about little. I look forward to the day when an Anglican bishop in full ca-

nonicals will attend a humanist rally on the South Downs, or a Salvation Army band lead a procession of Young Atheists to lay a wreath on Karl Marx's grave in Highgate Cemetery. It cannot be long delayed, if it has not happened already.[176]

Although the main interest of the "44" movement was Lutheran union in America, it was not here that the decisive breakthrough occurred. The first Ecumenical engine to breach Missouri's walls was a most unlikely one: the so-called "EKiD" (Evangelical Church in Germany), a Lutheran-Reformed-Union church-body formed in 1948 out of a post-war emergency council. Professor Sasse, whose conscience now compelled him to renounce his Erlangen University post and his membership in the Lutheran Church of Bavaria, saw clearly that EKiD was simply the extension of the Prussian Union to the whole of Germany. He wrote: "In Eisenach, at the foot of the Wartburg, the Lutheran Church of Germany was buried in 1948. Loehe's dream-vision of the interment of the Lutheran church by its own pastors had become a reality."[177] Incredibly, leading St. Louis seminary theologians could and would not see the point. In 1947 the *Concordia Theological Monthly* (*CTM*) was full of warnings about EKiD developments and defended Sasse.[178] But there is a strange note already in the Foreword to the 1948 *CTM*: "some of the great men of God were considered liberals by many of their contemporaries." By the September issue we have the announcement: "It can now (middle of August) be reported that the Eisenach meeting of the EKiD resulted in a federation, and not in a Church."[179] Sasse, who had been writing in the Wisconsin Synod's journal, is allowed one final say in the 1949 *CTM*—while an editorial note disagrees with his position[180]—and then disappears from the *CTM* until 1959! Behind the scenes things were even worse, as we shall see.

How could seasoned, conservative theologians, men like Graebner, F. E. Mayer, and William Arndt (two of them, by the way, among the original "44"), fall prey to such a tragic, far reaching misjudgment? A large part of the explanation is very likely to be found in the "Bad Boll" meetings which began in 1948.[181] These were large-scale theological conferences at Bad Boll, Germany, sponsored by the Missouri Synod for the purpose of establishing contact with Lutheran pastors and theologians, particularly in the state-supported churches. There is no doubt that Missouri's testimony made a positive impact on many individuals, who spoke with deep gratitude of this experience.[182] It also seems clear that the impact on the Missouri participants was not inconsiderable, and led to an overly optimistic evaluation on their part of the German church scene. It must be remembered that Missouri also had partner, churches in Europe, the "Free Churches," which were not in fellowship with the Ecumenical Lutheran bodies. Representatives of these free churches, who, after all, had a realistic grasp of the local scene, were quite dismayed at some of the positions taken by the Missourians. That dismay is, understandably, barely hinted at in the official reports,[183] but is quite explicit in the correspondence of that time.

Most distressing of all, theologically, was the strange new doctrine of the church propounded by Dr. Theodore Graebner. His starting point was the truism that *congregations* (regular assemblies of Christians around the means of grace administered by a divinely called public ministry) exist by divine command, whereas *synods* and other larger organizations of congregations exist by human right and arrangement. Hence, argued Graebner, only congregations are really churches, but synods are not—as if congregations lose their churchly character when they act together as churches in synods! In his 1949 Bad Boll essay, "Church and Churches," Graebner expressed himself very pointedly:

> The preliminary result of our considerations is that neither Lutheran World Council (sic), nor EKiD, nor VELKD (United Evangelical Lutheran Church of Germany), nor the territorial church of Saxony or of Hannover, nor the Synodical Conference, nor the Missouri Synod, are *church* . . .
>
> If single congregations by combining with others form larger unions—synods—territorial churches—or, through delegated authority, alliances like EKiD or World Council, then they have that right from the same authority (I Cor. 3:21) of their members; but what they form are not churches. Their purpose is not the fulfillment of a divine commission, but the solution of a problem posed by time and world.[184]

The printed version, published as a tribute to the Swedish Bishop Nygren, omits these statements but retains the gist: "We can say, synod, territorial church, a formation like the EKiD belong to Christendom, are a part of it, but are not church."[185] It is easy to see why from this point of view there was not much wrong with EKiD, nor with the newly formed Lutheran World Federation. Indeed, Graebner publicly stated that given a few constitutional amendments Missouri would be able to join LWF. This was of course highly offensive to the free churches. It became an issue at the French-Belgian convention at Strasbourg. And the pastors of the Finnish and Alsatian Free Churches sent circulars to all affiliated presidents and to leading theologians asking for doctrinal clarification of these and other issues.[186] Graebner died before anything came of it.

Meanwhile Professor Sasse and Pastor Hopf had left the Bavarian state church. Invited to St. Louis for a quarter in 1948, Sasse spoke up for the free churches and against the state churches in Europe. His testimony was far from welcome. To a free church friend in Europe Sasse wrote despondently, having noted good and bad points: "The most shattering [experience] for me is St. Louis. It is a chain of humiliations and deliberate unkindnesses which I here experience at the hands of the leadership of the seminary, aside from the many kindnesses and the human goodness of individuals. But Sieck, L. Meyer, and Fred Mayer are, with others, determined to go the way 'out of the ghetto,' that is, into unionism."[185] On the other hand, the President of the Synod, "Dr. Behnken was quite friendly and open, when I recently spent two days with him and made clear to him the constitution of EKiD. Yes, he was deeply shocked." Dr. Behnken became, indeed, a faithful friend and supporter of Dr. Sasse, and over the years backed Sasse's testimony with his vast personal prestige. As for the pro-EKiD theologians, said Sasse in the same letter, they imagined that the encounter with Missouri at Bad Boll "was *the* turning point of German church history! What a delusion, when one considers that simultaneously the Lutheran church was being buried in Eisenach!"

Missourians at Bad Boll were openly critical of Sasse's and Hopf's testimony against EKiD. Graebner even went so far as to write repeatedly to leaders of the Bavarian state church, including Bishop Meiser himself, dissociating himself from Sasse's and Hopf's and the free churches' judgments.[186] The propaganda value of such prestigious Missourian endorsements of EKiD was considerable. Yet history has repeatedly, and through the "Leuenberg Concord" conclusively, confirmed the faithful Dr. Sasse's clear perception of EKiD.

Graebner was not alone in his misconceptions. O. P. Kretzmann's 1945 paper on "Organization and the Church"[187] may well have been "the most notable contribution to the thinking of the Forty-four."[188] He also attacked "the distinction between the visible and invisible church"[189] Decades later Kretzmann expressed some surprise at the reaction to the "Statement of the 44": "Perhaps the strangest thing about it is that the most 'dangerous' theses are not considered at all by the brethren who are hollering their heads off. Such a simple thing as the interpretation of Romans 16, 17 and 18 we had to defend with our very lives."[190] One of the most "dangerous" theses, though hardly noticed at the time, was Thesis Six:

> We affirm the historic Lutheran position concerning the central importance of the una sancta ("one holy" Christian church) and the local congregation. We believe that there should be a re-emphasis of the privileges and responsibilities of the local congregation also in the matter of determining questions of fellowship.
>
> We therefore deplore the new and improper emphasis on the synodical organization as basic in our consideration of the problems of the Church. We believe that no organizational loyalty can take the place of loyalty to Christ and His Church.

That the purely external, organizational trappings of synods are only of human origin and authority is perfectly true and needs to be stressed. But the further implication that synods involve *nothing more* than "organizational loyalty" is as false as it is disastrous. We have here the germs of the Graebner concept: confessing, confessional *churches* are reduced to mere *human organizations*, which dissolve, theologically, into a mass of footloose congregations and even individuals. These separated congregations and individuals are then defenceless before the imperialism of Ecumenical unionism—for each of its engines. WCC, LWF, EKiD, and the like, thereby assumes the harmless guise of but one more of the same "human organizations!" Doctrine and creeds are then devalued. In place of an awesome, sacred *confession* before God and man, even unto "the judgment seat of Jesus Christ,"[191] we are given worthless "denominational tags!"[192] Who could possibly take any serious notice of such plastic trinkets. much less die for them?

Although it came to be taken for granted by many that "Synod is not a church in the theological sense"[193] and that this was the historic "Missourian" position, the facts show the contrary. The original (1847) constitution[194] of the Missouri Synod opens with a chapter on "reasons for the formation of a synodical union." The very first reason is "the example of the apostolic church (Acts 15:1-31)." Other reasons include "preservation and promotion of the unity of the pure confession" (2) and "joint extension of the Kingdom of God and realization and promotion of special churchly purposes" (6). It is clear that *only a church* can do such things, viz. teach, confess, build the Kingdom, and the like. No mere business concern or human organization can do it. Chapter Four of the Constitution explicitly assigns the following roles to Synod's "sphere of activity:" "1. supervision of the purity and unity of doctrine within the synodical boundaries. . . . 3. joint defence and extension of the church. 4. publication and promotion of an ecclesiastical (*kirchlich*-churchly) periodical. . . . 6. administration of the ecclesiastical (*kirchlich*-churchly) ordination and installation into office. 7. education of future pastors and teachers for the service of the church . . . . 14. connection with the Lutheran church overseas." Indeed, so self-evident was the churchly character of the Synod, that the official "clarifications" attached to the Constitution spoke of the application, to an offending pastor or teacher, of "the steps of admonition according to Matthew 18, 15-17 within the congregation first of all, as well as on behalf of the synod."[195] Also the "introduction" to the Constitution makes quite clear the deep and emphatic "churchliness" of the founders' thinking. The Synodical Constitution was deliberately designed to prevent the Confessions from being a mere "signboard," without bringing to bear "an ordering and shaping force on the whole constitution and on the church's entire manner of acting." Rather, the Constitution was to be one "which would prove in its whole execution that all parts of it are borne and permeated in a living way by the uncorrupted Confession and the pure doctrine of the church, so that the confessing and teaching church can devote itself to the realization and promotion of every special churchly purpose!" The whole argumentation of Walther[196] and Pieper[197] for Missouri's particular style of church government presupposes that it is *the church* which is here being governed, and that this must *therefore* be done with God's Word alone, and not with human rules and regulations! Hence also the great emphasis on doctrine and the Word at Missouri Synod conventions. This must be the main concern of the "representative church," for "decisions of synods (i.e. councils) are decisions of the church" (Tractate).[198]

This deep seriousness about the church evinced at the time of the founding of the Missouri Synod was a far cry from the light weight slogans, a century later, about mere "human organizations" and "denominational tags!" Of course the early Missourians knew perfectly well that neither their little synod nor the Lutheran church as a whole was the one holy Christian church! Yet they also knew that the only proper way of dealing with that one church is by faith, which means simply clinging to the pure marks of Christ's church (Gospel and Sacraments). Blind human sight leads not to Jerusalem but to Babylon. The moment we let go of modest faith and depend on arrogant sight, we begin to hanker after numbers and outward grandeur. Then the boundaries between orthodoxy and heterodoxy, Gospel and pseudo-gospel, confession and denial, become confused, and we are ready victims for the spectacular counterfeit church of the great Ecumenical Compromise. Under the hypnotic spell of glamorous Ecumenical mirages and siren songs, mistaken for the one, holy church of Christ, formerly solemn confessions appear as mere "denominational tags," and a confessional fellowship guided strictly by the pure marks of Christ's church seems like a petty, "man-made"[199] substitute for and obstacle to the glorious New Testament reality! The basic issue is very simply this: Is outward, organizational bigness, or confessional faithfulness and truth fulness the real key to the mystery of the New Testament church? The Lutheran Confessions (Augsburg Confession and Apology VII and VIII) give one answer; the modern Ecumenical Movement gives a radically different one. One must choose between the two. It would be difficult to find a single sentence more expressive of the un-Lutheran Ecumenical intoxication of our time than this statement from the prefatory report to the celebrated "Mission Affirmations," by their chief author, Martin L. Kretzmann: "In our time God has brought into being various empirical manifestations of the body of Christ in the form of ecumenical organizations such as the Lutheran Council USA, the National Council of Churches of Christ in the USA, the Lutheran World Federation, and the World Council of Churches."[200] So it is "the body of Christ" which is providing arms to Marxist cut-throats in Africa to terrorize black civilians! Are these the new marks of the church? Are we to shout again for Barabbas?

A strange paradox emerges from the phenomenon of "44": Graebner's rejection of synods and federations as real churches culminates in Kretzmann's embracing of LWF and WCC as "manifestations of the body of Christ!" Perhaps this is the nature of all transitional positions—unacceptable elements of new thrusts are suppressed until a changed situation permits them to surface. Those who refuse the proper honour to "constitutional" (that is, objectively, Biblically normed) orthodoxy are doomed to become the slaves of a totalitarian normlessness. The last state of that church is worse than the first. Still, it must be pointed out that the new Ecumenical outlook never did gain complete control of the Missouri Synod. Despite decades of ardent propaganda, in the *American Lutheran* and elsewhere, in favor of joining both the Lutheran World Federation and the World Council of Churches, those two objectives were never attained. But there is no doubt that things were moving in that direction. The 1955 *Report on Lutheran World Federation* prepared by M. Franzmann, L. B. Meyer, and M. J. Naumann still found the LWF unacceptable, since the latter had "functions and activities which are churchly in character," yet gave "equal room and scope to orthodox and heterodox churches and their proclamation. The ultimate question of truth or error, of orthodoxy or heterodoxy, is being bypassed" (p. 5). By 1968, however, at the Cambridge conference of Missouri-related churches, LC-MS delegates Gaertner [201] and Wolbrecht lobbied energetically for LWF membership. "The Missourian delegates, especially Dr. Wolbrecht, stressed very strongly the new opinion that we can belong to a greater assembly of churches without becoming co-responsible for what the other member-churches do . . . And he invoked to our regret the unhappy post-war definition or theory spread by the late (and declining) Dr. Theo. Graebner: that larger bodies and denominations, beyond the local congregations, are not properly 'churches,' but merely '*Zweckverbaende*.'"[202] Actually, the clearest possible definition of the whole issue had already been given in the 1965 *Document of Union* of the two merging Australian Lutheran churches: "Can a federation with a specific doctrinal basis act in essential church work (*in sacris*) on behalf of its member-churches without itself assuming the character of church in the New Testament sense?"[203] But whatever wants to be church must submit to Christ's own strict controls: His pure Gospel and Sacraments as the marks of the church.

Official Missouri responded to the lure of the Ecumenical fleshpots only very reluctantly. Probably cresting in the "Mission Affirmations" (1965) and LCUSA (1965-1967), Missouri's liberal movement summoned all its failing strength to push the Synod into fellowship with the ALC[204] at Denver (1969) and then collapsed. A sober theological re-thinking[205] has already begun with the production by the Commission on Theology and Church Relations of *A Lutheran Stance Toward Ecumenism* (1974).

Whatever may have been the illusions of individuals, it can hardly be denied that objectively the Ecumenical infatuation meant a radical retreat from the Lutheran Confessions. Let us assume that the endorsement, in a "Seminex" journal book review,[206] of pulpit exchanges between Jewish rabbis and Lutheran pastors was a momentary lapse. But we can hardly assume the same about the outspoken article by Dr. B. H. Jackayya of India, entitled "The Relation Between Doctrinal Consensus and Church Fellowship."[207] With full editorial approval the article defends the proposition: "We should STOP insisting on doctrinal consensus as a pre-requisite for fellowship and extend the hand of fellowship to all Christians who believe in Jesus Christ as their Saviour!" And the whole context makes it plain that what is meant is fellowship with churches as such, not simply with Christian individuals. Nor was this simply an isolated personal opinion. Jackayya echoed the anti-Confessional stand of his mentor and one-time predecessor as president of Concordia Seminary, Nagercoil, Martin L. Kretzmann. Writing in *Lutheran World*, the journal of the LWF, Dr. Kretzmann, who was then an official of the Missouri Synod's Mission Board, had stated in 1969: "it is imperative that we stop playing the 'church game' at once and declare ourselves in fellowship with all who bear the name of Christ, of whatever branch of the church they may be, and openly declare our commitment to the fullest cooperation in the mission of Christ without concern for what may happen to a particular ecclesiastical institution."[208] No doubt this is the real meaning of that oft-quoted statement in Kretzmann's "Mission Affirmations," now enshrined in the constitution of AELC: "The Evangelical Lutheran Church is chiefly a confessional movement within the total body of Christ rather than a denomination emphasizing institutional barriers of separation."

In plain language, this assertion means that the Lutheran church is not a church but one party, school, or opinion among others within the same church. But this is the traditional Reformed understanding of the church. The Reformed did not ultimately regard differences on the Sacrament as divisive of church-fellowship. They had no objections to fellowship with the Lutherans, even if the latter did still cling to a few pre-Reformation "superstitions" like the Real Presence! The Prussian Union embodied this Reformed-Calvinistic understanding of the church. So did the Evangelical Church in Germany (EKiD). So also did Schmucker's "American Lutheranism." And now "Seminex"-AELC, with their Jackayya-Kretzmann doctrine, are attacking the Lutheran Confessions in the same way.

Since the new Ecumenical doctrine of the church is obviously not that of the Lutheran Confessions, the latter have to be quietly adjusted, that is, denatured: "With this understanding of the mutual relationship of the parts of the body of Christ to one another we must look upon the Confessions of the church not as standards by which we exclude ourselves from others but as witnesses to the activity of God in Christ."[209] This "bold, positive, evangelical use of our confessional heritage" (Kretzmann) means that the doctrinal condemnations contained in the Lutheran Confessions are simply set aside. The "Seminex" confession, *Faithful to Our Calling*, says the same thing: "our Confessions, however, are not intended to be barriers between denominations, but bold affirmations of Christ, His Gospel and the unity of His Church."[210] Compare this with what the Formula of Concord says about the Augsburg Confession: "This symbol distinguishes our reformed churches from the papacy and from other condemned sects and heresies."[211] How is it possible, indeed, to confess without rejecting denials and deniers of what one confesses? In the light of the well-known stand of the Confessions themselves, one can only marvel at the self-contradictory gymnastics performed editorially by the former *Concordia Theological Monthly*: "It is no part of the doctrinal content of the Lutheran Confessions (which alone is binding) *that they are to be used today as a rule and norm for Christian faith and life.*"[212]

This modern abandonment of the Confessions, moreover, involves not "secondary" points of doctrine but something which is quite central and crucial in the Confessions: the Sacrament of the Altar. Whole chapters or articles are devoted to this subject. In both Catechisms the Sacrament is treated as one of the "chief parts" of Christianity. The Augsburg Confession and its Apology treat it explicitly in Articles X and XXIV. The Smalcald Articles stress it very strongly, and the Formula of Concord devotes its longest article (VII) to this matter. The Augsburg Confession and the Apology also treat this Sacrament, together with Baptism and the Gospel, as constitutive of the church and of her oneness (VII). To give equal rights to Reformed confessions which deny the Real Presence (Westminster Confession, Thirty-Nine Articles, etc.), is to abandon the Augsburg Confession and the *Book of Concord*. Yet this was done in agreements reached between Indian Lutheran churches and the united Church of South India. 213 Again it was Dr. M. L. Kretzmann who had for years advocated union with the Church of South India (a Presbyterian Congregational-Methodist-Anglican-Swiss Reformed merger) —at first, it is true, with serious reservations.[214] At one point, Kretzmann even employed the quaint argument that the Church of South India was "not a union nor even, in a certain specifically Lutheran meaning, a Church!"[215] It is not surprising that when Dr. Behnken had Prof. Sasse's essay, "The Confessional Problem in Today's World Lutheranism" (*Letters to Lutheran Pastors*, No. 43), translated and published in *The Lutheran Layman*,[216] the same Dr. M. L. Kretzmann, seconded by other Missouri liberals, mounted a public attack on Sasse's Confessional stand.[217]

Nor was the Sacrament at stake only in far-off India. The Presbyterian-Lutheran discussions in America concluded in 1965 "that 'no insuperable obstacles to pulpit and altar fellowship' existed. This statement took on special significance because the Missouri Synod had participated in this and subsequent dialogues."[218] In 1970 a number of Missouri Synod "moderates," including St. Louis seminary professors, published "A Call to Openness and Trust." This document includes a brief list of "items" which "should not divide the Christian fellowship" nor exclude anyone from membership in the Missouri Synod. Among the examples given is not only "the question of factual error in the Bible" but even *"the definition of the presence of Christ in the Lord's Supper!"* If this language means anything at all, it means that the *Book of Concord* has simply been swept aside with a few bland phrases. Yet the December 1972 *CTM* editorially treated the document as an instance of "loyal opposition" for which there ought to be room in the Synod!

After the New Orleans Convention (1973) had rejected certain doctrinal positions associated with the St. Louis faculty majority, support for that faculty was expressed from all sorts of strange quarters. Eden Seminary in St. Louis, belonging to the very liberal United Church of Christ, bestowed an honorary doctorate on President John Tietjen on September 9, 1973. Eden Seminary President Robert Fauth explained that Eden had always favoured an ecumenical approach, and praised Tietjen's "co-operative spirit." The Eden faculty regretted that Tietjen's "administration at Concordia has evoked severe criticism within his own denomination. Particularly in the light of that, we feel constrained to express our appreciation of his leadership."[219] Unlike his predecessor, C. F. W. Walther, who, as we have seen, declined a similar honour from a much more conservative institution (Goettingen), Tietjen accepted. Responding to the gesture at the opening service of Eden Seminary's academic year, Tietjen delivered a ringing defence of the new Ecumenical orientation, citing as a major proof-text the "Mission Affirmations'" notion of "a confessional movement within the total body of Christ" and of the Lutheran Confessions as "not intended to be a kind of Berlin Wall."[220]

By "Berlin Wall" apparently is meant any Confessional restriction on altar and pulpit fellowship! But if the Confessions no longer indicate the boundaries of church fellowship, then they have simply been thrown to the winds—in this case the winds of Ecumenical "dialogue." Certainly the Confessions, as we have seen, do not understand themselves as one of many optional currents in an endless stream of chatter! Officially ELIM-AELC are, for understandable reasons, still a bit coy about tearing down the "Berlin Wall," that is, the Confessions: "The Body of Christ is ... the unity which is ours through Christ and ... is open to careful reexamination of the sharing of the Sacraments with the broader Christian community."[221] But in practice ELIM-AELC are publicly committed to the fullest church-fellowship with both ALC and LCA, the latter of which has already adopted in a "working document" the anti-Confessional policy that "whenever the Sacrament is celebrated it should be open to all communing Christians present."[222] A sad illustration of this completely unprincipled practice occurred in the closing weeks of the Tietjen administration at the funeral of Dr. A. C. Piepkorn. On the occasion of this "requiem Eucharist" all and sundry were admitted to the Sacrament, without regard to their confession. The principle so freely surrendered here was the very one for which Doctors Piepkorn and Martin Scharlemann had valiantly and successfully contended within the Armed Services, as Dr. Scharlemann pointed out to the Missouri District President in an energetic protest.[223]

This reference to the military may serve as a convenient reminder of yet another vital aspect of the doctrine of the church which is in dispute today. The "Mission Affirmations" include the disastrous proposition: "That we affirm that the church is Christ's mission to the whole society."[224] Various qualifying statements, though inadequate, indicate that the proposition was felt to be disturbing. Dr. M. L. Kretzmann's commentary is far from reassuring: "As the body of Christ in the world, the community of the new creation, the church has a corporate responsibility towards the structures of society."[225] Despite lip-service in the "whereases" to Luther's distinction between the two kingdoms—the spiritual and the political—the statements cited effectively wipe out any such distinction. Indeed, this confusion is presented as a virtue ("holistic and dynamic") and as quite deliberate by former mission executive James W. Mayer.[226] The "Seminex" confession, *Faithful to Our Calling*, also speaks of the church as "Christ's mission to the whole person, the whole Church, the whole society and the whole world."[227] This unbiblical, Calvinistic formulation at once threatens to distort the Gospel into a "Social Gospel," a danger strongly suggested in the further statements that God in Christ "now promises to free us from any force that enslaves us . . . Rejoicing in this Promise, we fight against the imposition of any ecclesiastical, political, or social power that negates, threatens, or minimises the freedom we have in the Gospel."[228] Civic and spiritual, natural and supernatural, temporal and eternal, church and state, Law and Gospel are here lumped together in a mischievously un-Lutheran manner. (Compare Articles XVI and XXVIII of the Augsburg Confession and the Apology.) Such confusions are rampant also in Lutheran circles today, but the fact remains, as Prof. H. P. Hamann has pointed out in an illuminating essay, "Part of its sharp and careful distinction between Law and Gospel is the Lutheran Church's doctrine of the Two Kingdoms."[229] Social political programmes, world development, and the like are, if anything, Law, not Gospel; whereas the church's proper work is the distribution of the eternal treasures of the Gospel. Hamann writes:

> The church's mission in the world is declared to be wholly, or in great part, or at least in some part, the undertaking of

responsibility for the world, the providing of aid in the solution of its big problems, the support of endeavors being exerted for world development. In direct opposition to this description of the mission of the church, it is the concern of this essay to show, first, that the church has only one aim and world development is not part of it, and, secondly, that by devotion to and concentration on its proper task the church will not only be preserved as church but will also render signal service to the world.

Finally, despite all these criticisms, one cannot but sense and appreciate in formulations like the "Mission Affirmations" and M. L. Kretzmann's explanations a pained exasperation with the shallow pettiness and organizationalism of so much of modern church-life, and a deep yearning for something better, something a bit more obviously like the virile and vibrant New Testament reality. Indeed, many grass-roots "moderates" who care nothing about what they regard as the "finer points" of doctrine, imagine that they are simply exchanging the dry, dreary, and deadly routines of a stale traditionalism for the promised land of a vital, dynamic, exciting Christian fellowship. This is perhaps a sedate version of the "Age of Aquarius" fantasies. The tragedy is that in their eagerness to manifest the glorious Body of Christ—which in this age must remain an article of faith, hidden under many of fences—men become impatient with and surrender the crucial distinction between orthodoxy and heterodoxy, truth and error, Gospel and pseudo-gospel, confession and denial. But "cutting corners" is nowhere more hazardous than in the realm of the spirit. Without a firm hold on the objective Gospel, mere idealistic escapes from creaky parochialisms lead straight into the clutches of well-oiled global enterprises. The glib marketing of philosophies ("life-styles," in faddish lingo) and religions by the pied pipers of the modern mass-media manipulates millions on a scale that dwarfs the tragic Children's Crusade, in which many thousands of starry-eyed youngsters full of religious zeal ended up in the ready ships of Arab slave-traders!

In the face of the exotic attractions of cultists and occultists of all descriptions, much Lutheran practice seems humdrum and spiritually unexciting to many Lutherans themselves. Hence the frantic attempts at "warming up" chilly liturgies—even with the strange fires of the "charismatic" or neo-Pentecostal movement. Muggeridge wrote of "unspeakable clergymen with twanging guitars." There is considerable truth in the shrewd observation by Gritsch and Jenson:

> Despite the Lutheran denominations' greater official fervour for their dogmatic tradition, the *Book of Concord* has little greater communal effect among them than do the Thirty-Nine Articles among Episcopalians or papal decrees among American Roman Catholics. The Lutheran denominations live—or do not live—by the same mixture of fundamentalism, helplessness before every wind of doctrine, tag-ends of denominational tradition, and occasional saving theological and proclamatory miracles as do the other American denominations.[230]

Dynamic movements like neo-Pentecostalism cannot be resisted with mere decrees or prohibitions—though these too have their place. The appeal of cultism is a warning signal that an inner emptiness exists into which demons are wont to rush. If people truly understood and appreciated the grandeur of God's gift in His Gospel and Sacraments, no one would pay the slightest attention to all the froth and bother of the "tongues," "healings," or "Late-Great-Planet-Earth" excitements. But such living appreciation cannot come from books alone, though they are necessary. It is not enough to confess the *Book of Concord* in theory—it needs to be put into practice. Preaching and the Sacraments are to be *done* aright, not merely thought about. How can we expect Lutheran people to have a high regard for the Gospel and Sacraments, when in our parish life we so often disguise our high "theory" with Reformed or revivalistic practices which suggest a *low* view of the Means of Grace? If we expect people to have some regard for the Augsburg Confession's Biblical position on the Real Presence (Article X), then we shall have to express and implement this evangelical mystery in our public worship and church life (Article XXIV). In the New Testament as in the Lutheran Confessions the Sacrament is a vital and central part of Christian worship. Our actual practice often suggests the Reformed-pietistic notion of the Sacrament as an occasional "extra." Solzhenitsyn wrote that the Liturgy he heard and saw celebrated in church during his childhood made such a deep and lasting impression on him that no amount of intellectual argument or personal suffering later was able to erase it. There is no reason why Lutheran worship, taken seriously, should not affect men similarly. But who would expect the same from a rousing chorus of

"Pass It On"—with or without hand-clapping? If we foster a taste for spiritual marijuana, we need not be surprised if many go on to the "fuller" heroin of Pentecostalism. And if parishioners are not earnestly warned against seeking nourishment from a version like the "Living Bible," which deliberately changes the great texts about Baptism and the Holy Supper into mere picture language, how can we expect them to grasp or retain the sacramental teaching of the New Testament? Nor, of course, are people likely to be inspired in that direction if the Christian mysteries are celebrated with all the fervour of a stock-exchange report—collections being more prevalent than communions—or with the gabby folksiness of daytime television.

Even our best efforts, of course, cannot do justice to the full splendour of the Gospel of God (2 Cor. 3 and 4). But if people are clear about the treasure, and about their desperate needs as sinners, they will not be put off by the earthenness of the vessels. Christians must be taught to see themselves not as whimsical patrons or "customers" of the church, waiting to be pleased and pampered, but as sons and daughters of the living God, "like newborn babies" craving for the Source of Life in Word and Sacrament, despite all the obstacles, offences, and absurdities of men. After all, even during the earthly life of Jesus people who came to Him had to put up also with Judas, the ill-will of the Temple authorities, desperate tax-collectors, hysterical mothers, and the Lord's own deep lowliness, even to the point of the Cross. Then as now many turned away, discouraged. Still He gently invites: "Blessed is he who does not take offence at Me" (Matt. 11:6)!

3. The Use of the Confessions As a Rabbit's Foot

As we have already seen,[231] the old General Synod tried to cover its doctrinal nakedness with the fig-leaf of a formal "confessional subscription" to the Augsburg Confession. But "undisturbed liberty" was granted to interpret the Confession more or less as anybody might please. The General Council, and of course Missouri, strongly challenged this confidence trick, insisting that "the unity of the Church does not consist in subscription to the same Confessions, but in the acceptance and teaching of the same doctrines." Today the General Synod's "legal fiction" approach to the Confessions has become common church-political coin within official world "Lutheranism."

After unsuccessful attempts (1936-1940) to reach doctrinal agreement with the old ALC on the inspiration and inerrancy of Scripture, the then ULCA (now LCA) retreated to its 1934 "Savannah Resolution," holding that, since the "separated Lutheran church bodies all subscribe these same Confessions," this was sufficient for union and there should be no further doctrinal statements.[232] This ULCA-LCA union-policy based on the formality of "Confessional paragraphs" in constitutions became the major thrust of John Tietjen's programmatic book, despite a few verbal reservations. That the reservations were not meant seriously has become clear since. At an LCA function in 1976, for instance, Tietjen stated about the Missouri Synod conflict: "Lutheran relationships are very much at the heart of the controversy." He went on to say with obvious relish: "The Lutheran Church in America, at its last convention, very delicately had its say to the Lutheran Church-Missouri Synod about doctrinal statements, indicating that for the LCA the Scriptures and the Lutheran Confessions were enough."[233] And, of course, the new AELC is in fellowship with all and sundry.

"What right," asks Tietjen in his book, "does any Lutheran church body have to deny the hand of fellowship to those whose espousal of the faith of the Lutheran Confessions marks them as fellow Lutherans?"[234] This is precisely the view of the Lutheran World Federation, which holds that because all member-churches accept the "Confessional paragraph" of the LWF's constitution, they are thereby professing doctrinal unity and ought to show it by formally acknowledging church-fellowship with all other member-churches.[235] This approach invites at least a threefold objection.

First of all, the whole situation is patently untruthful. What is the meaning of all this solemn talk about the Lutheran Confessions if member-churches of the LWF, in fact, practice official intercommunion with Reformed churches, which deny the Real Presence of Christ's body and blood in the Sacrament? Or why did the LWF go to all the constitutional trouble, at its Helsinki Assembly in 1963, of adding the Apostles', Nicene, and Athanasian Creeds to its "Confessional paragraph," if there was not the slightest intention to exclude, curb, or ban even the wildest Bultmannian attacks on these very Creeds? Asmussen, a former president of the chancery of the Evangelical Church in Germany

(EKiD), has described the situation as follows: "But this is in fact the picture of wide sectors of our Lutheran Church today: clergymen read aloud the Christmas story, which they consider a fairytale. They read aloud the Easter story, to which they find access only after several reinterpretations. At the grave, they witness to the resurrection of the dead, which they consider a myth."[236]

The "No Other Gospel" and "Churchly Gathering" movements in Germany arose to combat the historical-critical assault on the most basic Christian truths. At an international conservative meeting in Sittensen, Germany, a Swedish participant asked an official LWF representative what would happen if the faithful Lutherans would be forced out of the Church of Sweden (a member-church of the LWF). Would the LWF then side with those who represented the doctrinal position of the Lutheran Confessions, or would it dismiss them as a "sect"? The LWF man could not answer. The report continues:

> It became clear that in accordance with its whole structure as a federation of existing, historical institutions with a common "doctrinal basis"—but no doctrinal authority—the LWF could only, in the acute case of a division, side, without regard to truth and confession, with the official institution, which continues the established historical tradition.[237]

The real value of all the lip-service to the Confessions in that case in nil. Nor are things very different in America. What is the meaning of a "consensus on the doctrine of the Gospel and the meaning of confessional subscription" being "sufficient"[238] to warrant co-operation in the Lutheran Council in the USA (LCUSA), if that body's Division of Theological Studies could issue a report[239] advocating room for "a variety of positions"—including attacks on Christ's Godhead and Atonement? Again, presumably all the seminary faculties of the ALC and the LCA would publicly pledge allegiance to the Lutheran Confessions. Yet their joint publication, *The Lutheran Quarterly*, printed without any public rebuke, a blatant denial of the Holy Trinity and of the Divinity of Christ, which blasphemously portrayed the Transfiguration as "an occasion on which Jesus, who had deep rapport with his psychic disciples, hypnotised them, and presented them with illusions of Moses, Elijah and the Voice of God, in order to convince them of his unusual messiahship . . ."[240] How can this sort of thing be related meaningfully to any alleged "consensus" about the "Gospel" or "Confessional subscription" or for that matter about any grain of Christian truth, however minimal?

If bodies like the Lutheran World Federation are neither able nor willing to do anything about the mockeries perpetrated by an unbelieving university "theology," why the hollow pretences about the exalted status of the Bible, the Creeds, and the Confessions? Of course, it will be said, no one who is "in the know" will have any illusions on this score. Very well, but why mislead the simple? Is this not "lying and deceiving by God's Name," contrary to the Second Commandment?

Secondly, the "orthodoxy-by-constitutional-paragraph" idea reduces Article VII of the Augsburg Confession to a legalistic, formalistic caricature. By 1969 the doctrinal conflict in the Missouri Synod was public and widespread enough to cause a dramatic change in the Synodical presidency. Yet this is how John Tietjen described the situation in that crucial year, which saw also his own accession to the presidency of the St. Louis seminary :

> Has there been a change in the theology of The Lutheran Church-Missouri Synod? Has its doctrine changed? To both questions some answer yes and are vehemently critical. Others vigorously deny the assertions, claiming there has been no change. Both, of course, are right. If "theology" and "doctrine" mean the Missouri Synod's confessional position as stated in its constitution, of course there has been no change. If the terms refer to ways of expressing or formulating the gospel, there has indeed been change.[241]

No creeds and doctrines are absolute, argues Tietjen; hence theological variety is healthy. Even the Bible contains "different 'theologies,'" although its formulations "help!" Nor are only "minor points" involved. The Nicene Creed itself is not exempt from the radical implications:

> Our task is to express the truth which those phrases affirm about God and about Jesus Christ and their significance for us in the language and thought forms of our day. For us "begotten" and "substance" will not do. The same could be said for other creedal formulations, even so crucial a formulation as the one dealing with the Holy Trinity or with justification.

What, then, is the unifying force in all this swirling variety? In the final analysis, apparently, it is no more than the formality of Confessional "subscription":

> The purpose of creeds is not to enforce theological conformity but to serve church unity. Together we accept the creeds as statements of the truth of the gospel. Ours is a confessional unity. Within that unity there is room—lots of it—for theological variety. While we each go about the theological task of articulating the gospel for our time, we are united by our common subscription to the creeds as witnesses to the gospel proclaimed in the Scriptures.

This fascination with the outward technicalities of constitutional paragraphs leads to a double distortion of theological vision: On the one hand, real attacks on the substance of the Confessions (for example, the 1970 "Call to Openness and Trust") are not perceived as such, so long as there is lip-service to the formality of the "Confessional paragraph." No matter what people actually teach and do, there is no change of doctrine as long as Synod's "confessional position as stated in its constitution" remains the same. On the other hand, however, any attempt to confess and safeguard the real doctrinal substance of the Confessions by distinguishing the Confessions' own genuine sense from false and invalid interpretations or distortions read into them is now perceived as "narrowing" the church's confessional base, as "adding" to the Confessions, etc. To "cow's eyes" (Luther) new documents appear as new doctrines. Hence the successful agitation against the famous "Resolution 9" of the San Francisco Convention (1959), which had held that Synod's pastors, teachers, and professors were to "teach and act in harmony with" Synod's official doctrinal decisions. It must be admitted that the resolution was not as precise as it might have been.[242] And so the next Convention (Cleveland, 1962) threw out this attempt to "hold the line," as "unconstitutional!" The attempt to make binding decisions about what the Confessions really said and meant was regarded as "amending" the unalterable "Confessional paragraph!" The real meaning of what had happened was blurted out naively in the *St. Louis Lutheran*: "Declaration of the resolution as unconstitutional did not alter the Missouri Synod doctrinal stand but removed its binding force!"[243] But what is a "doctrinal stand" without "binding force?" What is a "confessional position" the meaning of which cannot be officially fixed? Is it not simply a rabbit's foot—a good-luck charm—and no more?

Of course, the constitutional argument was merely a tactic.

The real objection was to the doctrinal content of documents like the Brief Statement. Lutheran union had become the fetish of Synod's new theological "elite," and all obstacles had to be moved out of the way. Martin E. Marty's piece ("Missouri's New Direction, 1962") for the official organ of the ALC explained the significance of the "scrapping" of San Francisco's Resolution 9:

> Some of the documents in question would have been insurmountable barriers to future inter-Lutheran theological unity because they belonged to the private experience of Missouri, were coloured by the scholastic bent and expression of its greatest dogmatician, and would prove uncongenial to many non-Missourians (as they are to some Missourians) were they to be imposed as confessions.[244]

Missouri's own *Lutheran Witness* celebrated the Cleveland Convention with a triumphant three-page editorial entitled "Turning Point."[245]

The same constitutional *Blitzkrieg* was tried before, during, and after the New Orleans Convention (1973) against President J. A. O. Preus' "A Statement of Biblical and Confessional Principles," but this time unsuccessfully. People could no longer ignore the obvious. It is amazing that to this day the New Orleans "Statement" continues to elicit much more constitutional paragraph cavilling and legal-procedural maneuvering than plain, sober doctrinal discussion of the document's actual content!

But this is just the point: Are the Confessions themselves interested in "subscription" formalities or in actual doctrinal content? Clearly the latter. The much-tortured seventh article of the Augsburg Confession insists that "the Gospel be unanimously preached in its correct sense and that the Sacraments be administered according to the divine Word." In other words, the Christian doctrine ("in all its articles," Formula of Concord, S.D., X, 31) must be actually proclaimed, the Sacraments actually administered. The living, dynamic Gospel cannot be imprisoned like a museum display in some "constitutional paragraph." Such formalities on patient paper mean nothing unless they are actually put into practice, that is, confessed. Doctrinal substance is primary, all else is secondary and subsidiary. Article VII demands not mere lip-service, but the actual sway of the pure doctrine in pulpits and conferences, seminaries and publications, synodical conventions and fellowship connections. Since the Missouri Synod's "confessional paragraph" (Article II) was deliberately designed not to muzzle the church's Confessions nor to let them be exploited as a mere "signboard," but, on the contrary, to insure their exclusive sway in actual church-life, it is clear that the Synod has the right and the duty to implement the doctrinal content of Scriptures and Confessions as circumstances may require. Such implementation has in the past required and may in the future require the formulation and adoption of new documents to distinguish genuine Biblical-Confessional doctrine form falsifications—for instance, the *Thirteen Theses* of 1881, the *Brief Statement* of 1897 and 1932, and *A Statement* of 1973.

When false Lutherans, who denied the Real Presence and other New Testament teachings, tried to turn the Augsburg Confession into a rabbit's foot by insisting on their "subscription" of it, even while they continued in their errors, the Lutheran church ended the pretence by adopting the Formula of Concord, which defined the real meaning of the Confession against distortions. Whoever, therefore, rejected the doctrine of the Formula of Concord could not be regarded as adhering in good faith to the Augsburg Confession. This is the Lutheran church's own official answer to Tietjen's question: "What right does any Lutheran church body have to deny the hand of fellowship to those whose espousal of the faith of the Lutheran Confessions marks them as fellow Lutherans?" For he meant, of course, "formal subscription" and a constitutional paragraph, *a la* ULCA-LCA and LWF.

Thirdly, there remains a yet more fundamental point. The current distaste for clear-cut doctrinal definitions and statements may, on the face of it, look like special piety and devotion to the Lutheran Confessions which one does not want to pollute with "additions." It is usually nothing of the kind. Behind it rather lurks the tragic "Ecumenical" inability to take a decisive stand on any doctrinal issue. "We have lost the Word of God and cannot find it again," lamented one Protestant academic.[246] Dr. H. Hamann, Sr., the leading theologian of the former Evangelical Lutheran Church of Australia, put it like this:

> On the other hand, we must expect to find, and we assuredly do find, great unwillingness on the part of men to commit themselves to any precise and clear-cut doctrinal statement and to confess such doctrines as divine truth, where the position over against the Holy Scriptures is radically wrong or is vitiated in various ways . . . Confessions that are made from such pre-suppositions are usually of the

vaguest and most general kind and are, besides, very flexible because they are open to personal, individual "interpretation".[247]

A perfect case in point is John Tietjen's previously cited article, "The Gospel and the Theological Task." Unlike the Lutheran Confessions, which identify the Gospel with "*doctrine* . . . in all its articles" (Formula of Concord, SD, X, 31), Tietjen separates them. Having, with the acknowledged aid of that anti-Christian philosopher, Paul Tillich, spun a terrible tissue of slippery uncertainties, where no "theology," creed, confession, dogma, or doctrine could ever be "absolutely final," Tietjen declared: "Once more the point: The church's creeds, critical as they are for theology, are themselves the product of theology and therefore not to be equated with the gospel message to which they point!" No wonder Tietjen was able to congratulate the unionistic General Synod for having "recognised the relativity of all human creeds as vehicles for expressing truth."[248] The new celebration of doubt had been put even more boldly in an amazing issue of the *Lutheran Witness* (April 20, 1963), the year after the great Cleveland "Turning Point":

> To the question, Is there no absolute truth? Are we always simply seekers after truth? *Dialog* replies vigorously: "To the first we answer: Yes, there is absolute truth. To the second we answer: Yes, *we* are always simply seekers after truth."
>
> With stimulating candor the editorial supports its answers: To the believer, "Jesus Christ, a *person*, and the event in which He confronts us is the absolute Truth." If He is the Truth, then ideas, however true, are only relatively true. In this light even "theological propositions read straight from the Bible" are only relatively true.

All this has nothing whatever to do with the Lutheran Confessions, but has been lifted bodily from Barthian "neo orthodoxy":

> In recent Protestant theology . . . a new conception of revelation has appeared . . . The scholastic conception of revelation has generally been accompanied by the theory of the plenary, verbal inspiration of the Bible.. .. The theory of God-acting-in-events has other implications. Since God confronts us through the meaning of events, any report or comment which powerfully conveys that meaning may be divinely inspired, whether or not it is factually inerrant. The

Bible can thus convey a true revelation of God, and its writers can be God's inspired interpreters, while at the same time they are thoroughly human and fallible.[249]

Karl Barth himself, of course, knew and understood—as his Lutheran admirers often do not—that his approach radicalized a Reformed-Calvinistic legacy and was profoundly incompatible with the Lutheran Confessions. Wrote Barth:

> ... in the truest sense there is no such thing as Reformed doctrine, except the timeless appeal to the open Bible and to the Spirit which from it speaks to our spirit. Our fathers had good reason for leaving us *no* Augsburg Confession, authentically interpreting the word of God, *no* Formula of Concord, *no* "Symbolic Books" which might later, like the Lutheran, come to possess an odour of sanctity. They left us only *creeds*, more than one of which begin or end with a proviso which leaves them open to being improved upon in the future. The Reformed churches simply do *not* know the word dogma, in its rigid hierarchial sense.[250]

Today even Lutheran churches are in full flight from dogma, that is, from the very idea of God-given truth and doctrine. The time was when those wishing to escape from the dogma of the Augsburg Confession restricted it to "fundamentals" (e.g., the General Synod) or to some central Gospel core, which would then be "enough" for true unity. This jubilee year of the Formula of Concord (1577) can note a decided advance on this technique. A new book from the LCA's Gettysburg Seminary takes up the Augsburg Confession's distinction between the Gospel (in which there must be unity) and ceremonies (in which there is freedom), and then classifies dogma or doctrine under "ceremonies," which are "the responsibility of free human creativity!"[251] There are of course qualifying statements and genuinely valuable and illuminating observations in that book, but the reduction of dogma to "ceremonies," even if only meant half-rhetorically, signals nothing less than the death-rattle of contemporary "neo Lutheranism." Certainly it would be difficult to imagine a more un-Lutheran notion than such ceremonial, paper-tiger "dogma." Luther reacted sharply to the shallow, anti-dogmatic, common-sense tolerance of the great humanist scholar Erasmus, because the Reformer saw that it amounted to a plea for scepticism and agnosticism:

> To take no pleasure in assertions is not the mark of a

Christian heart; indeed, one must delight in assertions to be a Christian at all . . . Away now with Sceptics and Academics (Platonists) from the company of us Christians; let us have men who will assert, men twice as inflexible as very Stoics! . . . Nothing is more familiar or characteristic among Christians than assertion. Take away assertions and you take away Christianity . . . What Christian can endure the idea that we should deprecate assertions? That would be denying all religion and piety in one breath—asserting that religion and piety and all dogmas are just nothing at all . . . The Holy Spirit is no Sceptic, and the things He has written in our hearts are not doubts or opinions, but assertions—surer and more certain than sense and life itself.[252]

How would Luther have responded to the utterly nihilistic sentiments contained in the address of World Council of Churches Central Committee Chairman M. M. Thomas at the 1973 Bangkok conference on "Salvation Today"? Said Thomas:

We are living at a time when we are deeply conscious of pluralism in the world—pluralism of human situations and needs, of varied religions and secular cultures, with different traditions of metaphysics, ideologies and world views, in terms of which Christians themselves seek to express their commitment to and confession of Christ. So much so that any kind of a unity in the doctrine of Christ or of salvation in Christ, which has been the goal of traditional Christian churches, is to my mind impossible even of conception except in religious imperialistic terms. As a historian of religion, Wilfred Cantwell Smith, has recently said on the grounds also of the loss of authority of the established churches today, "the old ideal of a unified or systematic Christian truth has gone. For this the ecumenical movement is too late," leaving a situation of "open variety, of optional alternatives," everyone choosing what suits him best . . . [253]

This is the real destination for the sake of which Lutheran churches are being asked to "die a painless and edifying death in the hope for a glorious resurrection in the great Ecumenical Church of the future" (H. Sasse)![254] All who play rabbit's foot with the Lutheran Confessions contribute to this end. Even the very anti-Missouri *Forum Letter* can see the handwriting on the wall of the "moderate" AELC: " 'We are bound only by scripture and the confessions.' In fact the statement is being reduced to an empty cliche, being negatively asserted against the bad experience in Missouri but not positively articulated in terms of theological subscription and substance."[255]

To reassure nervous conservatives, the face of doubt puts on the veil of humility. Is not our doctrinal knowledge imperfect? Is not orthodoxy an impossible demand, like perfect sanctification? Is perfect doctrine any more feasible than sinless life?[256] This demand for a wrong kind of doctrinal "humility" must be corrected by the great Reformer's reminders about the nature of Christian truth:

> In philosophy a small error in the beginning leads to a very large error at the end. So in theology a small error overturns the whole doctrine. Therefore doctrine and life must be rigorously distinguished from each other. Doctrine is not ours but God's, Whose called servants we merely are. Therefore we may not yield or change even one tittle of it . . . Accursed be that love which is preserved to the detriment of the doctrine of faith, before which all must yield, love, apostle, angel from heaven, etc . . . If they believed that it is God's Word, they would not play with it like this, but hold it in the highest honour, and accord it faith without any disputation or doubting . . . For doctrine is our sole light, which enlightens and leads us and shows us the way to heaven. If it becomes wobbly in one part, it must necessarily become wobbly altogether. When that happens, love cannot help us. We can be saved without love and unity with the sacramentarians, but not without the pure doctrine and faith . . . Doctrine is heaven, life is the earth. In life there are sin, error, impurity and misery . . . But in doctrine, as there is no error in it, so also no need for forgiveness of sins. Therefore doctrine and life may by no means be equated. One tittle of doctrine counts for more than heaven and earth; therefore we do not tolerate that it be violated in the slightest. But when it comes to errors of life, we can overlook very much.[257]
>
> But doctrine must not be sin, nor guilty, and does not belong in the Our Father, when we pray: "forgive us our trespasses." For it is not our doing, but God's very own Word, Who cannot sin nor do wrong . . . Here it is not necessary, yes not good, to ask for forgiveness of sins . . . for it is God's and not my Word, which God neither should nor can forgive, but must confirm, praise, crown and say: You have taught

aright, for I have spoken through you, and the Word is Mine. Whoever cannot boast that of his sermon, let him leave preaching alone, for he certainly lies and blasphemes God . . . So life may well be sin and wrong; yes it is, alas, only too wrong; but doctrine must be absolutely straight and certain, without all sin. Therefore in the church nothing but alone the certain, pure, and sole Word of God may be preached.Where that is lacking, it is no longer the church, but the devil's school.[258]

Reformed theology's reliance, in the final analysis, on direct Spirit-action 25 tends to make objective Gospel-doctrine somewhat less crucial. But for the Lutheran church the loss of the objective, God-given doctrine of the Gospel is the end of everything. Lutheran theology dissolves into pointless word games, if the objective Gospel from heaven is sacrificed. "New look" Lutheranism is taking the suicidal plunge into the general dogmatic dissolution which holds that *"faith created the Gospel, not vice versa."*[260] No pietistic-charismatic flutterings with imaginary Spirit-feathers can rescue anyone from this pit. The genuine Lutheran church must with all Christians take her stand on that foundation against which the very gates of hell cannot prevail-Christ's own immovable, Biblically-fixed Gospel, utterly objective, *ante et extra nos*—that is, before and outside of us, independent of our faith, love, hopes, fears, feelings, moods, experiences, sins, etc.[261] "The kingdom ours remaineth!"

4. The Question of Church Politics

Church politics, like beauty, is largely in the eye of the beholder. My "politics" is likely to be somebody else's "responsible leadership" and vice versa. It all depends on whose ox is being gored. As long as there are outward structures, ways and means must be found to conduct their affairs "decently and in order." That makes virtually unavoidable arrangements like deliberative assemblies, delegates, elections of leaders, parliamentary procedure, and the like. These things are in themselves neither good nor evil but indifferent. Everything depends on the use to which this machinery is put. Given the machinery, *all* use of it is "politics"—the only alternatives being *good* politics or *bad* politics. (Only the invincibly ignorant could believe that "politics" was introduced into the Missouri Synod by J. A. O. Preus or, for that matter, by John Tietjen!) "Bad," moreover, could in this context mean either "evil" or else simply "incompetent" or "ineffective." Our main concern in the church must be with substantive, objective good and evil and with their irreconcilable difference, defined, of course, by reference to God's revealed will and Word. This paramount issue tends often to be clouded by useless wranglings about the character and qualities of individuals. Christian realism requires not only that we leave all ultimate judgments of hearts to God but also that we understand ourselves and others with humble, non-utopian sobriety (Rom. 12:3). On the one hand, the Christians' evil flesh (Romans 7) pollutes his best and finest works and service with injections of false, carnal motives. On the other hand, we can become the tools of objective evil despite our own best intentions and subjective sincerity (Matt. 16:22, 23). This Christian sobriety is quite unlike the sophisticated psychological claptrap which paralyses people into moral cowardice and a craven, "other-directed" spinelessness. On the contrary, Christian truth releases men for useful service to their gracious God, and to one another for His sake. For it means that what is good is good regardless of the human foibles and frailties of its servants and advocates. Evil, on the other hand, remains evil despite the good intentions and admirable human qualities of those who have been tricked into its service. We are not excused *from* truth and goodness by the unworthiness of their advocates, nor are we excused *into* falsehood and evil by any personal worth in their standard bearers. That is why Luther at the Imperial Diet of Worms (1521) refused to let his own faults in any way deter or distract him from the rightness of his cause:

> I confess that I have been more harsh against them than befits my religious vows and my profession. For I do not make myself out to be any kind of saint, nor am I now contending about my conduct but about Christian doctrine. But it is not in my power to recant them [the writings in question], because that recantation would give that tyranny and blasphemy an occasion to lord it over those whom I defend and to rage against God's people more violently than ever.[262]

This is not to say that church-political methods are of no importance. It is simply to place them into a churchly perspective, so that they are seen and judged not as ends in themselves, but as strictly subordinate means, serving the absolute primacy of the objective truth of the Gospel of Christ, that is, of the marks of the church. Church-government in the proper, Lutheran sense of the term is not "administration," but the tending of Christ's flock with Word and Sacraments by His called ministers, among whom presidents are first among equals.[263]

The worst church-politics is not honest, "divisive" leadership, but the unctuous Sadduceean "churchmanship" which sidesteps truth for the sake of togetherness, "peace," and, of course, the budget! And that remains the greatest threat to spiritual and theological integrity posed by the prevailing corporation-model of church structure:

> Reflecting the spirit of the times, the Church was becoming increasingly responsive to everything that made for effectiveness of action, and correspondingly allergic to any theoretical considerations that might hamper its vigorous activism . . .
>
> Following the dominant patterns of American life, there was an increasing tendency to think of the Church as a kind of business corporation chartered to do the Lord's work. The subordination of questions of truth—though only of those regarded as "unessential"—to efficiency of operation carries a recognisable suggestion of pragmatism.[264]

These significant sentences are taken from Loetscher's important book entitled *The Broadening Church*. The volume relates, with approval, the story of the U.S. Presbyterian Church's doctrinal collapse into modernism and indifferentism. This well-documented book's importance lies in the fact that, as the author says in his preface, much of the account "with appropriate changes of places and names—finds broad parallels in many another leading American Church. Its story is a kind of theological barometer of the times." Certainly the book presents many close parrallels to the Missouri Synod struggle some forty years later. The outcome, however, was totally different. In 1929 the liberals were in effective control of the Presbyterian denominational machinery, but were opposed by a conservative faculty majority at Princeton Seminary. The seminary was "reorganised," and the conservatives, under the brilliante J. Gresham Machen, founded the opposition Westminster Seminary in Philadelphia. In Missouri it was the other way around. In 1969 conservatives under Dr. J. A. O. Preus recaptured control of the synodical administration, while the liberals tried to safeguard continuation of the St. Louis seminary's "new direction" by installing the pro-Ecumenical Dr. John Tietjen as successor to President A. O. Fuerbringer. By 1974 the liberal faculty majority joined their deposed President Tietjen in "exile" at "Seminex." Why the difference in outcome? Why did the Missouri Synod become the only major American church-body to turn back the modernist tide? Part of the answer, under God's providence, doubtless lies in the fact that Missouri conservatives could truthfully claim that their position was not merely one strand or school among others, but the sole, authentic, and original confessional platform on which the Synod had been founded, and which it had consistently maintained since its 'inception. Presbyterian conservatives were not in that advantageous situation.

The church-political course of events in the Missouri Synod reflects at least two major distinct but closely related phases of theological struggle. The first phase was essentially over the quest for union with other U. S. Lutherans, particularly the ALC. This phase may well have been triggered by Missouri's rejection in 1929 of the Intersynodical, or "Chicago," Theses (1925), which had, after years of discussions, been agreed upon by the official representatives of the Buffalo, Iowa, Missouri, Ohio, and Wisconsin Synods.[265] Buffalo, Iowa, and Ohio formed the ALC in 1930, and many "progressive" Missourians not unnaturally felt a strong sense of kinship with that basically conservative body, and sought fellowship with it—at first undoubtedly with no thought of doctrinal change or compromise on Missouri's part. *The American Lutheran*, the organ of the American Lutheran Publicity Bureau (an unofficial organization within the Synodical Conference), became the standard-bearer of that point of view. By 1945, however, the "Statement of the 44" revealed, as we have seen, a significant shift in the doctrine of the church and of fellowship, and thus in the Confessional Principle itself. By the early fifties the Biblical Principle itself came under attack, inconnection with the "neo-orthodox" invasion, as we shall see in detail in the next section. This attack marked the second phase of the struggle.

Now the union-movement, in tum, became radicalized, aiming far beyond the ALC, at the pan-Lutheran LWF and also the WCC. The increasingly open attacks on Synod's traditional doctrine and the St. Louis seminary's obvious and leading role in the doctrinal changes, together with the most solemn official assurances that nothing like this was going on at all, resulted in a deep credibility crisis and produced a rising tide of conservative doctrinal concern which finally swept away the Harms administration in 1969, and the Tietjen administration at the seminary in 1974.

Any suggestion, therefore, that the whole thing was simply or even mainly "power-politics"[266] is false to the point of fraudulence. It is true that the "Preus forces" *tackled* the problem; but no one should pretend that they *created* it (I Kings 18:17)! What Preus brought was not revolution—that had happened long ago—but counter-revolution. The surprising thing, in view of Missouri's background, is not that the liberal invasion was finally repelled, but that it had been tolerated for so long.

Let us look more closely at three elements which had decisively shaped the pre-Preus situation: (1) the high priority of inter-Lutheran fellowship; (2) the conscious and crucial role of the St. Louis seminary leadership in reversing basic doctrinal positions; (3) the ostrich-like denials on the part of Synodical officials long after the situation had become perfectly obvious.

The centrality of the ALC-fellowship issue is hinted at in E. Clifford Nelson's probing questions:

> Did the ALC wooing of Missouri between 1959 and 1968 produce a backlash against "moderates" who were coming into positions of leadership? Did in fact the ALC create the phenomena of Jacob Preus and New Orleans? In other words, could the present (1973) polarization in Missouri have been avoided? Would the problem of organizational unity for the whole of American Lutheranism have been nearer solution? No one, of course, knows the answers, but the questions persist.[267]

Inter-Lutheran fellowship was clearly and explicitly a major concern already in the "Statement of the 44" (1945).[268] By 1961 liberal Missourian Martin E. Marty was publicly urging "the prophets" to work "from within" their denominations "for constructive subversion, encirclement, and infiltration, until anti-ecumenical forces bow to the evangelical weight of reunion."[269] This same approach some years later prompted *Christianity Today* to refer to Marty's endorsement of "ecclesiastical Machiavellianism" and to comment:

> Ministers who have taken denominational ordination vows are increasingly faced with the question of personal

honesty and integrity as they participate in a movement that explicity condemns denominations and aims at their merger into the ecumenical church. Applying the borrowed phrase "sociological Machiavellianism," Dr. Marty counsels a procedure that would actually promote "the ultimate death and transfiguration of these forms" while patiently "living in denominations and being faithful to their disciplines."[270]

Had Marty been speaking purely hypothetically, or was "constructive subversion, encirclement, and infiltration" against "anti-ecumenical forces" actually going on in his own Missouri Synod? The ranking theologian of the orthodox Lutheran churches in Europe, Prof. W. M. Oesch, observed in a comprehensive theological analysis, and precisely with reference to the same Martin E. Marty, "Missouri's young intellectuals are founding Jacobin Clubs behind the scene . . ."[271] Indeed, the liberal Prof. John Strietelmeier of Valparaiso University has gone even further. He admitted that there had been an actual liberal takeover which was then reversed at Denver in 1969:

> . . . for something like 25 years prior to 1969, the Lutheran Church-Missouri Synod was controlled by a coalition of Liberals and Moderates . . . . These years of Liberal ascendancy ended suddenly and decisively at the Synodical Convention in Denver in the summer of 1969 . . . Having come to power, the Conservative party did what the Liberals had done a generation before. They consolidated their power and began to divide the spoils.[272]

An insight into the origins and motives of this church-political manipulation of the Synod was given by another "insider," a prominent St. Louis seminary scholar (now at "Seminex"), who stated in a graduate class in July 1968

> . . . that the "progressive" movement got started in a smoke-filled pastor's office in New York City in 1930, when 3 LCMS pastors . . . decided, after Synod had turned down the Chicago Theses and had authorized the drafting of the Brief Statement, that they would start a movement to "change Synod." Their goals were to prepare the LCMS for outreach into America by use of English (vs. German), and by moving Synod toward a more open doctrinal stance. To attain these goals they urged the election of conservative leaders (e.g., Behnken) who would listen to their suggestions of names for seminary presidents, professors . . . and other

officials. [The professor] said he joined that growing underground movement in 1940.[273]

The point here is not to question the sincerity or even the real merit of much of this programme in its early stages, but simply to note the church-political implications, in view of the mischievous fable that church-politics entered Missouri only in the 1960's.

The pro-ecumenical "subversion, encirclement, and infiltration" finally came to fruition in the ill-fated Harms administration (1962-1969), which E. Clifford Nelson fittingly describes as follows: ". . . the synod elected Oliver Harms who was destined in the next seven years to lead Missouri into closer relationships with other Lutherans, including membership in the new Lutheran council, despite uneasiness among the traditionalists."[274] President Harms' single-minded determination to bring about fellowship with the ALC succeeded—though by a slim margin—in 1969, but at the cost of his own office. The St. Louis seminary had done what it could to support Harms, even sending him a formal letter of "loyalty" and "thanks" for his "leadership in the trying situations besetting the Church and especially in the progress toward fellowship with the American Lutheran Church."[275] But seeing the handwriting on the wall, the seminary administration moved swiftly, already in 1968, to insure itself against possible reversals at Denver. Dr. M. Scharlemann is on record to the effect that

> Dr. Repp one day suddenly announced to the faculty that we had better get a new president before the term of President Fuerbringer comes to an end. He suggested that the election of a new president ought to take place before the Denver Convention lest we get a man out of step with what was going on. I think you will understand how extraordinary such a suggestion is in light of the fact that new seminary presidents are not, as a rule, elected before the term of the previous one ends. I think it demonstrates a determination to prevent any possible change in what was going on at the seminary.[276]

And so Dr. John Tietjen was duly hand-picked as a suitable successor, despite the fact that he had received only a few congregational nominations, as compared with over sixty for Dr. M. Scharlemann and over a hundred for Dr. R. Bohlmann, the present incumbent.[277]

But there is no need to dig into obscure archives to discover the main reason why Tietjen was chosen for the important seminary post. The public record is perfectly unmistakable. Willmar Thorkelson, religion editor of the *Minneapolis Star* and a member of the ALC, reported in 1969, shortly after Denver:

> Besides the synod presidency, another key synod office was filled in 1969—the presidency of Concordia Seminary, St. Louis, where Dr. A. O. Fuerbringer retired. Named to succeed him was Dr. John H. Tietjen, former director of public relations for the Lutheran Council in the USA, who was expected to exercise strong leadership in the direction of great ecumenical involvement for the Missouri Synod, including LWF membership.[278]

What the religion editor of a secular newspaper knew must have been known also to the four electors whose votes secured the presidency for Tietjen: the Synodical president, the District president, and the chairman of the Board for Higher Education, and the seminary's Board of Control. Tietjen's book *Which Way To Lutheran Unity?* had appeared already three years before in 1966. The dust-jacket of this book described the author as a "Man with a View of Lutheranism's Momentum" and said of him:

> In 1959 he received his Th.D. from Union Theological Seminary, and began his editorship of the *American Lutheran*—first as managing editor, and then as editor from 1962 to 1966.. .. In September 1966 he became executive secretary, Division of Public Relations of the Lutheran Council in the United States of American (LCUSA).

The virulently pro-Ecumenical posture of the *American Lutheran* of those years is documented in virtually every issue. Nor did Tietjen himself make any secret of his pan-Lutheran viewpoint. All this must have been known to the electors who chose him; hence the only possible conclusion is that he was chosen to foster and protect the Ecumenical cause. His whole subsequent stand and behaviour have abundantly justified the confidence of those who elected him in his total dedication to the ecumenical programme and diplomacy.

With these considerations we have already entered upon the question of the St. Louis seminary's crucial leadership role. Synod's Board for Higher Education has officially found that there has been "a conscious effort over the years to change the doctrine of the LCMS by using the Synod's own schools to bring about change."²⁷⁹ How the St. Louis seminary fit into this general pattern became crystal-clear in Tietjen's own *American Lutheran*, which printed this triumphant editorial tribute in 1964:

> In recent years Concordia Seminary must be given credit for its share in the change that has been going on in the Lutheran Church-Missouri Synod. There are some who do not like to hear it, but the Missouri Synod has changed and is changing—in many ways—theologically too. The St. Louis seminary has helped produce the change. About the middle of the forties the Seminary itself experienced a change. With the passing of an older generation of professors younger men arrived on the scene, men who had studied in institutions outside of the Missouri Synod, men who had escaped from the cultural isolation . . . Quietly and unobtrusively the seminary faculty prepared the ministry of the future. Slowly the synod began to change. The Seminary alone is not responsible. Yet it has contributed to the change . . .
>
> Hounded by heresy hunters, its faculty members have had to cross every orthodox t and dot every doctrinal i in all of their public utterances . . .
>
> The time has come for Concordia Seminary to reclaim its role as teacher of the Missouri Synod. In ever so many areas the synod needs effective theological leadership. The faculty members of the Seminary ought to speak out boldly on the questions of Biblical interpretation, ecumenical involvement, confrontation with the problems of a scientific age, the relation of the Christian faith to social issues, and reforms needed in the Lutheran Church today. There are signs that members of the faculty are prepared to speak out. The responsible synodical officials ought to stand ready to support the Seminary in its exercise of leadership. And the church had better listen. Church is always in need of prophets. It may not always like what they say, but woe to the church when it fails to pay heed.²⁸⁰

These observations are more perceptive and revealing than the Seminary's understandably more reticent official history, *Log Cabin To Luther Tower*, by C. S. Meyer (1965). The book contains a wealth of fascinating details, but tends to skirt the larger issues. Pastor T. Baker's frankly polemical tract *Watershed at the Rivergate* (1973) is strewn with enticing clues which ought to be pursued by anyone seeking to supplement and update Meyer's book.

It is self-evident, especially in the circumstances which led up to Denver, that the Seminary was deeply involved in the Synod's political processes. Thus the *Faculty Journal* for May 28, 1968, states laconically: "Fuerbringer described the importance of good nominations for elections at the Denver convention." This involvement was intensified under the Tietjen administration, noted for its unprecedented intransigence and open defiance not only of Synodical officials, but of the Synod itself. Much was made of President Preus' exasperated pre-New Orleans remark that "Tietjen must go." Yet already a year before that the Tietjen administration had announced, in the *New York Times* of all places, that Preus must go! The four-column special dispatch from St. Louis, printed on June 11, 1972, stated:

> Faced with the loss of accreditation, the Concordia Seminary faculty and administration acknowledged this week that the school's future as a viable academic in situation depended on the Lutheran Church-Missouri Synod rejecting its conservative leader, the Rev. Dr. Jacob A. O. Preus, or in revising church laws to check his power...
>
> Many faculty members say privately that the ideal solution for the seminary is defeat of Dr. Preus...

The dispatch does not mention the curious fact that prominent Missouri "moderates," including Dr. A. C. Repp of the St. Louis seminary, were among the leading officials of the accrediting agency, the American Association of Theological Schools (AATS). The Tietjen administration had already tried in connection with President Preus' investigation of the seminary to frighten synodical authorities with the prospect of loss of accreditation.[281] Even more curious is the article's suggestion that the 1973 New Orleans convention should, beside defeating Preus, revise synodical regulations "to shore up the independent authority of the school's board of control." A few days earlier *St. Louis Post-Dispatch* religion editor James E. Adams had, under the dramatic heading, "Concordia President Seeks Aid of Synod,"[282] reported President Tietjen's plan more fully:

> The seminary has no alternative now except a program of making the members aware of the long-term threats posed to Concordia and the synod's 15 other institutions of higher learning, he said.

"In all likelihood, there will have to be revision of our by-laws to establish that our board of control actually has control of the institution," he said. "We can't do this without the help of the synod."

Either the seminary president was bluffing, or else he was being very naive in thinking that the Synod was in any mood to abandon the St. Louis seminary to its own devices. When the New Orleans Convention (1973) made short shrift of such illusions, Tietjen acted boldly to create a financial base for future theological independence in the form of the "Fund for Lutheran Theological Education" (FLUTE), with Drs. Tietjen, Damm, Krentz, and Bertram among the incorporators![283]

There is no need to pursue here every question of ad ministrative detail or even intrigue. An official White Paper will no doubt eventually document the record of those years. (So far the post-Tietjen Seminary in St. Louis has been prevented by the muzzle of Synodical By-law 5:31j from publishing its case against ex-President Tietjen. Since Tietjen and his partisans have exercised no such restraint, the general impression given to the church—both here and abroad!—may well have been confusing.) One question, however, ought to be faced. It has to do with the well-known claim of the "moderates" that they represent brotherly tolerance, healthy "diversity," "liberating unity,"[284] and the like, as opposed to the conservatives' penchant for narrowness, division, legalistic conformity, uniformity, etc. In actual fact, the liberal promotion of "diversity" was more rhetoric than reality, a tactic rather than a principle. It was resorted to in direct proportion to the liberals' loss of influence. The most fervent plea for the representation of "the complete spectrum of permissible opinion" in Synodical schools and agencies, by way of a "kind of evangelical balance-wheel operation" appeared in December, 1972.[285] By that time the liberal movement was pleading for its own survival. While it had been in power it certainly had not demonstrated any great concern for fairness of representation. Will anyone argue that Tietjen was chosen as president—over Bohlmann and Scharlemann—to reflect the general convictions of the Synod? Or that *C.T.M.* editorial policy on ALC-fellowship, for instance—rotated to the sweet harmonies of an "evangelical balance-wheel"? And why, when the "crunch" came, were there only *five* tough-minded conservatives on the St. Louis faculty—out of a total of 48? Even these five were more survivors from former times than "token" acquisitions, since most of them had joined the faculty already in the fifties, and none of them after 1963! Was this an example of "liberating unity"?

Nor is it at all likely that even these "minority five" would have been allowed to function without let or hindrance, had the Tietjen-administration succeeded in maintaining control of Concordia Seminary. The formal division into majority and minority parties must be traced to the watershed faculty meeting of April 16, 1970. This meeting had been called to condemn Martin Scharlemann, in his absence, for having dared to take the seminary's problems to the President of the Synod—basically the same crime for which Herman Otten was made to languish in synodical limbo these many years. Scharlemann had for several years expressed misgivings about the seminary's drift away from Synod's confessional stand. Convinced that seminary-sponsored discussions were becoming "a game we were playing," Scharlemann acted, thus triggering President Preus' fateful decision to appoint a Fact Finding Committee. Scharlemann reports:

> The time had come, I concluded, to prepare a formal request to the President of Synod that official inquiry be made into the situation at the seminary. That letter was sent to President Preus on April 9, 1970. It described, under ten points, the strong kinds of doctrine that students were hearing and telling. My request suggested that whatever committee was to be appointed should be given authority to insist on straight answers. I indicated that I felt such an inquiry needed to be made in order to clear the name of the seminary and to certify to the church that what was being taught was, in fact, Lutheran theology.
>
> The response of the administration came in the form of a most vicious personal attack during a special faculty meeting called for that purpose for April 16, 1970. In this meeting—the subject of which the president refused to announce ahead of time!—the carbon copy of my letter to President Preus was read to the faculty, in my absence and without my permission . . . The faculty itself passed a much milder resolution than the administration had suggested, I might add. Three men among more than fifty had the integrity and courage to take exception to what was going on and had their objections as well as their negative votes recorded.
>
> Since I am sure that this matter would come before the

Board, I wrote President Tietjen at once, asking for permission to sit in the Board meeting to defend myself when his report on it would be made. This request was brusquely denied. In fact, I was accused of in subordination.

In time (as you know) the inquiry got under way. While professing all kinds of cooperation in public, the administration of the seminary used every conceivable device to call off or to frustrate the course of action determined by President Preus.[286]

Not everyone of course was as unintimidated as General (U.S. Air Force) Scharlemann, who had himself been at the heart of a synodical storm less than a decade earlier. It is said that Dr. A. C. Piepkorn wept openly as he was forced to choose between his comrade-in-arms and the seminary administration. Later, in his defence of Arlis Ehlen, President Tietjen enunciated the principle:

> If the phrase, "higher critical views", refers to the use of historical-critical methodology, then it is not possible for Dr. Ehlen to teach any of his assigned courses at a seminary level of instruction, thus taking the text of the Holy Scriptures with utter seriousness, without using historical-critical methodology. Nor is that possible for any other faculty member who teaches a course in Biblical interpretation, regardless of the department to which he may belong.[287]

Given the right circumstances, troublesome opponents of the historical-critical method might on this basis be considered "unscholarly" and dealt with accordingly. But a resourceful administration need rarely resort to the most drastic measures. More indirect ones will normally do. Take academic advancement. On November 17, 1970, President Tietjen announced to the faculty that Prof. E. Schroeder of Valparaiso University had been called to the seminary's Systematics Department.[288] Schroeder was at once given the full professorial rank denied to Bohlmann and Klann despite their qualifications and seniority.[289] Nor does it seem likely that the Autumn 1973 enrollment trends were altogether spontaneous: with six sections of Symbolics offered to first-year men, who presumably had as yet no real basis for judgment, only nineteen chose the normally popular Robert Preus, eleven took Wunderlich, and one took Klann, while the sections of faculty-majority members were overflowing beyond the usual limit of 30.

Of course it is only fair to observe that the Tietjen administration saw itself beleaguered from the outset. But could it ever have been different, given the alternatives imposed by the liberals' self-understanding: "perpetuating a legalistic immigrant sect or rediscovering a church that is essentially ecumenical, evangelical, and in perpetual need of renewal"?[290] Did not such a view necessarily call for a large dose of Marty's "subversion, encirclement, and infiltration"? And theological guerilla warfare never fosters parliamentary ideals of fair representation! Indeed, even the Federated Theological Faculty of Chicago, which had made "diversity" its very reason for being, found the principle difficult to apply:

> It contained unregenerate, modified, and neo-orthodox liberals. Indeed, there was a deliberate effort made in new appointments to maintain a diversity of views. But if this process of self-education on the part of the faculty was to be continued, it soon became clear that certain types of mind would not fit into the Faculty circle. A man, for instance, might be a notable scholar and highly prized as a possible member of the Faculty; and yet he would not be considered if he took the position that his ideas alone were valid or if he declined to listen to the voice of alternate points of view. A doctrinaire stance like that would quickly destroy the basis on which the Faculty conducted its common intellectual life.[291]

If even a half-secular interdenominationalism saw its insipid "diversity" threatened by dogma or conviction, how much genuine diversity could reasonably be expected from a movement dedicated to "subversion, encirclement, and infiltration"?

Finally, one needs to examine the growing incredibility of the official make-believe, to appreciate the utter exasperation that finally produced the conservative "backlash." As early as 1936 the newly elected President John W. Behnken received a detailed theological analysis of perilous trends from Pastor William Oesch, then in charge of Luther-Tyndale Memorial Church in London, the mother-church of the Evangelical Lutheran Church of England. Oesch warned against certain directions evident, above all, in the *American Lutheran*:

> Crypto-Calvinism, an externalised and enthusiast conception of the Church for which the pure Means of Grace are not pivotal and the [civic and churchly] spheres blurred; but

also Crypto-Romanism, to make what had been reduced to less, in essence, look more, in appearance, and thus to cheat the devil. The statement was that these two strands were converging toward a version of the Social Gospel.[292]

Later Pastor Oesch published three numbers of *The Crucible*, which continued the careful theological analysis. The outbreak of World War II in 1939 ended the venture. The cause was taken up again in America in 1940 by *The Confessional Lutheran*, which battled on valiantly for nearly three decades under the energetic editorship of Pastor Paul Burgdorf. Dr. Behnken, as his memoirs indicate,[293] saw little merit in those early warnings and responded accordingly. This tragic absence from the outset of any real meeting of the minds between the synodical administration and conservative critics was to cost the Synod dearly. Positions hardened, relations deteriorated, the theological situation worsened, yet remedial action was postponed. By 1959 the Synodical administration itself appeared worried, hence the ill-fated "Resolution 9" of the San Francisco Convention, seeking to "hold the line," above all, on the *Brief Statement* of 1897/1932.

The years 1961 and 1962 saw two "State of the Church" conferences, with several hundred people taking part. Although the meetings were organized privately by conservatives, Dr. Behnken sent Dr. L. B. Meyer as his personal envoy to observe the proceedings. Meyer issued a formal "evaluation," which did its best to allay concerns and was sent by Dr. Behnken to all pastors and teachers in the Synod. Out of these meetings there issued a permanent organization, its publication *The Faithful Word*, and two wide-ranging *Books of Documentation* full of photo-copied evidence of varying quality and relevance, concerning the progress of liberalism and ecumenism in the Missouri Synod. All this turmoil could hardly have arisen quite suddenly, without any warning. Yet the 1960 convention of the Western (now Missouri) District of the LC-MS had been edified with the following incredible "Respectful Observations" by its public relations committee:

> The Lutheran Church-Missouri Synod by general consensus has done well in keeping pure the Bible doctrines in its teaching and preaching. With the present group of Synod's and the Western District's officials, and the Western District clergy, the best indoctrinated of all churches in the world, there is no particular need for worry in this regard. However, let us earnestly ponder upon the question:

How Can We Better Our Public Relations?
For this self-analysis much helpful information can be received if we all take as our key question: *"How can the church have more popular appeal?"*[294]

In 1962 Oliver Harms was elected president, upon the retirement of John W. Behnken, after a long and fruitful tenure. ("The Romans have their John XXIII," it was quipped at the time, "but we have our John the everlasting.") Towards the end of his presidency Dr. Behnken had become very troubled about the situation, and he made no secret of it. At a theological conference in Thiensville in 1960, which sought to avert the imminent breakup of the Synodical Conference, Behnken said, sadly but with deep humility and honesty, that Synodical Conference principles had been violated in Missouri and that "some of these men have not been disciplined as firmly and as quickly as they should have been." He continued:

> Our meetings . . . and also this conclave have convinced me all the more that it is necessary to emphasize and put into practice firmer discipline . . . We realize that the independent action on the part of a few—who by some are called intellectuals—has caused misgivings in the minds and in the hearts of our brethren within the Synodical Conference. We are sorry for these actions and we beg your pardon. [295]

But the full extent of the deterioration became clear to Behnken only after his retirement. He complained to friends that he had been misled by the St. Louis seminary administration. Only such a conviction on Behnken's part can account for what must surely be regarded as a drastic step for a man of his standing. Having received no satisfactory response to a series of twenty eight pointed questions about the historicity of persons and events in the Old Testament, which Behnken had submitted to the seminary president (Fuerbringer) in 1966, he now (March 6, 1967) treated his document as public, and sent it to all District Presidents, seminary faculties and boards of control, and to others.[296] Most of the questions were spiked with a blunt question: "If so, why? If not, why not?" Behnken's "earnest, request and fervent plea" was that he "be given frank, conscientious answers on the basis of Scripture, God's holy Word." The St. Louis faculty minutes for March 28, 1967, reveal no response except polite contempt: "Dr. J. W. Behnken has directed some questions concerning phases of interpretation of Genesis to the faculty and to many others. Copies of his questions were distributed." Period. Finish. And that was that! Fuerbringer, of course, had had the questions already since the previous summer, but they are not mentioned in the official record of his report to the faculty's opening retreat in September, 1966:

> Conditions in Synod are a little less troublesome, although pockets of disaffection continue . . . The faculty should be thoughtful concerning nominations for synodical offices. They may be cleared with the President's office if desired . . . The influence of the State of the Church Movement and the Wisconsin Synod is lessening. The group is recognising that its own structures are beset by the same problems of which they accuse us. There may be possibility of bringing these men back into the main stream of Lutheranism.[297]

At any rate, officially it was Dr. Harms' problem now. He was personally committed to orthodoxy. But he could never overcome the predicament illustrated by an incident which had occurred already half a year before his election. The District presidents and theological faculties had heard and considered Prof. Robert Preus' penetrating analysis of "Current Theological Problems Which Confront Our Church,"[298] namely the doctrine of Scripture, the historical-critical method, and the ecumenical movement. Harms himself had closed with a plea for "complete faithfulness to the Word" and for "integrity without 'double talk through use of unclear language.'"[299] Yet the same *Lutheran Witness* article which reported Harms' remarks, concluded with this soothing untruth: "Above all, our District Presidents can assure their people that despite certain liberal developments among some Lutheran theologians, our Synod's seminaries stand squarely and surely on the foundation of the Bible and the Lutheran Confessions." The same technique was used by the *Luthern Witness* the year after Harms' election. A candid-sounding "Synodogram" ("From Synodical Headquarters") assured readers that the obvious changes in theology were matters of wording only, not of content. The article concluded:

> Because it is generally known that the Missouri Synod is wrestling with theological problems, this question is asked: "Have we changed our doctrinal position?"
>
> The answer is no . . .
>
> Says Dr. Harms: ". . . Our studies will make it clear that

the Word of God with all its doctrines is our sure and immovable constant. . ."[300]

And so it went. Concerned inquirers were assured by Harms "that in my frequent conversations with professors who are in question in the areas you mentioned, I have the insistent statements and confession that they promote completely, and wholeheartedly our traditional position on inspiration, inerrancy, and revelation."[301]

Two "bomb-shell" pronouncements date back to those early Harms years. The first was a decision of the Texas District Board of Appeals, handed down on July 3, 1963:

> We believe the defendant supplied and has presented a preponderance of evidence to accentuate a situation in Synod that amounts to liberality [sic] and treason. . .
>
> We believe there is a situation in Synod similar to that which prevailed to and even during the Reformation period, when the Roman Catholic church excommunicated men such as Luther for being too catholic, while it retained in its fellowship the skeptics and scoffers, since they did not attack nor defy authority . . . the defendant presented sufficient evidence to sustain the charges of liberality [sic] and treason in some quarters of Synod . . .[302]

Even more pointed was Synodical Vice-President Dr. R. Wiederaenders' statement to the District presidents and the seminary faculties on December 2, 1963:

> Despite repeated efforts we have not dealt honestly with our pastors and people. We have refused to state our changing theological position in open, honest, forthright, simple and clear words. Over and over again we said that nothing was changing when all the while we were aware of changes taking place. Either we should have informed our pastors and people that changes were taking place and, if possible, convinced them from Scripture that these changes were in full harmony with "Thus saith the Lord!" or we should have stopped playing games as we gave assurance that no changes were taking place. With increasing measure the synodical trumpet has been giving an uncertain sound.[303]

The level of Synodical unrest reached a new high in 1965, with the rise of the "Faith Forward-First Concerns" movement. Unlike previous groupings, such as the "State of the Church" conferences, the new movement included among its active participants not simply "grass-roots" elements, but District presidents and others who wielded considerable in fluence. New and powerful pressures were now exerted on President Harms to do something about the St. Louis seminary. Harms himself gave a few potent examples in his letter to President Fuerbringer of December 17, 1965, which initiated a remarkable series of exchanges now on file in the archives of synodical headquarters. Among other things the letter mentioned a group of concerned District presidents, a District in which fifteen out of sixteen circuit counselors faced the problem of contributions being withheld, a Chicago-based conservative action group formed by prominent laymen, specific protests against public statements by seminary professors and others, and the open amusement in some circles over the forty-million dollar offering campaign. To help him meet this barrage of criticism, directed largely at the seminary, Harms suggested "that perhaps a statement with which the faculty would agree but prepared and signed by the department heads would help. This statement should be a short statement, a simple one, one that addresses itself very directly to the points at issue . . . very straightforward, synodstanced, and in complete agreement with Holy Scripture and the historic Lutheran Confessions, the Lord guiding us."

Under date of January 20, 1966, the faculty responded with a two-page letter which affirmed central Christian truths on the basis of Scripture, creeds, and confessions, but in phrases which, however excellent in themselves, were nebulous in the context of the synodical controversy. On February 15, Dr. Harms thanked Dr. Fuerbringer for the assurances which "under ordinary circumstances should make the hearts of people glad." He found, "however, that our present needs perhaps need some kind of a statement which denies the contrary to what you have said so well in the letter from the faculty." Harms then expressed the hope that the faculty would be willing to add clear rejections of errors which had been attributed to them, for example, that "the factuality and truthfulness of Scripture is denied," that "the Bible contains errors," and the denial of "the historical correctness of Genesis 1, 2, and 3" in deference to evolution. Harms even prepared a sample formulation, showing how his suggestions for clear rejections of errors might be incorporated into the text of the faculty statement of January 20. The gist of Fuerbringer's reply, on April 11, 1966, was contained in this paragraph:

By and large, neither the Sacred Scriptures nor the Lutheran symbolical books speak directly enough to some of the issues that your letter raises to enable our faculty to make the kind of statement that you desire without a great deal of careful reflection. Much of the discussion that is going on in our church-body and elsewhere in Christendom centers around the meaning of terms like "factuality", "historical correctness", "error", "flesh", and "evolution". I believe that it will unquestionably be possible to formulate a consensus among the members of the faculty on any of these issues and we propose to address ourselves to them. At the same time, this will not, in my opinion, take place within any time limit that would be of help to you in your present situation.

Harms was no doubt thoroughly disillusioned but took no steps to provoke a head-on collision with the seminary. Perhaps he simply became preoccupied with other pressing concerns, such as the campaign for fellowship with the ALC. Publicly the synodical administration closed ranks with the seminary, continuing to maintain as a united front that there was no false doctrine.

By this time an impressive list of outside opinions, judgments, and warnings were on record. Fraternal relations were suspended in 1955 by the Evangelical Lutheran ("little Norwegian") Synod and in 1961 by Wisconsin—largely because of Missouri's unionistic direction.[304] The ultra-liberal journal *Dialog* commented that "Wisconsin was ultimately forced to conclude that the representatives from Missouri either were incredibly ignorant of the state of affairs in their own churches or were deliberately glossing the troublesome differences and making promises they could not, or did not intend to, keep".[305]

The leading dogmatician of the European Lutheran free churches, Dr. William M. Oesch, published the first part of his thorough analysis, *Memorandum Inter Nos*, in May, 1960. In 1962 the Evangelical Lutheran Church of Australia took the unprecedented step of addressing formal letters of fraternal concern to both Missouri and Wisconsin, in the wake of their separation. The most serious admonitions by far were addressed to the Missouri Synod. The seven specific concerns included toleration of "destructive Biblical criticism, " and "What appears to be uncertainty of the Lutheran conception of the Church as expressed and confessed in Augustana VII and VIII, and in the corresponding

Article of the Apology, with the result that the distinction between orthodox churches and heterodox churches also practically goes by the board." Moreover, there was "the seeming failure or inability of officials, district synods, and the general convention to deal effectually with these extremely grave phenomena."[306] Although the letter was addressed directly to "The Lutheran Church-Missouri Synod, assembled in regular Convention at Cleveland, Ohio, June 20-30, 1962," it was never given to the convention, but only to a committee.[307]

There were other Australian efforts,[308] including finally a public plea by Prof. Sasse not to establish fellowship with the ALC or membership in the LWF in 1969. Another 1969 document, in the same vein as Sasse's, originated in Australia but was signed by distinguished Lutheran free church leaders in Germany, France, Belgium, and Finland. It was published as "Occasional Paper No. 1" by *Balance*, later to evolve into *Affirm*. The Finnish church had sent in a detailed plea and protest already prior to the 1967 New York convention. By the time of Denver, 1969, "all the continental European sister churches of the LC-MS" had "officially intervened," reports Dr. Oesch in his wide-ranging Bethany Reformation Lectures on the state of Lutheranism.[309]

The sensation of Denver is well known. It is not true, however, that Dr. Harms was the first incumbent Missouri Synod president to be voted out of office. It had happened before—when Behnken replaced Pfotenhauer in 1935. Of course, no one imagines that such things happen, even humanly speaking, entirely by accident. The pro-Preus movement had been spearheaded by the *Balance* group, which seems to have grown out of "Faith Forward-First Concerns." Among its highly-respected leaders were Pastor William T. Eggers, editor of the *Badger Lutheran*; Prof. Walter A. Maier of Concordia Theological Seminary, Springfield, a son of the *Lutheran Hour* preacher; Prof. Robert Preus of St. Louis, the redoubtable authority on, and champion of, Lutheran Orthodoxy; Dr. Waldo Werning, author and administrator; and Dr. Eugene Bertermann, editor of the *Lutheran Layman*. Yet it seems at least doubtful whether events would or could have taken this course without the long and lonely years of courageous idol-smashing carried on by Pastor Herman Otten's *Lutheran News* (1962), which became the weekly *Christian News* in 1968. It has been a remarkable phenomenon. Feared, ridiculed, hated, and condemned it was; but ignored, hardly ever. Always independent, no matter who was in power synodically, *Christian News* pursued its own prophetic mission without fear or favor. And one does not expect "fairness" or diplomacy from prophets or gadflies! Errors of judgment occurred, of course, but no other paper was as open to correction as *Christian News*. Blunt and abrasive the paper was and is—but for examples of real "lovelessness" and personal malevolence one must turn to the unbelievable letters of its critics.

Like Luther, *Christian News* was plain-spoken. But without this dogged plain-spokenness would the Missouri Synod ever have woken up? Of course, the open appeal to the grass-roots[310] was in the nature of the case more obvious, more public than the quiet manipulations and machinations of privileged elites behind the scenes in the ivory towers of seminaries, colleges, and bureaucracies. But was it therefore more "political"? If anything was "political," it was the underhanded takeover and exploitation of Missouri Synod institutions by those who, however sincere, were subverting the Synod's declared doctrinal stand while pretending otherwise. Open appeals to rank-and-file pastors and people in the name of truth—with no reward except hatred and contempt—are in the best of churchly traditions. Effeminate sentimentality and a spineless roundaboutness are simply not the same as Christian love at all. Such considerations no doubt prompted Dr. H. Sasse—who could never uncritically embrace Missouri's entire theological heritage, much less *Christian News*' unbending version of it—to write shortly after the conservative triumph at Denver, 1969: "Somebody should rise and publicly thank Herman Otten for his brave fight. We all were sometimes not fully agreed with him. He has made blunders. But why was it left to a young pastor to speak where others should have spoken?"[311]

Denver was but the prelude to New Orleans, 1973. The root of the trouble was at the St. Louis seminary and had to be faced there or not at all. The new Tietjen administration tried the same nonchalant policy of "hear no evil, see no evil, speak no evil," which had worked so well for so long. But without the active support of the synodical administration, things became rather more difficult. It was so typical of the seminary to seek refuge in public relations. A $5000 survey by a professional public relations firm revealed that fully one third of the pastors polled would not agree that the seminary was "true to sound Lutheran principles."[312]

President J. A. O. Preus' Fact Finding Committee, having interviewed the St. Louis faculty members between December 11, 1970 and March 6, 1971, submitted its report to the President of Synod on June 15, 1971. He, in turn, issued a full Report to the church on September 1, 1972, after the seminary's Board of Control had had a chance to act on the Fact Finding Committee's findings. This presidential report fully establishes, from the actual interview transcripts, the alarming doctrinal deteriorations, particularly in the areas of Biblical authority versus historical criticism, and of church fellowship and doctrinal latitude. The seminary's own counter production, *Faithful To Our Calling, Faithful To Our Lord*, which the author has analyzed elsewhere,[313] was designed to offset the negative impact of the investigation, but its admissions, evasions, and omissions really had the opposite effect. Despite the mounting evidence, Tietjen continued to make glowing public pronouncements. For example, several discussions in 1969-1970 between the seminary's departments of systematic and exegetical theology had revealed such serious disagreements that the secretary was directed to "prepare a statement of divergent positions" by February 18, 1970.[314] When the statement was presented and discussed at the interdepartmental meeting on that date, "President Tietjen asked the members of the departments to keep that document confidential because, he claimed, it would be 'disastrous' if it got out into the church."[315] Yet when the "minority five" of the faculty on November 4, 1970, publicly dissociated themselves from a faculty statement because of "basic theological differences within the faculty," Tietjen stated in the *Lutheran Witness Reporter* (November 15, 1970): "this is the first time it has ever been formally brought to my attention that some faculty members claim there are basic theological differences"! Nor were these differences minor. In a small group discussion on May 6, 1970, of Tietjen's suggestions for interpreting the seminary to the Synod as soundly Lutheran, the chairman of the exegetical department

> stated that every member of his department operated on the assumption that the Bible contained serious contradictions and that our exegetes could no longer employ the method of harmonising the Biblical records. He referred to the people in the synod who opposed the historical-critical method as "harmonisers". His illustrations of alleged differences within the Bible made it clear that he was talking

about major theological emphases rather than mere discrepancies in detail. He also stated that one reason for the difficulties in the synod on this matter is that members of his department operate on the assumption that the positions of Pieper and the *Brief Statement* have long ago been overcome.[316]

Yet as late as April 11, 1975, writing in *Christianity Today*, Tietjen accused President Preus of creating a "smokescreen" with the claim that the authority of the Bible was at stake, and said; "The authority of the Bible is not at issue in the Missouri Synod . . . I fully accept the authority of the Bible. I am totally committed to the Bible as the inspired and infallible Word of God."

The New Orleans Convention, despite impassioned rhetoric against the move, adopted the meticulously reasoned and documented Resolution 3-09, which declared certain positions associated with the St. Louis faculty majority to be "false doctrine running counter to the Holy Scriptures, the Lutheran Confessions, and synodical stance," which therefore, in the words of the Formula of Concord, "cannot be tolerated in the church of God, much less be excused and defended."

Since then, it is true, the fight has been mainly about bylaws and administrative procedures. This unpleasant situation has been forced on the Synod quite deliberately by the "moderate" leadership's steadfast refusal, in their continued public relations program, to come clean on the serious doctrinal differences. Even the liberal *Forum Letter* (May 1975) commented on "Seminex" tactics at the April 1975 theological convocation:

> As one Seminex prof remarked, "I'm not sure from day to day what our approach is. One day we're going to candidly state our differences and let the devil take the hindmost. The next we're trying to demonstrate that we believe the same thing 'old Missouri' always believed about inerrancy and all the rest." Seminex reps at the convo tended to take the second tack, as they did at New Orleans in 1973. Of course Seminex has a continuing concern about placing people in LCMS parishes.
>
> . . . But Seminex credibility is strengthened by candour, not by pretending there are few if any significant differences. If, for example, the historical-critical method doesn't make that much difference in what one believes about the Bible or how one does theology, why bother everybody by in-

sisting on using it?

Still more remarkable was the conclusion of Dr. Milton Nauss of St. Louis that, while charges of "injustice and lack of integrity" against conservatives are "justified to a degree," the "Moderates are even more guilty of these same things, however, in a more sophisticated fashion."[317] He explained:

> It was the Moderates who inaugurated the Synodical controversy in the late 1950's and early 1960's when they introduced a new mode of Biblical interpretation which began casting questions upon traditional ways of accepting the Creation account, the Fall into sin, the Jonah account, certain miracles and statements of Jesus Christ, etc . . .
>
> When various lay people, pastors and professors called these divergencies to the attention of the Synodical Administration in the 1960's, they were assured that "nothing has changed" in our Synodical teaching. I believe this was a cover-up—likewise a serious lack of integrity.
>
> When the Concordia Seminary faculty walk-out ocurred in early 1974, we were led to believe this was a spontaneous action. Actually, the fact of the matter is (as has been divulged) that this was a strategy which had been planned already some time prior. This too indicates a lack of integrity.

All the same, the endless preoccupation with by-laws is a danger-signal. Among Lutherans it is axiomatic that only "faith" (doctrine, sacraments), not "order" (administration, government) of itself can be church-divisive. In God's Word and doctrine there can be no yielding, but in outward matters, such as indifferent ceremonies or man-made regulations for good order, the rule is that love shall be supreme and consciences may not be bound. On occasion it may be the Christian duty of the majority to yield to the minority in such matters. Conservatives dare never absolutize the letter of human regulations, but must be ever mindful of their churchly intent. This means too that conservatives should beware of simply echoing liberal charges of "playing politics" every time an orthodox president of synod restrains the full use of his authority in order to avert greater harm among confused and excited people. "The salvation of the people is the ultimate law," says an ancient maxim.

Beneath the necessary church-political struggle, it must be remembered, there are unavoidable theological issues. Liberals may profit from the realism and conservatives from the magnanimity of O. P. Kretzmann, former President of Valparaiso University, who, though he was thoroughly out of sympathy with the direction of New Orleans, nevertheless had the greatness to write of it:

The Sound of a Scream—However else the sound from Rivergate is interpreted, it needs to be heard as a scream. The pain had become unbearable. Oppressed brethren answered in the only way they could. "Get off me, you are crushing me!" The scream sought relief—and with it a pardonable sense of momentary vengeance. "Let somebody else do the screaming for a change!"

Together with the great "credibility barrier," the "scream" is a phenomenon to be reckoned with. It can be explored by conversation with brethren who participated in it and felt the relief. The voice is there, ready to interpret. It says things like these:

"I am only a simple pastor, trying to do my work. The Seminary does not care about me. It talks down to me, makes me feel like a fool. The *CTM* is too hard to read, not worth the effort. Even if I had time to read it, it gives me nothing I can use where I am. It disturbs me, but fails to comfort me."

Again, "When the Seminary says 'un-Lutheran' to President Preus, it says 'un-Lutheran' to me. I identify with him, belong to the Missouri he describes. To attack him is to attack me. I stand accused, but cannot comprehend the accusation."

The Scream continues, "The Seminary has had it all its own way. Professors have felt free to pursue their exotic learning, to delight in new knowledge. But they are totally out of touch with me. They have no feeling for the church as I know it. It is supposed to be the church's Seminary. How can it be that, when I can no longer joyfully, confidently, proudly identify with it!" And again, "The Seminary has not been honest with me. It calls me 'un-Lutheran,' yet insists nothing has really changed. Well, I know that I have not changed! I am preaching and teaching faithfully the way the Pastor did who confirmed me, the way I was taught. If the Seminary cannot even realize that it has changed, it is either blind or dishonest."

"What else can I conclude!" the Scream says. "The abstract intellectualism at the Seminary is rationalism. The Seminary is evasive, not playing square with the church. Its responses all look defensive and tactical to me, as though designed to cover up a secret subversion of the Scripture principle by a specious use of the Gospel. What about the simple question of historicity, for example! Why cannot the Seminary understand that question, and give the church a direct, simple, and clear answer!"

The voice says, "You talk of suffering, of persons and families who will suffer. Have you no feeling for that minority on the Seminary faculty, for their pain, for what they have suffered? They have felt judged, excluded, accused, unwanted, unheard. I identify with them. Their pain is my pain. If they could not be loved and heard in the fellowship of the whole faculty, how can I expect to be loved and heard from where I am?" Therefore the Scream. It is more than theological. It is from brethren of ours, deeply wounded.

If that Scream can be heard now, and even welcomed for what it is telling us, that in itself could be seen as a gift of divine and necessary grace—and a little sign of hope for our beloved church's tomorrow.[318]

CENTER STAGE

IV. THE COUNTER-BIBLICAL (CRITICAL) ATTACK

1. *The Critical Contagion in Stages*: ULCA-ALC-LCMS

Although looser views of biblical authority, inspiration, and inerrancy were held already prior to World War I by individual theologians in the Iowa Synod, the General Council, and especially in the General Synod,[319] the Lutheran bodies generally presented a "solid front against the claims of critical study of the Bible."[320] "On the whole, Lutheranism in America looked upon scholars who used the historical-critical approach to the Bible as subversives" (Nelson).[321] Already in 1920, however, the newly formed United Lutheran Church's "Washington Declaration," in conscious opposition to what was regarded as "the exclusivist confessionalism" of the midwestern synods, "refused to speak of verbal inspiration and inerrancy of the Scriptures."[322] Still speaking of the ULCA, historian Clifford Nelson continues:

> By 1927-1930 individual professors of theology were taking positions incompatible with an orthodoxist view of scriptural inerrancy. They used the method of historical criticism and carefully distinguished between the Scriptures and the Word of God without separating one from the other.

Nelson also informs us that the pioneer and leading exponent of the new movement in the ULCA was the great T. E. Schmauk's successor in the Philadelphia (Mt. Airy) Seminary, C. M. Jacobs.[323] The latter followed generally in the wake of the German Erlangen University theology, which had discarded verbal inspiration and inerrancy "in favor of an emphasis on Scripture as the faithful witness of the early church to the revelation (Word) of God."[324] Both Walther and Pieper, as we have seen, protested most vigorously against the Erlangen approach, particularly that of its leading light, von Hofmann, who denied not only verbal inspiration, but even Christ's substitutionary atonement. Hofmann's radically unorthodox approach was recently, and most warmly, again *commended* by ALC theologian Gerhard Forde![325]

It is not surprising that the official discussions between Missouri and the ULCA in 1936 and 1938 came to nothing. They foundered on the ULCA commissioners' declared inability "to accept the statement of the Missouri Synod that the Scriptures are the infallible truth 'also in those parts which treat of historical, geographical, and other secular matters, John 10:35.'"[326] The ULCA men, however, attempted to hold on to the word "inspiration" while denying verbal inspiration and inerrancy as man-made "theories." This amounted, as Prof. Engelder of St. Louis put it so clearly, to "a clumsy form of sophistry. It deals with an 'inspiration' which is not real inspiration."

What may be less well known in the Missouri Synod is the fact that inspiration-inerrancy was the major source of division between the old ALC and the ULCA, and that their official representatives wrestled for years with this issue. Nelson has given the details.[327] Already the first ALC's basic theological document, the "Minneapolis Theses" (1925) accepted the canonical Scriptures "as a whole and in all their parts, as the divinely inspired, revealed, and inerrant Word of God." This statement asserted quite pointedly what the ULCA, as we have seen, had refused to say in its "Washington Declaration." That body also declined in principle to formulate new statements as a basis for fellowship. Nevertheless it participated for years in negotiations with the ALC which finally culminated in the schizophrenic "Pittsburgh Agreement" of 1940.

It may be of interest to note that the main champion of inerrancy in these discussions, after the death of the ALC's President Hein, was the Dubuque Seminary (Iowa Synod) theologian J. Michael Reu. Born and educated in Europe, this great churchman was open to the influence of Erlangen, which had honored him with the degree of doctor of theology. In the twenties and early thirties Reu had restricted the Bible's inerrancy to its saving message, and had opposed the strict definition of the "Minneapolis Theses." But by the time of the ALC-ULCA discussions (1936-1939), Reu confessed verbal inspiration and inerrancy and could not be budged from this stand by his opposite number from the ULCA, Prof. C. M. Jacobs. Jacobs and other ULCA men spoke of a "Christ centered view," distinguished between "Scripture" and "Word of God," and did not in principle oppose "higher criticism." Their view, so familiar today, was that "The Bible's authority lay not in its inerrancy but in its religious message . . ."

Again, "When we talk about the Word of God, then, we mean Christ, we mean the Gospel . . . The place where we get into difficulty is when we say the Scriptures are the Word of God because they are inspired." How ironic that this same ULCA view, rejected by the ALC as intolerably liberal, should have conquered, some thirty-odd years later, the very citadel of "Missourian" orthodoxy in St. Louis!

Reu continued to oppose the seductive "neo-Lutheran" rhetoric and insisted on the phrase "without contradiction and error." In the end, the ULCA's President Knubel suggested a compromise formula. Serving notice that the ULCA would never accept "a fundamentalist interpretation of inerrancy," he offered the term "errorless," although he admitted that the two sides would understand that word differently. Reu asked whether this term went "farther than your (Baltimore) Declaration," and was assured by Knubel that it did. Thereupon Reu yielded to the formulation "a complete, errorless, unbreakable whole of which Christ is the center." This was the crucial wording of what came to be known as the "Pittsburgh Agreement" of 1940. It shocked the Missouri Synod, which understood the document as a sellout to the ULCA. The latter body adopted the statement, but very half-heartedly, and not without placing the new document under, rather than over, its previous pronouncements. Nelson writes that the "significant minority" which opposed the Pittsburgh Agreement in the ULCA was "led by a young pastor named Franklin Clark Fry,"[328] who later became president of his church and rose to ecumenical prominence as "Mr. Lutheran" (LWF) and "Mr. Protestant" (WCC).

The Missouri Synod meanwhile presented its well-known solid front for inspiration-inerrancy throughout the thirties and forties. Even those who favored a softer line on fellowship, and especially towards the ALC, were quite unyielding on the matter of strict biblical authority. The "Statement" of the "Forty-Four" insisted in its second thesis on "the great Lutheran principle of the inerrancy, certainty, and all sufficiency of Holy Writ." Dr. William Arndt, St. Louis Seminary Professor, co-translator of Bauer's great New Testament lexicon, and one of the original "Forty-Four," continued to write books and articles[329] which not only defended verbal inspiration and inerrancy, but insisted that this matter was crucial to any proper doctrinal agreement among Lutherans. Another leading "Forty-Four" signatory, Prof. Theo.

Graebner, widely known for his scholarly anti-evolutionism (*God and the Cosmos*, Eerdmans, 1932, 1943, 1946), had made much of the inspiration issue in his quite outspoken *The Problem of Lutheran Union* (1935). In his later years Graebner was much more optimistic about U. S. inter-Lutheran prospects. This, however, was not because Graebner had changed his mind about inspiration, but because he felt American Lutheranism itself had become more conservative and was moving towards Missouri's stand on the Bible.[330] In support of this view Graebner pointed to a book he had helped to produce, *What Lutherans Are Thinking*, edited by the ALC's Dr. E. C. Fendt (1947). The essay on "The Word of God" in that volume did, indeed, take what Clifford Nelson has called the "old Lutheran" stand, namely verbal inspiration and inerrancy. But the aging Graebner appears not to have noticed that other essays in the book followed a "neo-Lutheran" line, as Nelson has pointed out.[331]

What was this "neo-Lutheranism" which took U.S. Lutheran seminaries by storm after the Second World War? It was an intoxicating brew stewed together mainly from newly rediscovered European ingredients, with Barthian neo-orthodoxy as probably the chief catalyst. T. A. Kantonen's bibliography in the Fendt volume reflected fairly well the influence now coming to the fore: the Reformed neo-orthodox thinkers Karl Barth, Emil Brunner, and John Baillie; and the Swedish neo-Lutherans or "Lundensians," Bishops Gustaf Aulen and Anders Nygren of the University of Lund. Many Lutherans simply lost their critical faculties on encountering this brilliant galaxy of theological celebrities. They assumed that since Barth was railing against the old-style optimistic liberalism, and with singular success, therefore he represented a return to the Reformation—hence the term "neo-orthodoxy." And, indeed, many were stimulated by Barth to study Luther and thus get back to the foundation itself, Scripture. But Barth himself, and his movement, deliberately avoided any return to the old Reformation position on biblical authority and inspiration. The situation, therefore, was that, while Barthianism represented a distinct improvement[332] over the old liberalism (inasmuch as there was a conscious attempt to get back to basic Christian concepts such as sin and grace, redemption, justification, etc.), the move from historic Lutheran orthodoxy to Barthianism meant an abandonment of biblical authority, hence a huge leap into liberalism. To use a geographical illustration, if I start out from Moscow for New York, then London indeed represents considerable and encouraging progress. But if I started out from Hackensack, New Jersey, with New York in mind, and then found myself in London, I would be foolish to congratulate myself upon my progress; I might well be on the way to Siberia! Barthianism proved to be not only the "London" halfway house of our illustration, but also one in which no one could stay permanently. To vary the figure, it was like being half-way down an inclined plane on roller-skates. As subsequent events showed, one either had to crawl all the way back up to a stable orthodoxy, or else slide all the way down into the liberal abyss, e.g., Bultmann, and the "death of God" fad.

Barth's system seemed more biblical than it was. The Swedish scholar Wingren observed airily: "Barth has the ability to a very large degree of being able to employ the language of scripture in a system that is totally foreign to the Bible."[333] Barth realised that the historical-critical method could produce nothing but a few dead bones. But he thought that one could—indeed must—keep the method, and then pack living flesh and sinews onto the dead bones by means of "theological interpretation"—hence the "New Hermeneutic." Barth demanded "that we endeavor to see 'through and beyond history into the spirit of the Bible, and then offered an interpretation that did not inquire about Paul's message to his original readers, but related the biblical text directly to the situation in which modern man finds himself."[334] Since for Barth, however, the actual biblical text was fully human and therefore full of errors, his "interpretation" necessarily meant reading his own ideas into the text. And Barth's basic idea was the "dialectic" or tension, a restless back-and-forth between two poles, time and eternity. Nothing earthly, concrete, historical—hence no doctrine, statement, or book—could ever be absolute, since God remained "wholly other" and His Word ultimately inexpressible. According to Barth, therefore, the Bible "never stiffens into positive or negative finalities . . . It always finds as much and as little in the Yes as in the No; for the truth lies not in the Yes and not in the No but in the knowledge of the beginning from which the Yes and the No arise . . . Biblical dogmatics are fundamentally the suspension of all dogmatics."[335] This deeply anti-incarnational thinking was a radical adaptation of a philosophical notion basic to Calvinism, as J. W. Montgomery has pointed out in a most incisive essay on "Lutheran Hermeneutics and Hermeneutics Today."[336]

Barth's high-octane flow of words[337] caused befuddlement among lesser lights, and encouraged an unclear style which evaded precision and definition with an over-heated pietistic rhetoric. Theology had fallen into a confusion of tongues. Old words were used in new and vague senses. Even liberals on occasion felt threatened by the all-enveloping double-talk:

> Today's seminary student is likely to have gained the impression that liberal theology has been utterly discredited. (It may not be quite so clear to him that about 85 per cent of liberalism's initial accomplishments and attitudes are taken for granted by his teachers)...
>
> ... it is possible to recognise as one of the perils in the present situation the danger that the vital, creative movement from within liberalism which has been unhappily dubbed "neo-orthodoxy" may unintentionally issue in a caricature of itself—a sort of spongy orthodoxy or spineless fundamentalism, a biblicism without guts.[338]

Whatever the intellectual and theological merits of the new approach, it certainly conveyed a sense of excitement. Therein probably lay its chief appeal. The familiar old ways seemed like stale beer by comparison, and the injection of new froth was most welcome. An intriguing article in 1949 referred to the neo-orthodox fever as "The New Crisis in American Lutheran Theology,"[339] and reported that at a gathering of theological leaders "from most of the Synods in the United States, held at the Chicago Lutheran Seminary in 1946, probably 18 out of 20 of those present definitely spoke the language of neo-orthodoxy."

A good indication of the new trend was ULCA theologian Joseph Sittler's 1948 book *The Doctrine of the Word*. The liberal Reformed-Barthian thrust is unmistakable:

> For if we equate the Word of God with the Scripture, we are confusing things heavenly with things historical. The Unconditioned is by such an identification delimited by the conditioned...
>
> The cosmology of the Bible was shattered by the work of Copernicus, Galileo, and Newton. Its chronology was brought under severe question by a critical science of history and the pursuit of critical paleontology...

To assert the inerrancy of the text of Scripture is to elevate to a normative position an arbitrary theological construction.[340] Not surprisingly, Sittler's view of Christ plummeted together with his view of Scripture.[341]

By 1955 the ULCA was making national news with the heresy proceedings conducted by its Northwest Synod against three young pastors, Crist, Gerberding, and Wrigley. Some of these men's theological statements were blatant denials of such essentials of the faith as the atonement, resurrection, ascension, the divine nature, and even the continued personal existence of Jesus![342] Historian Clifford Nelson gets over the disturbing implications with a few cheerful generalities about "an unfortunate ecclesiastical backlash" and the relations between facts, history and faith.[343] That arch-enemy of orthodox Christianity, *The Christian Century*, pointed out at the time: "The trouble with Crist and Gerberding and Wrigley is that they believed what they were taught in their Lutheran seminaries. And those seminaries are related to the whole church."[344]

The most shocking aspect of the whole spectacle was the fact that the ULCA's official paper, *The Lutheran*, gave vigorous editorial support to the heretics, and repeatedly and prominently featured Reinhold Niebuhr's spirited defence of them, once under the revealing title: "Symbols of the eternal must be taken seriously but cannot be taken literally":

> Heresy trials almost inevitably revolve, as the Wisconsin trials do, around peripheral articles of the faith. The young men are accused, among other things, of not believing in the virgin birth of Jesus or in his "physical resurrection" or ascension. Are these beliefs really tests of the quality of the faith?
>
> Does any church which insists upon them really do justice to the quality and character of faith as an encounter between God and the soul? Does it understand the symbolic character of a great deal of religious truth? Could it maintain that the Lordship of Christ is really effectively witnessed by belief in his virgin birth or ascension?
>
> Does not any interpretation which makes acceptance of miraculous historical events the test of faith reduce the spiritual quality of that faith, and does not the application of such tests brand as heretics all but a few literalists and fundamentalists?
>
> The issue raised in Wisconsin involves the validity of the religious symbolism. All symbols of the eternal, particularly

those which assert the divine validity and revelatory power of events in history, must be taken seriously but cannot be taken literally. The well-known German theologian Rudolf Bultmann has made this issue central in theological thought both in Europe and America . . .

These accusations therefore embarrass the whole portion of the Christian ministry which would have to say, "If they are guilty, so am I."[345]

Less forthright but highly significant was the collective reaction to the controversy by sixteen ULCA seminary professors.[346] The neo-orthodox orientation of this interesting document becomes clear in such features as the shift from the *fact* of the virgin birth to its "theological significance"—hedging on the bodily resurrection, ascension, and sacramental presence—and the weasel-words about Scripture: "The Bible is the Word of God as the human record through which the Holy Spirit bears witness to God's redemptive act in Christ."

With the ULCA's official theological circles at the bottom of the hill, the ALC and later Missouri came tumbling after. Already in 1950 the ALC-related *Lutheran Outlook* published a very critical review of F. Pieper's *Christian Dogmatics*. The article included this revealing assertion: "Nowadays the combined weight of the Luther-scholar is on the side that the non-verbal-inspirationists are more '*Luther*'an then the hitherto orthodox Lutherans."[347]

In 1960 the old ALC joined with the UELC and the large Norwegian-background ALC to form The American Lutheran Church. This transformation illustrated the futility of administrative measures alone, apart from theological solidity in the seminaries, in safeguarding a church's doctrinal stand. The leadership had succeeded in writing into the constitution itself a strong confession of the Scriptures "as a whole and in all their parts, as the divinely inspired, revealed, and inerrant Word of God."[348] But this provision was a dead letter from the beginning. Of the large ALC component of the new church Clifford Nelson has recently written:

> By 1956, when the proposed constitution of the new American Lutheran Church was voted on by the Evangelical Lutheran Church, several if not most of its professors of theology were teaching a view of Scripture at variance with the statement on the Bible in the new constitution. That is,

while church administrators sought to uphold "old Lutheranism", many college and seminary professors were teaching "neo Lutheranism

Jeffrey Hadden's survey in 1968 showed that only 23 per cent of the ALC's clergy accepted the Bible's full inspiration and inerrancy, whereas 76 per cent of Missouri's pastors still did so.[350] No wonder ALC President F. Schiotz found himself compelled to reinterpret the ALC's constitution: "The ALC holds that the inerrancy referred to here does not apply to the text but to the truths revealed for our faith, doctrine and life."[351] The irony was that Schiotz' "interpretation" was the very view which the ALC's consitutional wording had been designed to exclude! A lonely voice of protest is being maintained by *Lutherans Alert-National*, with a seminary in Tacoma, Washington.

Among the first public symptoms that the neo-Lutheran, historical-critical contagion had reached the Missouri Synod was the publication in 1950, and by the Synod's own Concordia Publishing House, of *From Luther to Kierkegaard,* written by the young intellectual Jaroslav Pelikan. With supreme confidence in the prevailing winds of doctrine, the book announced that the Lutheran Church had been set on the wrong philosophical track already by Chemnitz and the Formula of Concord, that the German philosopher Immanuel Kant had destroyed the foundations of Lutheran Orthodoxy, and that Lutheranism now needed a new philosophy, namely that of Kierkegaard, to wit: "Only that is true which is true for me." Such glib "trendiness" came now to dominate a new breed of Missouri Synod scholarship which stressed breadth rather than depth. Lutheranism's stately and venerable old doctrinal edifice was no longer seen from within, but only from the perspectives of its avowed enemies. Hence it was no longer understood. External, superficial neglect and dilapidation were mistaken for structural weakness and collapse. And so the rambling old mansion was condemned unsentimentally to be bulldozed in order to make way for some streamlined "contemporary" abomination, a la Barth, Aulen, or Tillich. Indeed Pelikan himself came to pay glowing tribute to Schleiermacher, who figures as arch-heretic in Pieper's *Christian Dogmatics*, and even to the neo-pagan Paul Tillich, whose "Protestant principle" abolishes the whole idea of God-given truth and doctrine.[352]

Pelikan served on the faculty of Concordia Seminary, St. Louis, from 1949 to 1953.[353] It may or may not be a coincidence that student unrest about verbal inspiration came to a head in the 1953-1954 school year. "The chief questions of the students centered in the extent to which the Scriptures themselves and the Confessions of the Church teach a doctrine of Verbal Inspiration and what the function of that doctrine is."[354] The faculty responded with a series of special presentations and discussions, initiated by the dying Prof. F. E. Mayer. The main essays, attempting with varying degrees of success to "hold the line," were presented by Profs. A. C. Piepkorn, M. Franzmann, and W. Roehrs. In the event, the effort proved too little and too late. A perusal of the student journal, *Seminarian*, for the next few years shows that magazine to have been in the hands of a self-perpetuating clique of propagandists for neo-orthodoxy and ecumania. The scandal was merely underscored when, in a well-meant attempt at fairness, the *Seminarian* in 1955 started to print also a few orthodox articles—but in a kind of conservative ghetto under the quarantine-flag "Another Voice!"

The influence of the leading theological graduate schools here and abroad was well assessed by Clifford Nelson:

> Many of these men, who found their way into teaching positions in major colleges and seminaries of the Lutheran churches, *including Concordia Seminary (St. Louis)*, had been exposed to contemporary biblical research (Dodd, Hoskyns, Wright, Albright, Bultmann, G. Bornkamm, von Rad, *et al.*); to contemporary theologians such as Nygren, Aulen, Barth, Brunner, Tillich, and the Niebuhrs; and to the Luther researches of Swedes, Germans, Englishmen, and Americans (notably Wilhelm Pauck and Roland Bainton). *One result was that in the course of time students were exposed to a new brand of Lutheranism that was remarkably similar in all schools, whether in Chicago, Philadelphia, the Twin Cities, or St. Louis.*[355]

The considerable influence of the German (Erlangen) theologian Werner Elert on Missouri's new theology after World War II has been stressed both by "Seminex" Prof. E. Schroeder,[356] and by Springfield Seminary Prof. D. P. Scaer.[357] Sasse's judgment of Elert was: "There are excellent paragraphs in Elert's *Dogmatics*. But his doctrine on Holy Scripture is terribly weak."[358]

Barth, of course, was much worse. His impact on Lutherans, when popularized, came through as: "The Bible is full of errors. That is the Incarnation."[359] A 1959 article about Barth ("The Einstein of Theology") in Missouri's official youth magazine gushed as follows:

> But this man is different. This is Karl Barth, the Einstein of theology. More than any man since Luther he has guided and plotted the course of Christian thought . . .
>
> Barth has solid ground under his feet. He whole heartedly accepts the inspiration of Scriptures and in this respect he is a solid conservative . . .
>
> *Greater or lesser Barthians teach at almost every Protestant seminary in America, including our own.*[360]

In fact the Barthian penetration of the seminary had already gone beyond the classroom level. Since at least November 1, 1958, the St. Louis seminary's Curriculum Committee had been including this bit of neo-orthodox philosophizing in the "biblical languages" section of its annual report to the Board for Higher Education, *Able Ministers*:

> Thus "to know", *iadah* or *ginosko*, does not concern the comprehension of fact but the experiencing of and absorption into the One known. "Truth", *emunah* or *aletheia*, does not concern the veracity or factuality of a given idea, but it concerns the trustworthiness of God in bringing His plan of salvation in Christ Jesus to come true in the lives of individuals.

This pious nonsense, by the way, was thoroughly exploded by the University of Edinburgh's Professor of Old Testament Literature and Theology, James Barr. His book, *The Semantics of Biblical Language*,[361] also levelled some pretty fundamental criticisms in this connection at Kittel's prestigious *Theological Dictionary of the New Testament*.

Not till the Tietjen years, however, did the Curriculum Committee make bold to attempt a radical re-shaping of the seminary's theological curriculum along the "trendy" lines prevalent elsewhere. Formation of the Theological Education Research Committee (TERC) was authorized by the Board for Higher Education already in mid-1969. The resultant 1970 report, *Theological Education for Today*, sought with a vengeance to implement the thoroughly "ecumenical," that is, unionistic, implications of the Mission Affirmations, and virtually wiped out the very concept of doctrine and dogmatics. One submission sneered openly at preoccupation "with preserving 'purity of doctrine' " (p.132).

The unsung heroes of those years of the liberal take-over were the rank-and-file pastors and people who kept the faith despite the official vacillations and shenanigans. Leadership and encouragement were provided by theologians and officials who were not in sympathy with the new directions. Naturally it is quite impossible to include here an even approximately complete list of such men. A few representative examples will have to suffice. There were of course active conservatives on both the Springfield and the St. Louis theological faculties. Raymond Surburg had been analysing, with great learning and acumen, the historical-critical and hermeneutical issues since the early fifties, before he joined the Springfield faculty.[362a] Younger conservatives, like the indefatigable *Springfielder* editor, Prof. David Scaer, had to endure years of administrative chicaneries and "economic sanctions" for their forthright stand. Three Springfield conservatives who figured prominently in the final conflict with the Tietjen seminary were Prof. Harry Huth, noted authority on the Lutheran confessions, who produced much of the literature emanating from the Commission on Theology and Church Relations; the exegete Prof. Walter A. Maier, whose *Crossroads* letter mobilized the confessional forces for New Orleans; and the Luther-scholar Prof. Eugene Klug, who was the main author of the crucial Resolution 3-09. A leading conservative thinker was the St. Louis systematician with a Yale doctorate, Prof. Ralph Bohlmann, author of *Principles of Biblical Interpretation in the Lutheran Confession*, 1968. The major figure among Missouri's valiant defenders of the faith was undoubtedly St. Louis Prof. Robert D. Preus, whose 1955 vindication of *The Inspiration of Scripture* had done so much to rally the demoralized conservatives.[362b] The sudden appearance of the brilliant John W. Montgomery on the Synodical scene, with his penetrating *Crisis in Lutheran Theology* (1967), had a galvanizing effect which cannot be overestimated. Montgomery was able to turn the tables on the liberals in the manner of St. Augustine's demolition of his former Manichean heresy. Whereas Montgomery's opponents were adrift on liberal currents by way of reaction to their own orthodox background, he had travelled in precisely the opposite direction and had arrived in the harbor of orthodoxy after having already explored and experienced the hopelessness of the secular superstitions which seemed so alluring to the formerly orthodox! Now, like St. Augustine, he could explode their fallacies from within, as it were. In slightly different senses this was also true of the valuable contributions made by Professors Horace Hummel[363] and Martin Scharlemann.[364] The latter had gone through considerable trials and tribulations in connection with some disturbing essays which he formally withdrew in a dramatic act of reconciliation at the 1962 Cleveland Convention. And now it was he who, as we have already seen, directly precipitated the fateful investigation of the Tietjen seminary, thus decisively reversing neo-Lutheranism's brief triumph over the Missouri Synod. Without such men, and many others like them, who refused to be cowed by any self-proclaimed "wave of the future," the Synod as an institution would have been lost to the Lutheran Church. Humanly speaking, things already seemed hopeless when God in His mercy relieved and delivered His Zion on the Mississippi!

2. Historical Criticism: Definitions and Distinctions Lest We Fight About Words

The argument about the historical critical method is so central to the whole Missouri Synod dispute, that every effort must be made to clear up its nature beyond any reasonable doubt. Let us begin by noting an extraordinary paradox. On the one hand, everybody speaks and writes quite unhesitatingly about "*the* historical-critical method," taking for granted that the thing is a clearly understood entity differing in certain definable ways from other approaches. Barth obviously thought so. The prominent critical theorist Gerhard Ebeling entitled a whole lengthy chapter of his important book *Word and Faith* simply "The Significance of the Critical Historical Method for Church and Theology in Protestantism." Gerhard Maier entitled his recent book *The End of The Historical Critical Method*. The German Scholars Ferdinand Hahn and Peter Stuhlmacher had no qualms about referring to "the historical-critical method" in their incisive essays in a scholary journal.[365] The blatant Fortress Press book, *Miracles in Dispute*, seeks simply to explain "the historical-critical method." So does another Fortress book, *The Historical-Critical Method*, by "Seminex" Prof. E. Krentz. Any number of others could be cited to the same effect. One conclusion, at least, must surely follow from all this—there is such a thing as the historical-critical method.

But, on the other hand, when one gets into the thick of the argument about how this method that everyone is talking about is to be defined, one is faced with this baffling plea from the pro-"Seminex" camp: "It seems to be fruitless to debate 'the historical-critical method as universally understood in scholarly circles,' because our discussions in the ACDC [Advisory Committee on Doctrine and Conciliation] have proved to us again that *there is no such thing*" (italics added)![366] Instead, we are told, "since the historical-critical method is such a complex matter, it is much more to the point to talk about 'the historical-critical method as it is used by us Lutherans.' " But that merely adds one further complication -the need to define "us Lutherans." According to Missouri "moderate" Paul G. Bretscher even Bultmann, who rejected the whole Christian faith, was one of "us Lutherans" and submitted "altogether to the authority of the Holy Scriptures as the Word of God!"[367] Clearly something is awry when people at first insist on the necessity of the historical-critical method, and then, when challenged, argue that "there is no such thing"—even while they continue to talk about it! One may be pardoned for detecting in this evasiveness a strong suggestion of that very "anti-intellectualism" of which liberals regularly accuse the conservatives.[368]

Objectively, the problem is not so difficult to disentangle. It can be done in two basic steps. The first is an exercise in elementary semantics. Either the term "the historical-critical method" is meaningful or it is not. If it is meaningful then its meaning must be clearly distinguishable from others. If it cannot be meaningfully differentiated from or contrasted with other methods, then the expression "the historical-critical method" is a meaningless piece of nonsense and is semantically useless. But since people obviously do mean something when they say "the historical-critical method," we can go on to step two and ask what specifically it is that distinguishes this method from others. A common pitfall at this point is to assume that the method consists essentially of a number of specific scholarly "techniques" (e.g., form criticism, redaction criticism, and the like). This was evidently the assumption of the "Seminex" *Faithful . . . I* document (p. 41). This definition of the historical-critical method as so many techniques, however, is fallacious and singularly unfruitful. For one thing, most of the "techniques" can be used, up to a point, also by anti-critical scholars. For another, particular "techniques" come and go. They are discovered, have their heyday, and may be abandoned—but historical-criticism goes on.

Thirdly, the discussion does not gain from being abducted off the open road of first principles onto booby-trapped jungle-paths of esoteric "techniques." This encourages people to frighten themselves and each other with technical complications and counter-complications. In the end the wearied disputants are content to take refuge in the logical quagmire that since the "techniques" differ, and even more so their applications by individual scholars, therefore there is no such thing as the historical-critical method!

Once the "techniques" fallacy has been put aside, step two of our argument can be completed with dispatch. It is clear even from Krentz' short book,[369] and more so from standard authorities like the German scholar Hans Joachim Kraus,[370] that the historical-critical method arose out of the rationalistic Enlightenment and differs from traditional biblical scholarship in that it insists on treating the Bible not as an unquestioned authority, but as one ancient book among others. All biblical statements are therefore open to challenge before the court of sovereign human reason. Historical criticism understands itself simply as the general scientific method applied to past events, namely history. This means that the critic and his reason are judge and jury, while the Bible, like all other ancient documents, is on trial, whether as defendant or as witness; for even as a witness its credibility depends entirely on the findings of the critical "court." This situation, of course, represents a complete reversal of the classic roles of reason and Scripture in Lutheran theology. Under the new, critical regime, reason is master and Scripture is servant, whereas formerly it was the other way round. For this reason alone, as the author has shown elsewhere,[371] "using the historical-critical method with Lutheran presuppositions" is as futile and absurd an undertaking as eating ham with Jewish presuppositions! Krentz seems strangely unaware that what he rejects out of hand under the rationalistic propaganda label "sacrifice of the intellect"[372] is really the Lutheran-Christian attitude.

It is important to see that the uncompromising supremacy of "scientific" human reason in the historical-critical method is not an excess or an abuse which can somehow be tempered. On the contrary, it is of the essence of the method; indeed it is its basic point. Science has neither use nor room for privileged authorities or sacrosanct texts. It recognizes only observations, experiments, logical inferences based on them, and, reluctantly, whatever axioms or assumptions are necessary to sustain these operations.

That is why, in Krentz' understatement, "the method tends to freedom from authority."[373] Historical criticism cannot successfully ape scientific objectivity if it is caught flirting with authority-principles or making special allowances for some writings in preference to others. Here lies the historical-critical method's "innermost impulse of scientific questing and questioning,"[374] which it cannot give up without thereby surrendering its scientific pretensions, in short, its very reason for being. This state of affairs was grasped and formulated with exceptional lucidity in a series of theses presented for discussion in the University of Munich:

> If exegesis is to be practiced historical-critically, it must use the methods of secular historical science, i.e. criticism which allows only probable judgments, and the principles of analogy and correlation (cf. Troeltsch). Thereby it subjects itself in principle to secular-historical judgment.
>
> If historical-critical exegesis subjects its findings to secular-historical judgment, then the demand that it be bound to an ecclesiastical teaching office or to confessional writings contradicts its very starting point.[375]

Historical criticism, to be true to itself, must keep itself unfettered by any authority save that of human reason. But this very feature has condemned the method to ultimate sterility and bankruptcy. This approach to the Bible, based on unbridled human rationality alone, is now coming to be recognized as a blind alley.[376] One prominent critical scholar charges that there are "mutually exclusive opinions on every topic or question in the discipline,"[377] and then suggests that the solution lies in placing the historical-critical method "within the framework of a theology of the Third Article of the Creed."[378] But if this is to mean anything concrete, or to make any practical difference, it must involve some sort of doctrinal, theological controls or authorities—the very things which the historical-critical method cannot by definition endure. Its whole meaning and history have been emancipation from all such authorities! Any return to a decisive authority-principle would spell not modification but abandonment of the historical-critical method. It would lose its precious scientific independence and thus become indistinguishable from plain old traditional Bible study.

Still it is a fact that the supremacy of human reason means different things to different people. Some historical critics are obviously and dramatically more radical than others. For example, some think that miracles cannot and do not happen, while others leave the question open. Both types of critics take for granted that critical reason must sit in judgment over the claims of the biblical writers. Both agree that biblical reports of miracles may be challenged, cross-examined, and found wanting by the critical scholar. The only difference is that while some hold that sound human reason rules out miracles in advance, others consider this inference unwarranted. Thus Ernst and Marie-Louise Keller in their Fortress Press book *Miracles in Dispute* vehemently deny all biblical miracles on the grounds that miracles are impossible in the light of modern science. The great German preacher Helmut Thielecke, on the other hand, insists that "historical-critical Scripture research can be pursued with an entirely different motive from that of a possibly destructive Rationalism," and accepts miracles in principle. Even he, however, claims the right to leave undecided the question whether the Virgin Birth of Jesus really happened in fact, or "whether it was believing men who erected a sign," that is, invented the account to make a religious point![379]

The radical and not-so-radical critics do have points of agreement and points of difference. Is there a simple way to describe the relationship without joining in the fatuous refrain that "there is no such thing as the historical-critical method?" On the analogy of cosmology, or of special and general relativity, we might well distinguish between a "narrow critical principle" and "wider" one. The narrow critical principle is simply the acceptance of critical human intelligence or rationality as arbiter of knowledge, including, of course, biblical knowledge. This reason-as-master principle is in operation wherever and whenever scholars claim the right to "correct" or disagree with biblical statements, or to "cross-examine" the biblical witnesses with a view to separating fact from fancy. The wider critical principle would go beyond the bare authority of reason to the further assertion that reason in fact demands acceptance of something like "the scientific world view," by which is usually meant some sort of nineteenth century dogmatism about the impossibility of miracles. This latter, more rigid, and all-embracing "wider critical principle" seems to dominate much of the German understanding of historical criticism,[380] while the more "open-ended" British and American climate favors the "narrow critical principle," with much variety and flexibility of application.[381]

The dispute in the Missouri Synod is, in the main, about the narrow, not the wider critical principle. "Moderates" appear to assume that as long as they reject the radical anti-miracle bias of the wider principle, they have met the real objection to the historical-critical method.[382] That is an illusion. Lutheran theology has always opposed and continues to oppose the narrow critical principle, that is, the idea that the same liberties which one takes with ordinary books, viz. agreeing with some statements while disagreeing with others, may be taken also with the "divine writings" of the apostles and prophets. The unavoidable watershed issue here is inspiration-inerrancy, as we shall see. Missouri "moderates" themselves on occasion say as much:

> It is not enough to say that historical criticism means "discriminating appreciation." "The historian," says [David] Lotz, "must cross-examine, test, weigh, probe and analyze all written records of the past. If he fails to do this he *de facto* surrenders his claim to the title of historian!" In short, one cannot honestly practice historical criticism and be "under the Scriptures" in the sense that the Preus group means "under."[383]

L.C.A. theologian Leigh Jordahl agrees:

> The differences between the doctrines on Scripture of the "Moderates" and the "Conservatives" are absolutely irreconcilable. The classical Lutheran doctrine of verbal inspiration, as so vigorously articulated by Franz Pieper and Missouri's entire tradition, is utterly antithetical to the historical-critical method. Outside of Missouri I know of no theologian who even tries to hold to both views.[384]

But if the historical-critical method is by its very nature incompatible with inspiration and inerrancy, then it is deeply and tragically untruthful to portray it as nothing more than "neutral" scholarship. The persistent determination of "Seminex" to maintain this soothing fiction[385] has hardly helped to raise the levels of either clarity or charity in the Synodical dispute.

In sum, the historical-critical method cannot, without committing suicide, accept any restrictions except those imposed by the rules of scientific inquiry itself. Any method, therefore, which submits in principle to the divine authority (inerrancy!) of sacred texts is simply not the historical-critical method. On the other hand, any method which in principle waives the inerrancy of Holy Scripture cannot claim to be operating with Lutheran presuppositions. The loose, status symbol usage of the term "historical-critical method" to mean simply "competent, scholarly procedure," should be combatted as semantic humbug.

As this section began with a paradox, it may as well conclude with another one. From the foregoing discussion it follows that in one sense Lutheran scholars may not "use the historical critical method," while in another sense they must "use" it. Normally the word "use" in this connection would mean something like "accept and treat as valid." In this sense, of course, consistent Lutherans cannot "use" the method. But the word "use" might mean no more than "take into account the results of." In this sense no Lutheran theologician can afford not to "use" the method. Even the most ardent creationist, for instance, must, if he wishes to be taken seriously, understand the details of the evolutionary alternative. Christian schools must "teach evolution," not indeed to endorse it, but to refute it intelligently, which presupposes a basic grasp of the facts and arguments involved. Similarly it is unthinkable that a modern Lutheran seminary would not equip its students to cope with the issues posed by the historical-critical method. Pastors, as the public teachers of the church, must be competent to "refute the gainsayers" (Tit. 1:9). This they cannot do without a thorough grasp of the historical-critical leaven which, through popular journalism, now confronts and confuses also laymen everywhere. Such "use," of course, is designed to safeguard the church against the historical-critical fallacies, by enabling future pastors to spot, expose, and reject them. It is the very opposite of giving in to historical criticism by, for instance, the surrender of inerrancy.

3. Gospel and Incarnation: "Faith" without Facts? "Theology" without History?

Historical criticism, as we have seen, seeks to separate fact from fiction, wheat from chaff, by an impartial cross examination of all historical sources. But if the Bible is essentially different from all other writings, if as the inspired Word of God it is divine truth unmixed with human error, then it is in principle beyond the reach and scope of historical criticism. If the critical method is to have anything to work on, a wedge must first be driven between that which is Word of God in the Bible and that which is not. Once a more or less independent "human side" has been isolated, then criticism can operate on it without let or hindrance, while "faith" is left to tender its courtesies to an ever vaguer "divine side."

In practice this has meant a fatal split between facts and faith, between history and theology. The reason for this is not difficult to find. The critical method (precisely in its milder or "narrow" form!) can in principle question any and all biblical facts. Whatever scholarship regards as "established" today may well be challenged anew tomorrow. "The inevitable result," as the British scholar R.P.C. Hanson says,

> is that all the facts might as well be fancy because, while it is agreed that *some* of them are almost certainly facts, nobody can produce any satisfactory reason why his selection should be regarded as facts and not fancy, rather than that one, or that one, or that one. It is not merely that every critic plays the game differently from the others, but that every critic makes his own rules.[386]

Such treacherous quicksand could obviously not support any theological absolutes or certainties; hence "faith" had to look elsewhere for firm foundations. The whole realm of fact, history, geography, and the like came, therefore, to be regarded as the Bible's "human side," which could safely be abandoned to the tender mercies of historical criticism, while "faith" and "theology" went merrily floating off into the wild blue yonder of existentialist fantasies and mumbo-jumbo, that is, to the so-called "divine side" of Scripture! In this scheme the "divine side" reigns but does not rule. It has no independent dignity or substance at all, but is simply a sop and a pretence. Its boundaries are set unilaterally by historical criticism, which claims for itself whatever it wants. Anything left over, as it were, may then be appropriated, with meekness and gratitude, by "faith" and the "divine side."

Lest anyone think this description fanciful, let us translate it into the sober accents of scholarly jargon. A leading authority on the subject traces to the rationalist Semler "the critical splitting up into divine and human elements, whereby alone free biblical research is guaranteed."[387] Another recognised critical scholar has thus described the appalling "dilemma" into which theology has been forced by historical criticism: "The renunciation of the theological relevance of the factual element . . . has meant for exegesis something like a loss of reality . . ."[388]

What ought to be crystal clear is that any retreat from biblical facts and history as such is a retreat from the Incarnation itself. Any driving of wedges between the human and the divine in the Bible, between fact and faith, between history and theology, hits at the inmost nature of biblical Christianity. The written Word is about the Incarnate Word and is of a piece with Him. The Gospel is about the life, death, and resurrection of the Word-made-flesh (John 1:14) and is forever bound up with even seemingly minor details of the narrative: the Lord Himself decrees that the Bethany anointing will be reported "wherever this gospel is preached throughout the world" (Matt. 26:13). Without the earthly, historical, geographical facts and particulars there simply was no Incarnation. To say that the Lake of Gennesaret must be understood not as a geographical place but as a "theological place"[389] is to mock the Incarnate Son of God. To sacrifice facts and history is to sacrifice the Incarnation and change the Good News about Jesus into bloodless abstractions. This is the *spirit of antichrist, which denies that Jesus is come in the flesh* (I John 4:3). And this is precisely the spirit of historical criticism which, as the German Professor W. Kuenneth has pointed out, has reached "completion (*Zuendefuehrung*) and perfection" in Bultmann![390]

Yet Missouri's "moderate" party did not hesitate to follow historical criticism even into this deeply anti-incarnational tearing asunder of what God has joined together. Consider Dr. Paul G. Bretscher's forthright pronouncement:

> It is vital for Lutheran education to distinguish between the historical reality of Scripture (horizontal line) and the theological (vertical line) . . . Lutheran education will recognize that the revolution in Biblical studies is a gift from God to be accepted without fear and used to His glory . . .
>
> Certain areas in which contemporary Biblical studies have seemed to pose so great a threat are well known in our Synod. They have to do with the authorship of Biblical books, with the formation of the Pentateuch in the Old Testament and of the Gospels in the New, with the use the New Testament makes of Old Testament texts, with the understanding of literary forms, with *the historicity and facticity of persons and events, with the authenticity of Jesus' own utterances* in relation to the voices of witnesses who breathed His Spirit and spoke in His Name, and with the interchangeable iden-

tification between Jesus and His Church.

Through the purifying, Lutheran education will understand that *all such questions have to do with the "historical reality"* of Scripture. In terms of our diagram they belong to the horizontal line and not to the vertical. *It is not appropriate, therefore, to approach such questions by appealing to the Bible's inspiration and authority* [italics added].[391]

All historical facts are here in principle detached from God's Word and revelation (the "vertical line") and relocated in a different dimension—the "horizontal line," where "all such questions," including "the historicity and facticity of persons and events" belong. If this language is meant to be taken seriously, it must mean that the Bible's own authority cannot settle any of these questions, since the entire "horizontal line" is the rightful domain of historical criticism! But since critical scholarship in principle leaves all such questions permanently unsettled and uncertain, Christian faith and doctrine must here be thought of as being entirely independent of historical facts. The biblical Incarnation-Gospel is thereby thrown to the winds. Indeed elsewhere Bretscher explicitly rejects the proposition that "the historical framework . . . in Scripture is an essential part of the Word of God!"[392]

The "Seminex" confession, *Faithful . . . I*, though understandably not as outspoken as Bretscher, also takes for granted the fatal historical-critical disjunctions facts/faith, history/theology, human/divine. Hence the critical slaps at "an absolute acceptance of each detail of the miracle, precisely as it is reported" (p. 19), and at insistence "on a public acceptance of the historicity of every detail of the life of Jesus as recorded by the evangelists, as if that were a test of our faith" (p. 25—shades of Reinhold Niebuhr's defence of the ULCA heretics!). This orientation shows itself further in perverse oppositions like "central meaning of the miracle accounts for us" vs. "dwelling on the authenticity of isolated miraculous details" (p. 19), "the need for historical factuality" vs. "the primary need for Christ" (p. 23), "promise of a faithful God" vs. "the accuracy of ancient historians" (obviously meaning the New Testament writers!) (p. 26), and "the Promise" vs. "the historical authenticity of every detail of the Scriptures" (p. 26).

Of course, the historicity of Adam and Eve is openly given up (pp. 15-17)—despite the fact that St. Luke traces the Lord's own human ancestry back to Adam, and despite the fact that St. Paul in Romans 5 and I Corinthians 15 rests the whole foundation of Christ's redemptive work on the creation and fall of Adam as the real, historical progenitor of the human race. Here doctrine and theology are quite radically separated from their factual-historical moorings. The pretence that the whole thing is purely a technical argument "about the kind of literature involved" (p. 17) is threadbare. A painstaking German monograph about the origin of the concept of "myth" in modern biblical scholarship has shown that the surrender of the factual-historical content of Genesis was prompted not by any textual, literary, exegetical considerations, but simply by the "incompatibility of biblical proto-history with the newly won scientific and historical understanding regarding the primordial condition of the world and of mankind."[393] Once admitted into Genesis, the mythological virus could not be contained there, but relentlessly infected the entire biblical organism. For as Valparaiso University Professor N. Nagel once quipped in connection with the deteriorations in Anglican Christology, "when the Old Testament springs a leak, the water is soon seeping into the New."[394]

Of course, Missouri "moderates" fondly imagine that among "us Lutherans" historical criticism is used quite differently and is therefore harmless. Since the "moderate" forces are also firmly committed to inter-Lutheran church-fellowship here and now, they must regard all the LCUSA member-churches as being "us Lutherans" together. We have already noted the historical-critical devastations within the LCA especially, but also in the ALC, which is in full church-fellowship with the LCA. The LCA's Fortress Press has published many books advocating historical criticism, including *Miracles in Dispute* (1969). The latter book particularly takes pride in the starkest horrors of criticism without any attempt at concealment, and with full awareness that historical criticism *"makes a difference to the way one think s of Jesus"*:

> If the miracle stories of the Bible are to have a meaning today it must be sought for on a different plane of reality. For miracles cannot be retained on the level of historical fact . . .
>
> It makes a difference to the way one thinks of Jesus. Is he a mighty being of superhuman power, who can manipulate the elements as he wills, stilling the storm and the waves, conjuring fish into the fisherman's net, abolishing the force of gravity, and altering his own material substance so that

at one moment he is a man who can be touched and can eat and drink, and at the next a spirit who can pass through closed doors? Or is he an ordinary man who did nothing like this at all and never wanted to; a man whose enormous significance expressed itself not in any physical abnormality but merely in his behavior and in his destiny?. . .

The four evangelists report things in the most matter of fact way which today neither historical scholarship nor general opinion can accept as facts, but to which the Church none the less clings when in its creed it proclaims that Jesus was conceived by the Holy Ghost, born of the Virgin Mary. . . rose again from the dead, ascended into heaven . . .

There is an explanation, which has been discovered through the unqualified and consistent application of the historical-critical method. Criticism means separation, division, and also distinction. Those elements which are probably historical are divided and distinguished from the unhistorical ones according to the standards of our present knowledge and in analogy with the experience which is general in historical scholarship as a whole . . .

The [historical-critical] method releases us from the necessity of believing the incomprehensible and the improbable out of devotion to the church; for it makes proper understanding possible.[395]

So much for the harmlessness of historical criticism among "us Lutherans." But what if we restrict our field of vision to Missouri Lutherans only? It has been very confidently maintained by representative "moderates": "we *categorically deny* once more, that practitioners of the method within the Synod have denied such doctrines as the Virgin Birth, the Resurrection of our Lord, or Original Sin"[396] (emphases in original). The facts, however, do not warrant such optimism.

Already in 1962 Dr. Robert Scharlemann had followed "contemporary German theology" in driving a wedge between the Resurrection and the Empty Tomb. Defending this theology in general and Bultmann in particular, Scharlemann thought it a misunderstanding to see in these views "a subversion of the Christian faith."[397] In April 1972 Prof. W. Bartling, then a member of the faculty majority in St. Louis, stated in an address before the Louisiana Pastoral Conference: "I believe that many of my Christian brothers have problems with the virgin birth, real presence, bodily resurrection . . . I can't bear the burden of Scriptural infallibility." Even the Lutheran Confessions' doctrine of the two natures of Christ was criticised by River Forest Prof. W. Bouman, and that much more fundamentally than he was willing to admit.[398] The notorious Concordia Publishing House course for high school students, *Out of the Desert*, even went so far as to treat Judaism, Christianity, and Islam as equally valid "ways" to the same God! "Moderate" spokesman Paul Bretscher illustrated historical criticism by interpreting the dove and the opened heavens at our Lord's Baptism simply as "a graphic literary imagery."[399] In the same essay Bretscher said of Bultmann, who rejected all Christian dogma as so much myth and legend, including the Trinity, the Incarnation, Atonement, Resurrection, and Ascension: ". . . as a Lutheran preacher Bultmann submits altogether to the authority of the Holy Scriptures as the Word of God . . . It is not Bultmann's intention to detach the Gospel from the history of Jesus. . ."[400]

One bizarre glimpse into the historical-critical bankruptcy was provided by Sten H. Stenson's Abingdon Award-winning book *Sense and Nonsense in Religion*. The book "defended" the validity of Christianity and other religions on the grounds of "the punlike character of miracle stories and religious legends." "Religious" language, in other words, is not to be taken literally, but is comparable to puns or "witticisms," which "are irrelevant to truth and falsity in the usual propositional sense." Stenson likens "religious" language "especially" to the theatre of the absurd (p. 232)! Of course, he applauds Tillich's rejection of all absolutes and Bultmann's notion that "it was not a historical interest that dominated the Gospel writers . . . 'but the needs of Christian faith and life' " (p. 153). Indeed, Bultmann is here cited to the effect that the evangelist St. John "while making free use of the tradition creates the figure of Jesus entirely from faith!" Stenson's total relativism is clear from these excerpts:

> If a Jew comes to understand Torah, he will, in a sense, have risen above it and can then throw it away . . . Likewise, when Christians come to understand Christ they will no longer need to cling to him as, literally, the only way to the Truth. This, among other things, is what the so-called death of God theologians have discovered.
>
> . . . both Judaism and Christianity are anti-idolatrous, self-destructive, and equally true in the manner of religious

"wit."[401]

But what has all this to do with the Missouri Synod? One of the judges who awarded the Abingdon prize was none other than Missouri "moderate" Martin E. Marty, who gushed: "It is a fresh presentation of the Christian faith, and of faith itself. I would be proud to hand it to bright people up and down my block and to colleagues in worlds of media or academy!" One is tempted to assume charitably that Marty was simply too busy to study the book he praised so lavishly. But that disturbing little reference to "faith itself" in addition to "the Christian faith" suggests that he knew only too well what he was saying.

What parochial innocence, then, slumbers smugly in the conviction that "it can't happen here," that the Missouri Synod's magic touch can somehow tame the wild rapacity of historical criticism into a lamb-like "discriminating appreciation!" Hence Leigh Jordahl's gentle taunting of Missouri's "moderates:"

> Do you really believe that you have some special gift and grace so that even if you discard (as you most certainly are) that principle of an absolutely inerrant Scripture, you can somehow do what no other denomination has so far managed to do: keep your fundamental theological presuppositions even while you engage in a historical-critical methodology that must mean a recognition of relativity and, theological pluralism? Can you really, except by the most anti-intellectual gymnastics, adopt a method but purge it of those aspects which you term "negative" by the use of "Lutheran presuppositions?"[402]

4. Lutheran "Controls": Law/Gospel or Sola Scriptura?

The "moderate" professorial manifesto *Faithful . . . I* expresses the conviction that the historical-critical method can be kept under control by means of "certain presuppositions" about Scripture. "These include: 1) the centrality of the Gospel in the Scriptures; 2) the distinction between the Law, which always accuses, and the Promise, which always assures; 3) the Spirit's gift of faith . . ."[403] So far so good. But noticeable for its absence is any reference to verbal inspiration, inerrancy, and the "formal principle" or *sola scriptura*. This, of course, is no accident. Verbal inspiration and inerrancy stand and fall together—and inerrancy has clearly fallen in the document. As regards the "formal principle," the statement pointedly makes "the Gospel alone," not Scripture, "the governing principle for Lutheran theology."[404] And all this is obviously regarded as being so much more genuinely Lutheran than the "fundamentalism" of the Synod's official position.

This tissue of fallacies needs to be challenged from a number of angles. The first and most obvious point to be made is that any "Law and Gospel" separated from strict biblical authority hang in air and, far from "controlling" historical criticism, are in fact totally at its mercy. The standard defence of Bultmann, who gave up the whole dogmatic and historical content of the Christian faith, has always been that he insisted on the Law/Gospel distinction and on justification through faith alone, hence was really only extending Luther's own line of thought! This sophistry, moreover, has been seriously advocated not only in Europe,[405] 'but even in the Missouri Synod![406] The *Faithful . . . I* document itself inadvertantly admits the pointlessness of its notion of "Promise" by applying it to Adam and Cain (p. 28), whose historical existence had already been made a matter of opinion. Now, if this "Promise," the very anchor-concept of the whole production, cannot keep the historical-critical method from snatching away the historicity of Adam and Cain, how or why can it possibly be thought to protect the New Testament facts from being snatched away as well?

"Moderate" theology generally seems haunted by a deep confusion about the mutual relations among facts, faith, Scripture, and Gospel. *Faithful. .. I* seems to assume that the Gospel is one authority-principle (the "Lutheran" view), and the Scripture principle (inerrancy, etc.) is another (albeit an "un-Lutheran") alternative. Bretscher even imagines that by "formal principle" is meant the outward form or the words into which an idea is put![407] Nothing could be further from the truth. By "formal principle" is meant not the wording but the *authority* on the basis of which something is taught. The Scripture principle, then, is the Gospel's own authority principle and not something separate on the side! To put it very crudely, the "formal principle" or "Scripture principle" (that is, Scripture as sole authority, *sola scriptura*) is simply the door of the Gospel's hen-house. The door is there not for its own sake but precisely to protect the whole house. If it is gone, it would be foolish to say smugly, "O well, that was only the door—the rest of the hen-house is still safe!" Once the door is gone, the historical-critical fox is free to take whatever he pleases. The hen-house will be quite empty eventually, even if not after the first two or three visits!

The "moderate" approach suffers from split loyalties. On the one hand, there is the realization that the biblical Gospel is "grounded in historical events."[408] On the other hand the historical-critical commitment results in this terrible disjunction: "Our faith rests in the promise of a faithful God, not in the accuracy of ancient historians."[409] So, when it comes to their facts, the New Testament writers are simply "ancient historians," whose "accuracy" is not of primary or crucial concern to "faith!" And Bretscher, as we have seen, denies that "the historical framework . . . in Scripture is an essential part of the Word of God."[410] Similarly, Walter R. Bouman thinks that one should not speak of "an act of faith in the incarnation of our Lord."[411] Since the "act of faith" is "in" Jesus, we "do not make 'an act of faith in,' that is, entrust ourselves to, a doctrine about an historical incident." (Are we, therefore, wrong to confess with the Apostles' Creed that we believe *in* the holy Christian church, the communion of saints, the forgiveness of sins, the resurrection of the body, and the life everlasting?) Bouman says that calling our belief that "the incarnation and other events took place" an "act of faith" is an example of that historical faith "which the *Book of Concord* condemns!" This is a serious misrepresentation. The Confessions oppose not the acceptance of historical facts by faith, but the idea that faith is no more than such acceptance: ". . . here the term 'faith' does not signify *merely* knowledge of the history . . . but it signifies faith which believes *not only* the history but *also* the effect of *the history*, namely, this article of the forgiveness of sins" (*Augsburg Confession* XX).

The intimate link between facts and faith is embarrassing only if one has succumbed to the historical-critical infection. Krentz has no illusions about the heart of the problem: "Historical criticism produces only probable results. It relativizes everything. But faith needs certainty."[412] Taken at face value, these statements demolish the favorite "moderate" fallacy that since the Gospel is historical, it calls for historical criticism. The point is that faith and the Gospel deal only with *certainties*, while historical criticism reduces everything to mere probabilities, in short to doubts and uncertainties. Facts which are merely probable are of no use whatever to the Gospel, which asserts not human guesswork but divine revelation and authority. To argue, therefore, that the Gospel's historical element "invites" or requires historical criticism is as non-sensical as saying that aircraft are highly explosive and therefore require explosive detonation, i.e., being blown up! It is just *because* the Gospel is so historical that it cannot yield to historical criticism! The more faith treasures the Gospel-facts, the more it will resist with the tightest security measures, as it were, any infiltration of historical criticism, which is hell-bent on "exploding" these certainties into lifeless open questions. A "gospel" which surrenders the certainty of its facts and its biblical authority-principle is not the Gospel but a miserable stalking-horse for historical criticism!

A perfect illustration of all this is the fate of the Lord's Supper at the hands of the historical-critical method. One Missouri "moderate," though he admitted that "biblical criticism does change the rules and does change the character of biblical authority,"[413] cheerfully announced that "what higher criticism has revealed is that we may be confident that the Words of Institution are from Christ..."[414] But this is the very thing which historical criticism has most pointedly subverted! Concerning the Lutheran-Reformed agreement, or rather compromise, on the Sacrament embodied in the so-called "Arnoldshain Theses," we are informed that half the participants were "leading New Testament scholars," and that it was the historical-critical approach which "ultimately determined the course of the discussions and the formulation of the Theses."[415] Yet because of this historical-critical approach it was *"no longer possible to connect the institution of the Supper with the night in which He was betrayed!"*[416] In other words, the historical Jesus never instituted the Sacrament; instead, the account was created by the "faith" of the early Christians after their "Easter-experience." Such sinking sand cannot support any firm doctrine of the Sacrament, least of all the Lutheran Church's confident certainty that her sacramental teaching "rests on a unique, firm, immovable, and indubitable rock of truth in the words of institution recorded in the holy Word of God and so understood, taught, and transmitted by the holy evangelists and apostles, and by their disciples and hearers in turn."[417]

And what historical criticism does to the Sacrament, it does in principle to the entire Christian doctrine and to the historical facts in which it is grounded. If the Apostles' Creed were to be reworded to reflect honestly the prevailing critical opinion, it would "confess' about Christ something like this:

> ... Who was probably not conceived by the Holy Spirit or born of the Virgin Mary, was almost certainly crucified under Pontius Pilate, dead, and buried; on the third day or so He seems in some sense to have risen again from the dead, and was thought to have ascended into heaven; from thence, if the preceding is valid, he may or may not return ...

To object here that critical conclusions need not always be negative, but can also be very positive, is to miss the whole point—rather like the mouse which, accused by an elephant of being the tiniest, most insignificant creature he had ever seen, replied: "You must excuse me. I've been sick lately." Even the most positive critical conclusions cannot rise above mere probability, and are in principle open to challenge by any scholar at any time. A million critical assertions of "This is most likely true" do not add up to one single, simple catechismal confession: "This is most certainly true!" The chasm between them remains unbridgeable.

Krentz seeks to escape the calamitous consequences of his critical premises by turning a nasty necessity into an imagined advantage for "faith." If criticism destroys all historical proof and reduces everything to probabilities, he reasons, then so much the better for faith, which can believe all the better without such false props.[418] It almost seems as if Krentz here lets faith determine historical facts with divinely given certainty, quite independently of any historical criticism. That would be precisely the traditional, anti-critical stand. The appearance, however, is deceiving. In reality Krentz is here advocating a notion of "the true nature of faith" in support of which he cites Roy Harrisville's 1964 lectures at the ALC's Luther Seminary in St. Paul. Harrisville argued that faith cannot in principle be hurt by historical criticism even if one accepted, for instance, the critical view that Jesus Himself neither claimed to be nor thought of Himself as Messiah or Christ![419] But what kind of "faith" is this which can improvise and even "improve" on the historical Jesus? Faith, suggests Harrisville, is so independent of facts and doctrines, that it can face the historical-critical fires with serene indifference, letting "burn everything that will burn and without reservation wait for what proves to be unburnable."[420] But, of course, that "unburnable" residue would be especially useless to faith; for, as Krentz puts it, faith's kind of truth "disappears" if historical proofs are given! Did the truth of the Resurrection disappear, then, when Thomas and the others received the living proof of it (John 20)?

From such perspectives everything must appear topsy-turvy. "Moderate" theology imagines that its reckless gamble on historical criticism is a bold venture of faith, while plain old obedience to the biblical text is "subtly rationalistic." The mistaken supposition is that orthodoxy comes by its convictions through a "series of rational proofs" (as distinct from "a relationship of trust"), starting out with an attempt "to prove the Bible's factual inerrancy," and then proceeding to the Gospel from this un-Lutheran "prior truth."[421] This is why Scripture as "formal principle" appears, from the "moderate" point of view, as some kind of foreign body encroaching on privileges which belong to the Gospel alone. Orthodoxy here has been quite misunderstood. It is just orthodoxy which walks solely by faith, depending entirely on "a relationship of trust," whilst historical criticism insists on sight, rational proof, "the verification of historical details!"

Contrary to the tiresome caricature, orthodoxy insists not on the Bible but on Jesus as the crucial watershed for faith. F. Pieper, for instance, roundly rejects the suggestion that an unbeliever must be persuaded first of the inspiration of Scripture and then of salvation in Christ![422] Orthodoxy recognises that the Bible is seen in one way *before*, and in quite another way *after* one has come to faith in Jesus. For this very reason orthodoxy maintains so insistently the very necessary distinction between *apologetics*, on the one hand, and *theology* proper, or Christian doctrine, on the other.[423] Apologetics seeks merely to clear away the obstacles, that is, the false arguments, which keep unbelievers from giving serious consideration to the claims of God's own Law and Gospel; they alone can smite and heal the sinner. In this apologetic realm it is perfectly valid, indeed necessary, to reason from the common ground of public information and argument which the unbeliever too must acknowledge. But this is merely incidental to the proclamation of Law and Gospel which alone can convert. It is simply a service of love, a missionary accommodation, to deprive the unbeliever of his chief excuses for dismissing Christianity out of hand. It is purely "pre-evangelism," to secure at least external engagement with the Gospel, which will then do its own work. For example, if someone refuses to read the New Testament because he has been "educated" to regard it as a doubtful collection of old legends, it is helpful to demolish this objection by referring to books like London University Prof. J.N.D. Anderson's expert treatment of the Christian case as legal, documentary evidence.[424] Once a person is willing to consider the Christian message, it will win its own victories. No matter what one's previous theory of the Bible, the Gospel has the power to create in the Law-stricken sinner faith, that is, trust in Jesus, the Resurrection and the Life! At the same time the Word documents itself as being God's own. Once a man confesses Jesus as Lord, he cannot in principle reject what Jesus Himself teaches about the Scriptures of the Old and New Testaments. Hence the Bible which seemed, *before* faith, in the realm of apologetics, to be simply a venerable documentary record, is now, *after* conversion, known, seen, and confessed as God's own inspired, revealed, immovable, and life-giving Word. That is the realm of theology and Christian doctrine.

All this is simply childlike faith and has nothing to do with "a series of rational proofs!" The fallacy is to assume that because books on doctrine usually begin, very sensibly, with biblical inspiration as basis and authority for all doctrine and practice, therefore the intention is to "prove" inspiration in order then to "reason" oneself or others into faith in Christ. This is arrant nonsense. Detailed manuals on Christian doctrine are normally written to instruct future public teachers of the church in the church's biblical faith. The standpoint of faith and of theology, therefore, can and must be presupposed. The Lordship of Christ is already a certainty from the outset and determines the whole treatment of the Bible; faith in Christ is not something still to be established in the middle or towards the end of the volume or set! What apologetics can only show to be probable at best, or not impossible at worst, theology proclaims as divinely revealed truth and certainty, to be received in humble faith. Hence that "neutral," "objective" argumentation which is the essence of the "narrow critical principle" is perfectly proper in apologetics, but is quite out of place in the realm of theology itself, which stands fully committed to Him who said: "He that is not with Me is against Me." In apologetics a general reliability of Scripture may be all that can be shown. But "after faith," in theology, such a view is totally inadequate and sub-Christian; for here, as the distinguished Reformed scholar James I. Packer has put it rather well, anything short of unconditional submission to Scripture is "*a kind of impenitence.*"[425] Lutherans ought to see this point, if anything, even more clearly. When Krentz praises historical criticism for removing "the idolatry that confuses the temporal and the eternal,"[426] he is on thoroughly un-Lutheran, liberal-Reformed ground. Apart from firm facts, authoritatively "fixed" by divine revelation (Scripture principle), the Gospel itself decays into a Bultmannian "tissue of significances, it dissolves into a mere *significat* ("it signifies") and has lost the force of the est ("it *is*")".[427] Lutherans, above all, must recognise and exult in the incarnational and sacramental realism of the biblical narrative, in all its historical particularity and theological fulness. It is sacrilege to offer the seamless unity of this holy mystery to the profane claws and teeth of the historical-critical abomination of desolations.

The "formal principle" (or Scripture principle), then, is not something additional, above, and beyond the Gospel and forced onto it from without. It is rather the Gospel's own authority dimension, the criterion by which the Gospel distinguishes itself from false gospels (Gal. 1:8, 9; Eph. 2:20). Apart from this biblical criterion the "Gospel" becomes an undefinable slogan to which even the arch-liberal Harnack can appeal: "That alone is to be authority which shows itself to be such within and effects a deliverance, the thing itself, therefore, the Gospel."[428]

It is not, of course, the Gospel at all, but its mortal enemy, historical criticism which demands the surrender of the Scripture principle. As one of the main founders of the historical-critical method put it, "the root of the evil [in theology] is the confusion of Scripture and Word of God."[429] Historical criticism has been trying to correct this "evil" ever since. Missouri "moderates,"—like Krentz[430] and Bretscher[431] do not hesitate to follow suit. Nor can *Faithful . . . I* manage a stronger definition of inspiration than that it "pertains to the effective power of the Scriptures to bring men and women to salvation through the Gospel,"[432] This, however, is not in spiration at all, but efficacy! And why that vague word "pertains"? Inspiration "pertains" to many things, but what precisely is it? The confusion continues: "We affirm, therefore, that the Scriptures are the inspired Word of God." *Therefore?* Because of its Gospel-power? But, in that case, are not creeds, catechisms, hymn-books, and our own sermons equally and in the same sense the inspired Word of God? Indeed, such notions of inspiration were openly defended before President

Preus' Fact Finding Committee![433]

This new, historical-critical view of Scripture and inspiration is no longer that of the Lutheran Confessions. The Confessions do not hesitate at the equation, the Bible IS the Word of God. And they do not take the "is" with any grain of salt. Thus the Smalcald Articles, for instance, use "Scripture" and "Word" quite interchangeably in the paragraphs leading up to the classic assertion of the great Reformation *sola scriptura* principle: "The Word of God shall establish articles of faith, and no one else, not even an angel (II, II, 15). The Formula of Concord allows no fuzzy confusions on inspiration which might blur the absolute difference between Scripture and all other writings. The prefatory section on "Rule and Norm" (Solid Declaration) insists on a clean break "between divine and human writings" such that the former are "the Word of God" in contradistinction to "human being's writings," none of which "dare be put on a par with it"—even if they are Bible-based and Gospel-drenched creeds and catechisms (par. 9)! In short, it is *writings*—not simply "the Gospel"—which are "divine" and absolutely superior to all mere "human being's writings"! It is these *writings* moreover, and not a "Gospel" or a Law/Gospel distinction abstracted from them, which are the sole rule and norm of doctrine, in other words, the formal principle of theology. Of course justification, or the Gospel in its strictest sense, is the heart and soul of, and therefore also the key to, the entire Scripture.[434] A just *because* the Gospel permeates the entire Scripture (always presupposing the Law), the Scripture principle *is* Gospel authority. Hence it is always and only actual Bible texts, that is the "certain and clear passages of Scripture," and not some "Law and Gospel" floating above them, which constitute the *"rule"* for interpretation!"[435] So much so, in fact, that Abraham is praised for taking an express word of God literally, rather than looking for a "tolerable and loose interpretation," even though the divine command to sacrifice Isaac on the face of it ran counter "not only to reason and to divine and natural law but also to the eminent article of faith concerning the promised seed, Christ!"[436] Despite the obvious and terrible dilemma, Abraham rightly "gave God the honor of truthfulness."

This giving "God the honor of truthfulness" is the whole point of the much-maligned and misunderstood doctrine of biblical *inerrancy*. Without inerrancy the Scripture-alone principle becomes an empty pretence. If the sacred text is subject to error, then it is no longer the standard of truth, but is itself in need of one. It is no longer judge but defendant. Historical-critical counter-theology with its fallible Bible resembles an asylum in which the Bible is straitjacketed and subjected to "treatment" while the patients play doctor and nurses! And it is not a question of how much or how little—the situation is in principle wrong. The Formula of Concord's sharp distinction between "divine and human writings" merely echoes Luther's Large Catechism, on Baptism: "I and my neighbor and in sum all men are capable of erring and deceiving, but the Word of God can neither err nor deceive!" It is sheer nonsense to try to restrict inerrancy here to certain topics only, such as Baptism or "the Gospel." Luther argues obviously from inerrancy to Baptism, not from Baptism to inerrancy! The inerrancy attaches to God's Word as such, not to particular topics only (else why just these and not those?). The critical anti-inerrancy stand should frankly admit that it abandons the Confessions' teaching on this point, indeed the whole Scripture principle; it should not pretend to be subject to the Scriptures and the Confessions.

The main point to be kept in mind here is that inerrancy is not something over and above, or in addition to the Bible's inspiration and authority. It is simply part and parcel of any *bona fide* confession that the Bible, as God's Word, is the sole and decisive authority for faith, *sola scriptura*. Least of all is it some kind of obvious fact or feature which can be established by common sense, and which then "proves" that the Bible is God's Word. It is an article of faith, given with inspiration itself. Inerrancy is to the Bible roughly as His sinlessness is to Christ. If Christ sinned, then he could be neither Saviour, nor Son of God, nor Lord. But we do not "prove" His divine nature by first "proving" somehow that He was sinless! On the other hand, the sinlessness of Christ is a kind of test or criterion which shows whether one really accepts Him as God and Saviour, or whether one is simply mouthing beautiful, traditional, but meaningless words. Similarly, the most fervent professions of absolute and unconditional submission to the Bible as the inspired Word of God, etc., lose most if not all of their meaning if one at the same time rejects inerrancy. How can I seriously accept something as "absolutely authoritative" if I also believe it to be mistaken or in error? An example will illustrate the hopeless self-contradiction. A historical-critical commentator on the Gospel for Sexagesima (the parable of the sower, Luke 8:4-15) notes: "Since [St. Luke's] interpretation of the parable is not factually correct, it dare not determine the sermon. But since it is, after all, written there, it must also be heard and taken seriously as God's Word!"[437] How does one "hear and take seriously as God's Word" what one has just called a mistake? If truth is the same as error, acceptance the same as rejection, and submission the same as rebellion, words simply have lost their meaning and language has become pointless. "Inspiration" without inerrancy has lost its savour and is fit only to be trodden underfoot. This counterfeit "inspiration" must resort to just the sort of equivocations with which *Faithful . . . I* thinly veils its surrender of inerrancy in favor of historical criticism.[438]

To turn inerrancy into a scarecrow it is often suggested that the whole idea comes not from the Bible but from human preconceptions of what a perfect book must be like.[439] To remedy this alleged fallacy, we are invited to examine the Bible's own view of itself. Unfortunately this is usually taken to mean that one looks at a number of biblical difficulties, finds them to imply error or contradiction, and then announces this finding as the Bible's own view of itself![440] This is a total misunderstanding of what Christian doctrine is. Let us consider an analogy. The doctrine of the sinlessness of Christ rests on the clear texts which teach it, and on nothing else. We do not first examine actual samples of the Lord's behavior (for instance, His anger in the Temple, Matt. 21:12ff.) for "the qualities they themselves exhibit"[441] in order to determine on that basis whether He was or was not sinless. Before ever considering Christ's actions and behavior, in other words, a *priori*, we know that He is and was without sin, and we know and teach this on the basis of the clear texts of Scripture. The same holds true for every doctrine of the Bible, including the Bible's doctrine of itself. To determine this we do not examine for ourselves various features of the text to see whether they strike us as inerrant! (One might as well place a consecrated wafer under a microscope to test for evidence of the Real Presence!) We simply see how the Lord and His apostles treated and regarded the sacred text, and then we obediently go and do likewise. The present writer once attended a lecture on this subject by a Protestant Old Testament professor in Australia. In part one of his essay the lecturer showed conclusively from the New Testament that for Christ and His apostles the Old Testament was the unconditional and infallible Word of God. But in the second part of his lecture the professor asked whether we today were bound to agree with Christ and His apostles in this matter. This he then proceeded vigorously to deny on the grounds of our superior modern knowledge. Such a position in principle attacks not only the apostolicity of the church (Eph. 2:20) but the very Lordship of Christ, of whose words we are not to be ashamed (Mark 8:38).

The Lord Himself habitually uses particular biblical texts to settle arguments quite beyond appeal. For Him it is "the Scripture" as such, that is, the actual text, which "cannot be broken" (John 10:35), even on such a minor point as the exact wording of an obscure reference in the Psalms (82:6). It is not any Messianic or Christological content or prophecy—there is none in the verse in question—but biblical authority pure and simple which is here at stake. No questioning or disputing of the text can be entertained—not to speak of the outright rejection involved in the accusation of error, mistake, or contradiction. St. Paul too insists that he believes "*all things* which are written in the Law and in the prophets" (Acts 24:14) and that "*all* Scripture is given by inspiration of God" (2 Tim. 3:16). And what applies to the Old Testament Scriptures must hold all the more for the writings issuing from the very fulness of Pentecost itself, the writings of those to whom Christ promised His Spirit's guidance (John 14:26; 16:13), whom He appointed to serve as the very foundation of the church (John 15:20; 17:20; 20:31; Eph. 2:20), whose proclamation is couched "not in words taught by human wisdom but in words taught by the Spirit" (I Cor. 2:13). The apostolic Gospel is our absolute standard or norm, allowing for no disagreement (Gal. 1:8, 9). Today that apostolic standard is accessible to us only in the form of the documentary record (Luke 1:1-4; John 20:31), the New Testament. It is not surprising that I Timothy 5:18 already quotes St. Luke's Gospel (10:7) as "Scripture." Inerrancy then simply means no more and no less than the indisputable veracity which Scripture, as God's Word, claims for itself. Nor can one separate "earthly" from "heavenly" here (John 3: 12) or historical-factual from "theological" without in principle undoing the Incarnation.

To conclude, the Gospel's own "formal" or Scripture principle effectively excludes historical criticism. When this principle (including inerrancy) is surrendered, the Gospel itself is denatured and, far from "controlling" anything, becomes itself the plaything of the historical-critical will-o'-the-wisp.

5. *Theology of the Cross-Or Secular Cringe?*

In Romans 1:20 St. Paul writes that the existence of the Creator is plain from a consideration of the created universe. Any pagan and unbeliever can realise this fact—it is not faith but common "horse-sense." Yet many people imagine that this sort of thing is a proper and sufficient basis for religion. They fail to see that all this is mere "natural theology." There is no life-giving Gospel in it, the whole thing is Law, and leaves men dead in trespasses and sins. Luther took up this matter in his own powerful way in the famous Heidelberg Disputation of 1518. Against the reason-obsessed scholastics, with their haughty theological dream-castles, Luther hurled the thunderbolts of his nineteenth and twentieth theses:

19. Not he deserves to be called a theologian who sees the invisible things of God as being understood through those things which have been made.
20. But he who understands the visible and lowlier things of God, seen through sufferings and cross.

Not for a moment does Luther deny the natural knowledge of God "through those things which have been made." He simply points out that without Christ and faith this benefits no one but leaves men as they were. The new American Edition of *Luther's Works*, however, in a really terribly unfortunate mistranslation of the nineteenth thesis, makes Luther say something altogether different: In place of "those things which have been made," this version puts, incredibly enough, "those things which have actually happened" (XXXI, p. 40)! Here the whole connection with Romans 1 has been lost, and the impression is created that Luther was somehow belittling the importance of historical facts for Christianity! This is exactly the way in which a major Missouri "moderate" anti-inerrancy article has taken this mutilation of Luther, triumphantly citing it under the dramatic heading, "Needed: Luther's 'Theology of the Cross' "![442]

It is precisely the humble biblical narrative, Baptism, absolution, the Holy Supper, and above all, the divine-human Jesus Himself, the Word-made-flesh, that Luther means by the "visible and lowlier things of God" in which He wishes to be known and grasped with childlike faith. And it is just these "visible and lowlier things of God" which historical criticism subverts and treats with contempt, in the name of its god, Reason. It is tragi-comic to dress up historical criticism as "theology of the Cross." It is nothing of the kind. Criticism is inherently and radically secular, as Krentz also points out:

> It is difficult to overestimate the significance the nineteenth century has for biblical interpretation. It made historical criticism *the* approved method of interpretation. The result was a revolution of viewpoint in evaluating the Bible. The Scriptures were, so to speak, secularised. The biblical books became historical documents to be studied and questioned like any other ancient sources . . . The history it reported was no longer assumed to be everywhere correct. The Bible stood before criticism as defendant before judge . . .
>
> Biblical scholars use the methods of secular history on the Bible to discover truth and explain what happened. The methods are secular. The procedures may be modified to fit the Bible, but are not essentially changed.[443]

It is not the Cross but worldly wisdom which dominates this "theology of glory." A recent survey of U.S. Lutheranism concluded quite realistically:

> The data indicate that in Lutheranism a trend exists away from a belief system dominated by super naturalism to one dominated by a humanistic orientation toward life. The foundations of traditional Christianity increasingly have been challenged, especially by clergymen. For example, only one in ten LCA and less than one in five ALC clergymen view the Bible as God's Word and entirely true. More than three quarters of the LCA and more than half of the ALC clergy indicate that belief in the virgin birth of Christ no longer is necessary to be a good Christian. Nearly a third of the LCA clergy say that belief in Jesus Christ as Saviour is not essential to salvation.[444]

The Missouri Synod educator W. T. Janzow has produced a significant study of the Missouri Synod, entitled *Secularization in an Orthodox Denomination* (1971). Although the process of secularization is, of course, understood sociologically, the theological implications are nevertheless clear. Janzow shows, for example, that Missouri's "elite" (officials and professors) at the time of the study deviated considerably more from the Synod's traditional theology than did either the laymen or the clergy generally. Another sociological thesis incidentally documents the much higher degree of lib al penetration among graduates of the St. Louis seminary (before the "exile") than among those of Springfield.[445]

The distinguished Australian academic, Dr. Frank Knopfelmacher, has written a perceptive essay about the liberalization of the Australian Roman Catholic intelligentsia,[446] which is remarkably applicable to parallel developments among American (and Australian!) Lutherans. Knopfelmacher suggests that much of the liberal trend is basically a quest for social acceptance and advancement. Those who are moving up in the world are anxious to leave behind the stigma and isolation of the immigrant-culture, and to array themselves with the status symbols of the establishment. This easily produces "a groping, socio-cultural cringe to an amorphous reference group," namely to "the left-liberal, largely Protestant, intelligentsia and their activities, institutions, postures, rituals and prevailing political attitudes." Any suggestions of "fundamentalist, traditionalist, Catholic Irishness" must, of course, be scornfully repudiated—"they are the marks of the 'Irish peasant' who is not *salonfaehig* [socially 'house-broken']". Instead, social deference is paid to "universities and academic intellectuals, the bundle of projections and fantasies which Australian provincials tend to identify breathlessly with 'Europe,' and the causes and institutions of the Protestant establishment in pursuit of 'conscience' and 'charity.'" Lutheran applications shall be left largely to the reader's own imagination. Even (especially?) the sophisticated *Dialog* is not above an occasional strange obsession with immigrant "garlic and onions" (are they really Nordic?), from which, it seems, the late Franklin Clark Fry, beloved of "suburban, affluent, or on-the-way-up people," so happily delivered "Lutheranism in America!"[447]

Perhaps the most scandalous instance of uncritical deference being paid to secular superstitions was the craven cringe to evolution. This rather unholy sacred cow, now totally bereft of respectable intellectual foundations,[448] has been passionately embraced as a mark of intellectual respectability and good taste in many if not most Lutheran institutions of higher learning.

The cost was rarely considered, but has been appallingly high. Loetscher's *The Broadening Church*, describing the Presbyterian experience, does not exaggerate the impact of evolution:

> Of course, the most radical implications of evolution were not immediately drawn, nor were they everywhere accepted, but the disquieting and unsettling effects of the new doctrine were soon felt even in the most conservative circles. Evolution's challenge "to the creation narrative of Genesis was direct and immediate. The stimulus it gave to naturalistic developmental views of the Bible was soon apparent. Its implications for the traditional doctrines of the fall and sin and redemption were unmistakable. Was the Person of Christ to be excepted from naturalistic processes of development?
>
> ... Most ultimate of all was the threat of evolution to reduce the concepts of reality and truth themselves to sheer relativity.[449]

With evolution came the historical-critical destruction of biblical authority, which in turn promotes what Sasse has called "the decay of the doctrinal substance which can be observed in all denominations of Christendom."[450] Sasse continues:

> One has often the impression that the same spiritual disease through which the Greeks went in the 6th and 5th centuries B.C., and which began in India a little earlier, is now going through the "Christian" nations in the world. The faith of the fathers is dying and is being replaced by philosophical speculations or sociopolitical ideologies. The "God is dead" theology in America, the agnosticism which is openly confessed by Anglican priests in Australia, the transformation of the *sola fide* and the *theologia crucis* into a lifeless speculation in Lutheran circles, the New Hermeneutics which destroys the Word of God—"We have lost the Word of God and cannot find it again," as the leader of a Congregational College said—all this is indicative of a process of disintegration that is going on in all Christendom and leads not only to numberless personal tragedies, mental breakdowns and moral conflicts, but also to the dissolution of the churches. Like most of the great tragedies in the history of mankind, it is accompanied by a strange euphoria which accompanies certain lethal diseases. What actually may be the ruin of the Church is regarded as a wonderful renewal, an unheard of resurgence of the Church and its mission to the entire world.

"Law and Gospel" also have been turned into "a lifeless speculation." In *chic* Lutheran usage, "evangelical" means tolerant, and the "Gospel" is identified with a kind of secular permissiveness. That thought-provoking "profile" of U.S. Lutheranism, *A Study of Generations*, was led by poor theological advice to identify "Gospel-orientation" with a permissive moderation located somewhere between the "extremes" of liberalism and "fundamentalism;" holding positive, conservative beliefs for itself, but hesitating to brand their denial as heresy; open to change and variety.[451] The "hard line," by contrast involved doctrinal condemnations, "rigidity," stress on external authority, belief in a "true visible church," etc., and was described as "Law-orientation," hence "misbelief!"[452] If that were true, the mild Erasmus was "Gospel-oriented" and Luther, with his "rigid" doctrine and external authority (*Smalcald Articles* II, II, 15; III, VIII) a classic example of "Law-orientation." Not to mention Paul's dreadfully "Law-oriented" Gospel in Galatians 1:8, 9!

So ingrained is this confusion of the Gospel with a soft, secular sentimentality, that *Missouri in Perspective* could preach editorially about "Absolute Truth and Love" on the basis of a "text" from the Hindu Gandhi: "How can he who thinks he possesses absolute truth be fraternal?"[453] Another editorial opposed certain Synodical dismissals with this reasoning: "Jesus Christ came into the world, not to institute doctrine, but to save people (see Mark 2:27). And when people, bought by the blood of Christ, become expendable for the sake of what may (or may not) be pure doctrine, Christ's purposes are frustrated and that is sinful."[454] The secular assumptions here are essentially those which had surfaced in the old ALC, already a quarter of a century ago, in the following comment in a review of Francis Pieper's *Christian Dogmatics*: "One travels the old-fashioned roads of religion in this book, *when religion was the dominant interest in life*, and when all opposing ideas were roundly damned, from the Athanasian Creed to some of the documents issuing from the Predestinarian controversy"[455] [our emphases].

The neo-Lutheran "with-it-ry" is not the theology of the cross that it claims to be, but a cultural cringe to secular values. True, Aristotle, that idol of scholasticism, is generally booed—but mainly because he is out of fashion. The new Aristotles, evil geniuses like Darwin, Marx, and Freud, now set the tone.[456] While elsewhere persecuted Christians taste the cross to the full, we in the West accommodate ourselves more and more to the trendy gods denounced so eloquently, and from bitter experience, by men like Malcolm Muggeridge and Alexander Solzhenitsyn! How shallow is all our comfortable "relevance!" "Our business," wrote C. S. Lewis, "is to present that which is timeless (the same yesterday, today, and tomorrow) in the particular language of our own age." Is that not precisely what our new, "critical" theology is all about? Quite the contrary. Lewis continues:

> The bad preacher does exactly the opposite: he takes the ideas of our own age and tricks them out in the traditional language of Christianity. Thus, for example, he may think about the Beveridge Report [the basis of the British social welfare system] and *talk* about the coming of the Kingdom. The core of his thought is merely contemporary; only the superficies is traditional. But your teaching must be timeless at its heart and wear a modern dress.[457]

But without contempt of the world we cannot love, much less proclaim, the eternal things of God. Worldly "theology" leads instead to a despising of that very suffering and cross which open our eyes to the priceless grandeur of the "visible and lowlier" things of God! Is it our respect for suffering or our contempt for the sufferers, our other-worldliness or our love of convenience, that makes us so serenely indifferent to the torments of millions of our fellow-believers? In East Germany in August 1976 Pastor Oskar Bruesewitz burned himself to death in a futile attempt to draw the world's attention to the fearful oppression inflicted especially on young Christians under militant Marxism. He hoped no doubt by his own sacrifice to secure some relief for the weak lambs in his flock and elsewhere. Meanwhile, in New York and Washington other pastors used their freedom of action to speak out boldly—for the killing of the unborn in the name of "civil rights!" And in Minneapolis they explored the ultimate possibilities of self-indulgence through pornographic exercises in "human sexuality!" But, of course, it is all a matter of interpretation: "In the beginning was the Flesh . . ."[458]

V. EPILOGUE

No doubt the theological and historical contours sketched however inadequately within the brief compass of the preceding pages need to be supplemented or even corrected in various particulars. No one is more keenly aware of this than the present writer. He is convinced, however, that, whatever else can or should be said on the subject, the key to the Missouri debacle lies in the Biblical and Confessional Principles, which this little study has sought to spell out and apply. Explanations which fail to come to grips in any precise way with these principles may well be interesting, informative, and even witty, but can hardly be considered very relevant. On the other hand, all discussion leading to a further clarification of these principles should be warmly welcomed.

That the "moderate" theology runs afoul of "old Missouri's" most cherished convictions is so plain that it is really beyond dispute. More important are the wider implications of the Biblical and Confessional Principles. After all, whether something is genuinely "Missourian" or not is really of no theological interest except as it clarifies what is genuinely Lutheran; just as the question of what is really "Lutheran" is trivial and sectarian unless its intention is to make clear what is genuinely Christian.

The late Dr. Sasse, shortly before his death, wrote that "the present crisis in Missouri" was "the crisis of the entire Lutheran Church."[459] This is no exaggeration. The Biblical and Confessional Principles examined in the present treatise can be shown to have been shared in large measure by the antecedents of the present ALC and by the General Council elements of the LCA. Yet today Missouri alone among the three major U.S. Lutheran bodies stands officially for the "old Lutheranism" of their more or less common past. Is this significant? What can Lutheranism possibly be apart from "old Lutheranism?" How can it be defined or identified? Or is it simply an unprincipled growth, like cancer cells, jumping erratically from one current trend to the next?

In this time of chaos and dissolution we modern Lutherans need nothing more than a painstaking inspection of our roots. Glib "trendiness" cannot help us. For, to resume the quotation from C. S. Lewis with which this book began,

> sentences in a modern book which look quite ordinary may

be directed "at" some other book; in this way you may be led to accept what you would have indignantly rejected if you knew its real significance. The only safety is to have a standard of plain, central Christianity ("mere Christianity" as Baxter called it) which puts the controversies of the moment in their proper perspective. Such a standard can be acquired only from the old books.[460]

APPENDIX A
CHURCH AND FELLOWSHIP

(Excerpts from the Australian Lutheran *Document of Union* of 1966, as incorporated into the *Theses of Agreement*)

*

25. We uphold the distinction between the one, holy, Christian Church and the visible organised Churches.
We believe that the one, holy, Christian Church is present in those visible Churches where the marks of the Church are to be found, that is, where the Gospel of Christ is purely taught and the Sacraments are administered according to Christ's institution (Theses of Agreement, V).
26. We believe that true Christians are found in every denomination in which to a greater or lesser degree the marks of the one, holy, Christian Church are present, in spite of existing errors, and we rejoice in the unity of the Spirit that binds all true believers to their one Lord. Nevertheless, according to the Word of God and our Lutheran Confessions, Church fellowship, that is, mutual recognition as brethren, altar and pulpit fellowship and resultant cooperation in the preaching of the Gospel and the administration of the Sacraments, presupposes unanimity in the pure doctrine of the Gospel and in the right administration of the Sacraments.
27. We reject all religious syncretism or unionism (see Theses of Agreement, II, 2 and V, 14-15). Accordingly, we cannot acknowledge ourselves to be in fellowship with Churches with which we are not one in doctrine and practice.
28. We declare that wherever continued co-operation in the preaching of the Gospel and the administration of the Sacraments and worship exists, there we have a witness to the world of unity in the faith and a profession of Church fellowship.
29. There are, however, forms of co-operation between Churches not in Church fellowship that are not necessarily a witness to unity in faith. God's Word does not explicitly or categorically justify or condemn such co-operation in special circumstances. Therefore all such extraordinary cooperation must be determined from case to

case. Differences in judgment can be expected here and should be tolerated according to the law of love.

APPENDIX B
FELLOWSHIP IN ITS NECESSARY CONTEXT
OF THE DOCTRINE OF THE CHURCH

[produced in 1961 by European, South American, and Australian theologians in fellowship with the Missouri Synod to resolve the Synodical Conference deadlock].

*

1. The holy, catholic, and apostolic church is one body in Christ, incorporating all believers, whose faith is created, sustained, fulfilled, and known by God alone. The church and the faith of the heart (*fides qua*) are outside the competence and the direct comprehension of men.

(The following abbreviations will be used in the References to the various paragraphs)

SC	Small Catechism
CA	Augsburg Confession
AS	Smalcald Articles
Tractatus	Appendix to the Smalcald Articles
SD	Solid Declaration of the Formula of Concord
WA	Weimar edition of *Luther's Works*
par	parallels

    Matt. 16:16-19; Jn. 10:16, 27-29; Gal. 3:26-28; Eph. 1:20-23; 2:14,15; 2:19-21; 4:3-6,15,16 (Stoeckhardt, *Lehre und Wehre*, 1901, 97 ff.)—Nicene Creed; SC, Second and Third Articles; CA V and VII; Apology VII: 5-8.
    Jn. 6:44; Acts 13:48; Col. 2:12; 3:3, 4:2 Tim. 2:19.

2. Faith is created and sustained by God through the Means of Grace. Where the Means of Grace (Gospel and Sacraments) are in use, even where much impeded, there believers are present. We know this by faith, and not by empirical experience. This knowledge rests on the promise of God in the Means of Grace outside of us (*extra nos*) and not on criteria in us (*in nobis*): sanctification, or any assessment of men, their works, polity or discipline.

Is. 55:10; Lk. 8:11-15; Rom. 10:5-17; 1 Pet. 1:23-25; Tit. 3:5,6. CA V: "That we may obtain this faith, the ministry of teaching the Gospel and administering the Sacraments was instituted. For through the Word and Sacraments, as through instruments, the Holy Ghost is given, who works faith, where and when it pleases God, in them that hear the Gospel, to wit, that God, not for our own merits, but for Christ's sake, justifies those who believe that they are received into grace for Christ's sake." Apology IV:67, 346 (225); SC, Third Article (cf. Large Catechism, Third Article: 43-45); SD II:50; XI:29, 50—No other criterion: Apology VII:10,11,18,19.

1 Sam. 16:7; Acts 15:8.

3. Where the Means of Grace are in operation, there the church is to be found, whole, local, and tangible. The assembly regularly gathered about the pure preaching and the right administration of the Sacraments is called by God Himself the church at that place, irrespective of the hypocrites who may be attached outwardly to such assembly. This is no mere organizational form or association of individuals, but the one church that will remain forever (*Una Sancta perpetuo mansura*) in the exercise of its God-given, spiritual functions (Office of the Keys). This church is only one. Though locally apprehended, it must not be thought of as isolated, intermittent, or individual with reference to persons, time, or place.

Matt. 18:18-20; Acts 6:7; 12:24; 19:20 Eph. 4:3-16; 5:25,27 CA VII and VIII; LC, Third Article: 51-58, 61f.; AS, Part 3, VII; 1 Tractatus: 24, 67-69; SD X:9. —Luther (WA 18:652, 743): "The church is hidden, the saints latent... The whole life of the church and its being is in the Word of God." *Disputation of 1542* (Drews, 655f.) : "The church is recognized by its confession... it is in other words visible by its confession."

The addresses of the epistles and Acts, chapters 2-5; 9:31. Matt. 28:-20 par; Gal. 4:26-28; 1 Cor. 5:3-5; 1 Pet. 2:2-10.

4. The Means of Grace, which are the means of uniting the church to Christ, its head, are a given whole, inseparable from the total revelation of Law and Gospel as set forth in the Scriptures (cf. the whole definition in CA VII).

Jn. 10:34,35; 16:12-15; 17:20; 1 Jn. 2:26,27: Rom. 1:1,2; 2

Tim. 3:14-17 par.—AS, Part 2, II:15: "The Word of God shall establish articles of faith . . ." CA: first paragraph of transition from Art. XXI to XXII; SD, Rule and Norm. Note the singulars: 'doctrine', 'form of sound words', 'deposit', etc. 1 Tim. 3:15.

Lk. 24:47 and 1 Tim. 1:8,9 par.—SD V and VI.

5. The Means of Grace create the fellowship of believers with God and thereby fellowship with all believers. This fellowship is, accordingly, given by God, not achieved by any human effort. Its existence can be believed and known only on the basis of the marks of the church (*notae ecclesiae*).

Acts 2:42; 1 Cor. 1:7; 10:16, 17; 12:13; Eph. 4:3-6; 1 Jn. 1:1-4; 3 Jn. 3-8.—Apology VII:5 f., 12, 19,20.—Hollaz, *Examen* (1707 and 1750) p. 1300: "The inner and essential form of the church consists in the spiritual unity of those who truly believe, of the saints who are tied together (Jn. 13:35) as members of the church with Christ the head, by means of a true and living faith (Jn. 1:12; Gal. 3:27; 1 Cor. 6:17), which is followed by a fellowship of mutual love."

Gal. 2:6,9,11-14; 2 Thess. 3:14,15; 1 Jn. 1:5-7.—Apology VII: 22; SD X:3.

6. Where the marks of the church are opposed by false teaching, not only is this double fellowship (in the *Una Sancta*) endangered, but a power is set up which is in contradiction to the fellowship manifested on earth (see 12). Where the pure marks of the church (*notae purae*) hold sway, this disrupting power is repudiated and overcome through refusal to recognize its right to exist, for Christ alone must reign in His church through His Word. Where the sway of the pure marks of the church is rejected, the fellowship is broken. A rupture of fellowship for any other reason is impermissible. The restoring of a broken fellowship must be brought about by use of the pure marks of the church, as they cleanse out the impurity.

Matt. 7:15; 16:6; Acts 20:27-30; Rom. 16:16-20; Gal. 1:8,9; 5:9; 2 Cor. 6:14-18; 11:4, 13-15; Phil. 3:2; 1 Tim. 1:3, 18, 19; 4:1-3; 5:22; 6:3-5; 2 Tim. 2:15-21; 3:5,8,9; Tit, 1:9,10; 3:10; 1 Jn. 2:18-23; 4:1-6; 2 Jn. 8-11.—CA VII; SD XI:94-96. The negatives of all Symbols: CA XXVIII: 20-28; Apology VII: 20-22, 48-50; XV: 18; AS Part 2, 11:10: Tractatus: 38,41,42,71; Preface to SD: 6-10; X:5,6,31.

Acts 15; 2 Cor. 10:4-6; Eph. 4:11-14; 6:17. 1 Cor. 1:10; chapters 12-14.—CA VII:2,3; Apology IV:231 (110).

It is understood that the church takes action through the Office of the Keys committed to it by Christ (see 3).

7. Impurity can be discerned only by the standard of the pure marks of the church. The subjective faith of any man or group cannot be judged by us, but only what is actually taught or confessed, as it conforms or does not conform to the pure marks.

Jn. 8:31,32; Rom. 16:17; 1 Tim. 6:13,20; 2 Tim. 1:13.—The passages from the Symbols referred to under 4 and 6.

8. The purity of the marks is defended by the Symbols. The Symbols (*norma normata*) as the true interpretation of the Word of God (*norma normans*) are a continuous standard of public teaching in the church from generation to generation and bind together not only all true confessors of any particular time but those of all ages in oneness of teaching (cf. the durative present tenses in 'is taught' and 'are administered' and also the adverbs 'purely' and 'rightly' in 147 AC VII). In the Symbols we have a safeguard against those who hold God's Word to be present only as God wills from time to time, as they are also a safeguard of the truth against reliance upon a traditional exegesis and ecclesiastical success, and against a method of hermeneutics which uses the Bible as a book of oracles to the neglect of the rule of faith.

Is. 8:20; Matt. 16:16,17 par; 1 Cor. 15:1-5; 1 Tim. 6:12-14; 2 Tim. 1:13,14; 2:2; Hebr. 4:14.—Article 1 in each CA, Apology and AS; CA VII: "Also they teach that one holy church is to continue for ever. The church is the congregation of saints, in which the Gospel is rightly taught and the Sacraments are rightly administered. And to the true unity of the church it is enough to agree concerning the doctrine of the Gospel and the administration of the Sacraments. See also Formula of Concord, Norm and Rule, together with Prefaces.

Matt. 10:32.33,40,41: Rom. 10:9,10.

9. A quantitative approach is as misleading as an unhistorical one. The inexhaustible wholeness of the marks of the church calls for constant and complete submission and acceptance. The Symbols do not speak fully on every doctrine, but as presentations of the marks they have abiding validity, as have also their rejections of what they recognize as falsifications

of or subtractions from the marks.

Matt. 23:8; Jn. 10:5,27; 2 Cor. 5:18-20.—AS PART 3, VIII: SD X:31; Xl:95,96; XII:39,40

10. The faith which is taught in a church is first of all the formal and official confession of a church. This may, however, be called in question or rendered doubtful by actual or practical negation of it. In that case a distinction must be made between sporadic contradiction and persistent approval or toleration of contradiction. In the latter case, the official confession, no matter how excellent, is negated.

For Scripture passages see under 6 and under 8—SC, Second Commandment and First Petition: End of Preface to the *Book of Concord*; SD VII:I; X:5,6,10,11,28,29.

11. The marks of the church are all-decisive. Everything must be referred to them. This duty is hindered by presumptuous judgments or statements concerning the faith or lack of it in individuals. It is Enthusiasm to build on subjective faith (*fides qua*) and love, for faith is hidden and love is variable. Both are in man. The Means of Grace are objective, solid, apprehensible. Since these are God's own means, we must attend entirely upon them and draw from them the distinction between the orthodox church and heterodox churches.

See under 4, 6, 8, 10. Observe that of the abounding polemics in the *Book of Concord* more than one third is directed against pseudo-Lutheranism.

12. The fellowship created by Word and Sacraments shows itself fundamentally in pulpit and altar fellowship. It can show itself in many other ways, some of which, like prayer and worship and love of the brethren, the church cannot do without, others of which, like the holy kiss or the handshake or the reception into one's house, vary from place to place and from time to time. In whatever way the fellowship created by Word and Sacraments shows itself, all visible manifestations of fellowship must be truthful and in accordance with the supreme demands of the marks of the church. The "sacred things" (*sacra*) are the Means of Grace, and only by way of them is anything else a "sacred thing" (*sacrum*).

Acts 2:41-47; 1 Cor. 1:10 cf. 15:1-4; 10:16,17; 11:22-34; 12:13; chapter 14; 2 Cor. chapters 8 and 9. See also material under 2, 6, and 7.

13. Prayer is not one of the marks of the church and should not be coordinated with Word and Sacraments, as though it were essentially of the same nature as they. As a response to the divine Word, it is an expression of faith and a fruit of faith, and when spoken before others, a profession of faith. As a profession of faith it must be in harmony with and under the control of the marks of the church.

Dan. 9:18; Acts 9:11; Gal. 4:6; Rom. 10:8-14; 1 Tim. 2:1,2; Acts 27:35.—Apology XIII:16; XXIII:30,31: LC, Lord's Prayer: 13-30. Also see under 12.

This statement bears within it:

a) the implication that the member-churches of the Synodical Conference have not enunciated and carried through the principles outlined in it in their documents of fellowship with the necessary clarity and consistency.

and

b) the suggestion that the goal of the Synodical Conference discussion is to be reached by the traditional highway of the Doctrine of the Church. Since the premature turning off into the byway of fellowship has led to a dead end, it would seem best, first of all, to return to the highway and there move forward together guided only by the marks of the church.

Finally, the members of the Overseas Committee on Fellowship feel that they will not have done what is expected of them if they do not indicate, at least in a general way, in the concrete case of prayer fellowship how the approach here developed may lead to a happy solution of this vexing matter. It seems to them that statements in prayer fellowship like the following could be suggested as flowing directly from the principles enunciated:

1) Prayer between Christians belonging to churches which have a conflicting relation to the marks of the church must avoid the ever-present suspicion that the marks of the church are being disregarded.

2) "When joint prayer shows the marks or characteristics of unionism, it must be condemned and avoided. Such marks and characteristics of unionism are:

a) failure to confess the whole truth of the Divine Word (*in statu confessionis*);

b) failure to reject and denounce every opposing error:

c) assigning to error equal right with truth;

d) creating the impression of unity in faith or of church fellowship, where it does not exist." (Australian *Theses of Agreement*, II, 2)

These four characteristics of unionism are clearly negations of the marks of the church.

3) Joint prayer of the kind described in 1) cannot in the very nature of the case be normal or regular, but will rather be exceptional (see 2 d above).

4) Situations, however, can be imagined and have actually occurred in the history of the church where joint prayer of the kind mentioned in 1) can be practised, for it can be shown that the marks of the church have not or are not in such cases disregarded, jeopardized, or surrendered. These instances cannot be judged by a flat rule beforehand, for the situation differs with each case, and so a decision on the permissibility of joint prayer in any particular situation will have to be made by a fair and adequate judgment of that case. And in such individual cases one must reckon with the fact that Christians will differ in their judgment. Such differences in judgment will have to be tolerated in the church militant, as long as there is an evident loyalty to the demands of the divine Word and Sacraments.

Is. 59:2; Gal. 2.—SC, Commandments 1,2, and 3 and the First Petition; LC, Second Commandment: 53-56; First Petition: 39-48.

Gal. 5:1; Col. 2:16,20.—CA VII: 2,3; XV; XXVIII: 30 ff. and the correspondents in Apology and AS; SD X.

FOOTNOTES

1. C. S. Lewis on the need to read old books in order to understand the new. Introduction to *St. Athanasius on the Incarnation* (London: A. R. Mowbray, 1953), p. 4.
2. On even quite useful concepts like "triumphalism," "acculturation," "Americanisation," or "secularisation" in its sociological sense, cf. Jack Treon Robinson, *The Spirit of Triumphalism in the Lutheran Church-Missouri Synod* (Ph. D. thesis, Vanderbilt University Graduate School, Nashville, Tenn., 1972. University Microfilms); Alan Graebner, *Uncertain Saints* (Westport, Conn. and London, 1975); Walter Theophil Janzow, *Secularization in an Orthodox Denomination* (Ph. D. Thesis, University of Nebraska, 1970. University Microfilms).
3. Herbert Lindemann. "Personal Reflections on the Twenty-Fifth Anniversary of the Publication of 'A Statement,'" *Concordia Historical Institute Quarterly*, XLIII, 4 (Nov. 1970), p. 165.
4. See especially H. Sasse, *Here We Stand*, (Minneapolis: Augsburg:. 1946): *This is My Body* (Minneapolis: Augsburg, 1959); *In Statu Confessionis*, I (Berlin and Hamburg: Lutherisches Verlaghaus. 1966): II (Berlin: Die Spur, 1976).
5. See especially the literary deposit in *Lutherischer Rundblick* (1953-1976); also W. M. Oesch, *Solus Christus* (*Lutherischer Rundblick*: special jubilee issue, 1971); "The Present State of Confessional Lutheranism in America and the World," 1969 *Bethany Reformation Lectures* (*Lutheran Synod Quarterly*, X, XI).
6. H. Sasse, "Gedanken am Vorabend des Reformationsjubilaeums von 1967," *Lutherische Blaetter*, XIX, 89 (Dec. 1966), pp. 81-82.
7. Formula of Concord (FC), Solid Declaration (SD), Rule and Norm 9, Theodore G. Tappert, ed., *The Book of Concord* (St. Louis: Concordia, 1959), p. 505.
8. FC, Epitome, Rule and Norm 8. Tappert, p. 465.
9. FC. SD, Rule and Norm 10: cf. inexact rendering, Tappert, p. 506.

10. FC. SD, Rule and Norm 16, Tappert, p. 507.
11. Preface to the *Book of Concord*, Tappert, p. 11.
12. Apart from the Hay-Jacobs translation (1875, 1889, 1899) of Heinrich Schmid's *Doctrinal Theology*, these Lutheran classics have been virtually inaccessible to the English-speaking public. Robert Preus has undertaken the pioneering task of lifting these "sunken treasures" for our time. See his scholarly, sympathetic, but by no means uncritical, work in *The Inspiration of Scripture* (Mankato: Lutheran Synod Book Company, 1955); and *The Theology of Post-Reformation Lutheranism*, 2 vols. (London and St. Louis: Concordia Publishing House, 1970, 1972).
13. Bengt Haegglund, *History of Theology* (St. Louis: Concordia, 1968), p. 303.
14. Ralph Dornfeld Owen, *The Old Lutherans Come* (reprinted from *Concordia Historical Institute Quarterly*, April 1947), p. 5.
15. Theodor Hebart, *Die Vereinigte Evangelisch - Lutherische Kirche in Australien* (North Adelaide: Lutheran Book Depot, 1938), p. 26. Cf. H. Sasse, '"Das Jahrhundert der preussischen Kirche, "*In Statu Confesszonis II* (Berlin: Die Spur, 1976), pp. 184-193.
16. Theodore G. Tappert, ed., *Lutheran Confessional Theology in America 1840-1880* (New York: Oxford University Press, 1972), p. 7.
17. The leader of the Saxon immigration to Missouri, Martin Stephan, had originally planned to go to Australia, but was finally deterred by anti-British bias. See Carl Eduard Vehse, *Die Stephansche Auswanderung nach Amerika* (Dresden: P. H. Sillig, 1840?), p. 3.
18. T. Hebart, *op cit.*, p. 47.
19. Abdel Ross Wentz, *A Basic History of Lutheranism in America* (Philadelphia: Fortress, 1964), p. 93. Pennsylvania decided "That we will simply anticipate the future union with the Reformed Church." See S. E. Ochsenford, *Documentary History of the General Council of the Evangelical Lutheran Church in North America* (Philadelphia: General Council Publication House, 1912), p. 53.
20. Ochsenford, *op. cit.*, p. 63.
21. Vergilius Ferm, *The Crisis in American Lutheran Theology* (New York and London: The Century Co., 1927), p. 113.

22. The original constitution of the Missouri Synod in Ar. V, par. 15, provided for supervision of the pastors to see "whether they had allowed themselves to be misled into the use of the so-called 'new measures' which have become dominant here, or whether they carry on pastoral care in the sound, Scriptural manner of the orthodox church." An official explanation defined these "new measures" as the "arrangements, originating largely in the wake of Methodism, to achieve the quickest, most forcible and spectacular conversion possible ... e.g. camp meetings ... protracted meetings ... anxious bench, and others" (*Die Verfassung der deutschen evangelisch-lutherischen Synode von Missouri, Ohio und anderan Staaten, nebst einer Einleitung und erlaeutenden Bemerk ungen.* St. Louis: Weber & Olshausen, 1846, pp. 9,13). This is the background of the *Brief Statement's* rejection of "new methods" or "unchurchly activities, which do not build, but harm, the Church" (Of the Means of Grace, par. 22). CFW Walther in his *Law and Gospel* lecture series devoted the longest treatment by far to his 9th thesis, directed against the Reformed experience-theology, and pointing to the pivotal position of the Word and Sacraments (*The Proper Distinction Between Law and Gospel.* St. Louis: Concordia, 1928), pp. 127-210) !
23. Friedrich Lochner, *Der Hauptgottesdienst der Evangelisch Lutherischen Kirche* (St. Louis: Concordia, 1895), p. V. The Synod's original constitution explicitly provided in Art. V, par. 14, that it "regards this also as necessary for the purifying of the American-Lutheran Church, namely that the emptiness and poverty in the externals of divine worship be counteracted, which has here become dominant through the intrusion of the false, Reformed spirit" (*Die Verfassung*, etc., p. 8).
24. It is true that the Augsburg Confession was formulated before the rise of modern denominationalism. Yet the Lutheran/Zwinglian division had already occurred in 1529, not to speak of the Anabaptists.
25. *Luther's Works*, vol. 41, p. 211.
26. *Luther's Works*, vol. 39, p. 220.
27. Weimar edition, vol. 18, p. 633.
28. Preface to Revelation, *Saemmtliche Schriften* (St. Louis edition), vol. XIV, c. 139.

29. FC, SD, X, 31, Tappert, p. 616.
30. FC, SD, VII, 33, Tappert, p. 575
31. FC, SD, Introduction 9, Tappert, p. 503.
32. Preface to the *Book of Concord*, Tappert, p. 11.
33. FC, SD, Introduction and Rule and Norm, Tappert, pp. 502. 504. The Lutheran Confessions do not speak of a "Lutheran" church at all. The term "Lutheran" does not even appear in the index of the Tappert edition of the *Book of Concord*. The word is used however in the German version of Article XV, 44, of the *Apology*, where it is said of the opponents: "But of the knowledge of Christ, of faith, of the comfort of consciences they can preach nothing, rather they call this same blessed doctrine, the dear, holy Gospel, Lutheran."
34. Preface to the *Book of Concord*, Tappert, p. 11. Indeed, of the sincere and simple souls even in those churches with which agreement has not been established, but who "take no pleasure in blasphemies against the Holy Supper as it is celebrated in our churches according to Christ's institution," it is "to be hoped that when they are rightly instructed in this doctrine, they will, through the guidance of the Holy Spirit, turn to the infallible truth of the divine Word and unite with us and our churches and schools."
35. FC, SD, Introduction, Tappert, p. 501.
36. Preface to the *Book of Concord*, Tappert, p. 3.
37. Apology VII /VIII, 9 (German) .
38. *Luther's Works*, vol. 40, p. 233.
39. Vilmos Vajta and Hans Weissgerber, eds, *The Church and the Confessions* (Philadelphia: Fortress, 1963), p. 76.
40. John H. Tietjen, *Which Way To Lutheran Unity?* (St. Louis: Concordia, 1966), p. 150.
41. Walter O. Forster, *Zion on the Mississippi* (St. Louis: Concordia, 1953), pp. 523 ff.
42. Mundinger, *Government in the Missouri Synod* (St. Louis: Concordia, 1947), caricatures Luther's view by leaving out entirely Luther's insistence on the public ministry as a divine institution, not a mere arrangement of convenience (pp. 8-9).
43. Chr. Hochstetter, *Die Geschiche der Evangelisch-Lutherischen Missouri Synode in Nord-Amerika* (Dresden: Heinrich J. Naumann, 1885), pp. 184 ff.
44. Erwin L. Lueker, ed., *Lutheran Cyclopedia* (St. Louis: Con-

cordia, 1954), p. 148.
45. W. H. T. Dau's translation in Th. Engelder, ed., *Walther and the Church* (St. Louis: Concordia, 1938), gives only Walther's theses and biblical references, but not the citations from the Confessions and from theologians of recognised orthodoxy.
46. L. Fuerbringer, ed., *Briefe von C. W.F. Walther*, vol. I (St. Louis: Concordia, 1915), p. 99.
47. Hochstetter, *op. cit.*, p. 241
48. *Ibid.*, pp. 283-284.
49. Loehe to Iowa Synod President Grossmann, July 1, 1853, "Correspondence and Other Papers of the Rev. Wilhelm Loehe, Item 15," in the files of the Concordia Historical Institute, St. Louis.
50. FC, SD, VII, 33. 34. 41, Tappert, pp. 575-576.
51. Hochstetter, *op. cit.*, p. 251.
52. F. Pieper, "The Synodical Conference," *The Distinctive Doctrines and Usages of The General Bodies of the Evangelical Lutheran Church in the United States* (Philadelphia: Lutheran Publication Society, 3rd ed., 1902), pp. 139-140.
53. While refusing to regard any biblical teaching as an open question in principle, Walther said that "we by no means regard it as necessary in all circumstances to press the battle to the utmost for other Scriptural teachings, which are not articles of faith, much less to pronounce the judgment of condemnation over the opposing error, although we reject it, and to terminate fellowship with those who err only in this" (*Lutheraner*, vol. 27, p. 131, May 1, 1871, quoted in Sigmund und Gottfried Fritschel, *Iowa und Missouri* (Mendota: Iowa Synodalbuchhandlung, 1878), p. 182. See also "Important Explanations by Prof. Walther," in *Theologische Montatshefte* (edited by Pastor S. K. Brobst), vol. 4, no. 9 (Sept. 1871, pp. 272-273. Naturally, Walther presupposed that those who erred in such subsidiary matters or in points of "ethical casuistry" merely misinterpreted in good faith, but did not deny the inspiration and authority of the biblical texts.

The Smalcald Articles' opinion that St. Mary, the mother of Our Lord, remained perpetually a virgin (I/4, Latin) was never regarded by the Missouri Synod as an article of faith or as included in the Confessional obligation. The matter came up at the Missouri/Iowa Colloquy in 1867. See the somewhat different reports in Hochstetter, p. 289, and Brobst's *Theologische Monatshefte*, vol. 1, no. 12 (Dec. 1868), p. 375.

H. P. Hamann, in his incisive contribution to the Contemporary Theology Series, *Unity and Fellowship and Ecumenicity* (St. Louis: Concordia, 1973), restates essentially Walther's position when he writes: "Only what concerns the Gospel can be doctrine, only what directly belongs to it, only what directly impinges on it" (p. 42).

54. Tietjen, *op. cit.*, p. 154.
55. Brobst's *Theologische Monatshefte*, vol. 2, no. 9 (Sept. 1869), pp. 268-270. It is true of course that nothing could be more un-Lutheran than basing doctrine on Luther or even on the Lutheran Church and her Confessions, rather than on Scripture alone (Smalcald Articles II/II/15). If Mundinger's description (*op. cit.*, p. 2) of Keyl's Luther-fixation in sermon-writing is correct, there was indeed an unhealthy element of Luther-worship among the early Missourians. Fritschel seems to have documented the same on the question of interest-taking. But usury aside, it is impossible to read Walther without realising that he followed Luther not from hero-worship, but because Luther had convinced him with Scripture, and had thus taken his conscience captive to the Word. When a man of Walther's intellectual stature confessed himself simply "a student of Luther, and as I hope to God a faithful student," who had only "stammeringly repeated from this prophet of the last times everything he [Walther] had heretofore publicly said and written" (Hochstetter, p. 325; Mundinger, p. 3), then this should be taken as a token of great modesty and humility. How refreshing, in contrast to the contemporary arrogance which acts as if realistic and sober theological judgment had arrived on the scene only with our generation!
56. FC, SD, XI, 88, Tappert, p. 631.
57. FC, SD, XI, 58, 63, Tappert, pp. 625-626.
58. Luther to Capito, 9 July 1537, St. Louis ed., vol. 21b, c. 2176.
59. FC, SD, II, 44, Tappert, p. 529.
60. Gottfried Fritschel, "Zur Lehre von der Praedestination" Brobst's *Theologische Monatshefte*, vol. 5 (1872), no. 2 (Feb-

ruary). p. 49; no. 3 (March), pp. 82. 87-88; no. 4 (April), pp. 99-100.
61. FC II and XI.
62. Tietjen, *op. cit.*, pp. 59. 73. 76.
63. Theo. Tappert, ed., *Lutheran Confessional Theology in America 1840- 1880* (New York: Oxford University Press, 1972), p. 217.
64. *Ibid.*
65. J. T. Robinson, *op. cit.*, p. 64. See also Sydney E. Ahlstrom, *A Religious History of the American People* (New Haven and London: Yale University Press, 1972), p. 758: "In his most widely read work, *The Proper Distinction Between Law and Gospel* . . . Walther reveals himself as a truly 'Neo-Reformation' thinker, for he insists upon this distinction as the central problem in theology . . . Finally, he was led to so strong an emphasis on 'grace alone' that he was widely accused of being a crypto-Calvinistic predestinarian."
66. Herman L. Fritschel, *Biography of Drs. Sigmund and Gottfried Fritschel* (Milwaukee: privately printed, 1951), 135 pp.
67. See tripartite series "Vom Interessenehmen" in Brobst's *Theologische Monatshefte*, starting in vol. 2, no. 9 (September 1869), p. 268.
68. See the (German) preceedings of the general pastoral conference of 1880 (*Verhandlungen der Allgemeinen Pastoralconferenz . . . ueber die Lehre von der Gnadenwahl*. St. Louis: Concordia, 1880) and attached booklets by Walther.
69. Neve-Allbeck, *History of the Lutheran Church in America* (Burlington: Luther Literary Board, 1934), p. 241. Thus also in *Lutheran Cyclopedia*, p. 193. Theo. Graebner corrects "Romans" to "Ephesians" in C. T. M ., VI: 476 .
70. John Tietjen. *op. cit.*, p. 10.
71. *Ibid.*, e.g. p. 149.
72. *Ibid.*, pp. 125. 127. 153. 159, n. 4.
73. *Ibid.*, p. 151.
74. *Ibid.*, p. 158.
75. Ochsenford, *op. cit.*, p. 179.
76. *Ibid.*, p. 407.
77. *Ibid.*
78. *Ibid.*, p. 137.
79. Theodore E. Schmauk, *The Confessional Principle and The*

Confessions of the Lutheran Church as Embodying the Evangelical Confessions of the Christian Church (Philadelphia: General Council Publication Board, 1911), p. 890.
80. *Distinctive Doctrines, etc.*, pp. 94. 96.
81. *Ibid.*, p. 44.
82. *Ibid.*, p. 47.
83. Vajta and Weissgerber, *op. cit.*, p. 79
84. Tietjen, *op. cit.*, p. 71.
85. *Thesen fuer die Lehrverhandlungen der Missouri-Synode und der Synodalkonferenz bis zum Jahre 1893* (St. Louis: Concordia, 1894), p. 51.
86. Tietjen, *op. cit.*, p. 71.
87. Ochsenford. *op. cit.*, p. 181.
88. Vajta and Weissgerber, *op. cit.*, p. 77.
89. Vilmos Vajta, ed., *Church in Fellowship* (Minneapolis: Augsburg, 1963), pp. 5-6.
90. Adolph Spaeth, *Charles Porterfield Krauth*, vol. II (Philadelphia: General Council Publication House, 1909), p. 114. F. Pieper, *Christian Dogmatics*, v. I (St. Louis: Concordia, 1950), pp. 179-182.
91. Spaeth, *op. cit.*, pp. 218-219.
92. *Ibid.*, p. 236. See also another General Council voice expressing strong appreciation for Missouri, quoted in Graebner's *The Problem of Lutheran Union and Other Essays* (St. Louis: Concordia, 1935), p. 120.
93. E.g. the tasteless reference, in the immediate post-World War II atmosphere, to Walther as the "Fuehrer" of the Missouri Synod, p. 114, n. 9!
94. *Ibid.*, p. 181. Note also Walther's explanation: "The fact is that those who call our theology the theology of the 17th century do not know us. Highly as we value the immense work done by the great Lutheran dogmaticians of this period, still they are not in reality the ones to whom we returned: we have returned, above all, to our precious Concordia and to Luther, whom we have recognised as the man whom God has chosen to be the Moses of His Church of the New Covenant, to lead His Church out of the bondage of Antichrist, under the pillar of the cloud and the pillar of fire of the sterling and unalloyed Word of God. The dogmatic works of the 17th century, though storehouses of incalculably rich treasures of knowledge and experience, so that with joy and

pleasure we profit from them day and night, are nevertheless neither our Bible nor our confession; rather do we observe in them already a pollution of the stream that gushed forth in crystal purity in the sixteenth century." (Quoted in F. Pieper, *Christian Dogmatics*, vol. I, p. 166).

100. Werner Elert, *Morphologie des Luthertums*, vol. I (Munich: Beck, 1931), p. 160. The English translation by W. A. Hansen, *The Structure of Lutheranism* (St. Louis: Concordia, 1962), p. 183, gets this quite wrong: "a dogma which the ancient church, in addition to Scripture, presupposes as a source." Also, the central concept "evangelischer Ansatz" is not well rendered as "impact of the Gospel." This confuses cause and effect. "Ansatz" is a starting point, an "impulse" perhaps— "impact" is too much in the realm of result.
101. "Theses on the Authority of the Christian Church," St. Louis ed., XIX, 958.
102. St. Louis ed., XII, 1414.
103. Smalcald Articles, 11/11/15, Tappert, p. 295.
104. FC, SD, Rule and Norm 5. The same principle applies to the ancient creeds, par. 4, Tappert, p. 504.
105. *The Unity of the Church*: Papers Presented to the Commissions on Theology and Liturgy of the Lutheran World Federation (Rock Island: Augustana, 1957), p. 92.
106. A. C. Piepkorn, "The Position of the Church and Her Symbols, "*CTM*, vol. XXV, no. 10 (October 1954), p. 740.
107. Preface, 9, Tappert, p. 99.
108. Fred Kramer, "*Sacra Scriptura and Verbum Dei* in the Lutheran Confessions," *CTM*, vol. XXVI, no. 2 (Feb. 1955), pp. 81 ff. Cf. Holsten Fagerberg, *A New Look at the Lutheran Confessions 1529-1537* (St. Louis: Concordia, 1972), pp. 16 ff.
109. This oversimplification, subject to disastrous misconstruction, is criticised by Fagerberg, *op. cit.*, pp. 35 ff.
110. Paul G. Bretscher, "An Inquiry Into Article II," *Currents in Theology and Mission*, October, 1974, p. 42.
111. Paul G. Bretscher, *After The Purifying* (River Forest: Lutheran Education Assn, 1975), p. 63.
112. Fagerberg, *op. cit.*, p. 17.
113. A. C. Piepkorn, "What Does 'Inerrancy' Mean?" *CTM*, vol. XXXVI, no. 8 (September, 1965), pp. 577-593. Commented Sasse: "The term inerrantia cannot and should not be given up—the meaning is quite clear, the absence of real error in

the Bible. What Dr. Piepkorn in *CTM* wrote about the meaning of the word, he himself would not maintain after a thorough study of the "Thesaurus Linguae Latinae" and of the use of the word in the 19th and 20th centuries. What the defenders of 'inerrancy' want to safeguard is the truthfulness, authority and divine inspiration of the Bible" (Letter to J.A.O. Preus, February 24, 1970, copy on file in Concordia Seminary Library, Ft. Wayne, Ind., File 83).
114. Large Catechism, Baptism, par. 57, Tappert, p. 444.
115. FC, SD, Rule and Norm 9, Tappert, p. 505.
116. Vergilius Ferm, ed., *What Is Lutheranism?* (New York: Macmillan, 1930), p. 279.
117. Here too lies the deepest reason for the instant appeal of Darwinism: it was essentially a philosophical, even a theological appeal, not simply a scientific one. "The possibility, ever so distant, of banishing from nature its seeming purpose, and putting a blind necessity everywhere in the place of final causes, appears therefore as one of the greatest advances in the world of thought; from which a new era will be dated in the treatment of these problems. To have somewhat eased the torture of the intellect which ponders over the world problem will, as long as philosophical naturalists exist, be Charles Darwin's greatest title to glory" (Du Bois-Reymond, cited in John Theodore Merz, *A History of European Thought in the Nineteenth Century,* vol. II [Edinburgh and London: Wm. Blackwood and Sons, 1912] p. 435, n. 2).
118. See Hans-Joachim Kraus, *Geschichte der historisch-kritischen Erforschung des Alten Testaments* (Neukirchener, 1969), p. 254.
119. Edgar Krentz, *The Historical-Critical Method* (Philadelphia: Fortress, 1975), p. 55.
120. *Ibid.*, p. 30.
121. G. Eldon Ladd, *The New Testament and Criticism* (Grand Rapids, Eerdmans, 1967), p. 10.
122. Norbert Lohfink, *Bibel Wissenschaft Historisch Kritisch* (Butzon and Bercker, 1966), pp. 7-8.
123. Ochsenford, *op. cit.*, pp. 7-8.
124. August R. Suelflow, "Church Polity and Fellowship in American Lutheranism," *Springfielder*, vol. XXVIII, no. 1 (Spring, 1969), p. 5.
125. *Report of the Synodical President* (Blue Book, 1972), pp.

61-62.
127. Adolf Hoenecke, *Evangelisch-Lutherische Dogmatik*, vol. I (Milwaukee: Northwestern, 1909), p. 315.
128. Gerhard Forde, *The Law-Gospel Debate*, Minneapolis: Augsburg, 1969. See also Raymond Surburg, "Hofmann Redivivus," *Christian News*, April 26, 1976, pp. 8.
129. *Lehre und Wehre*, 1855, p. 248.
130. *Lehre und Wehre*, 1868, pp. 69. 101.
131. *Lehre und Wehre*, 1885, pp. 277-279.
132. Quoted in Th. Engelder, ed., *Walther and the Church* (St. Louis: Concordia, 1938), p. 15.
133. *Ibid.*, p. 14. See also the 1871 *Lehre und Wehre* series, "What do the newer, would-be orthodox theologians teach concerning inspiration?" Excerpts follow:

Basically Mr. Nitzsch is far from believing that the whole Bible is God's Word. But because of certain devout little old ladies in his congregation and because of a few other people he doesn't want to come straight out with it. But he gives a hint with the fencepost, as it were. Everything astronomical, physical geographical, ethnographic, in short everything scientific in the Bible—he says—is by no means revealed (p. 40).

Therefore Mr. Tholuck looks down, with a pitying smile, on the older exegetes, for whom, by virtue of their acceptance of an *inspiratio litteralis* (i.e. verbal inspiration) the absolute inerrancy of the New Testament stood firm as indubitable presupposition. For those fools the interpretation of the Old Testament given in the New Testament was normative!! While scientific exegetes like Tholuck have long ago given up this childish opinion, these redoubtable men explain the Old Testament without recourse to the New; they excuse the dear Apostles for not having interpreted quite scientifically, on account of their kinship with the rabbinical schools . . . For that Exodus 3:6 really refers to the resurrection of the dead, Mr. Tholuck by no means believes, although the living God Himself asserts it in Matt. 22:32. Rather, this man, who calls himself a doctor of divinity, dares to judge thus of the authentic explanation of his God: "One Old Testament interpretation has given the impression of rabbinical subtlety, not quite without reason. It is Matt. 22:32" (p. 42).

Of the five books of Moses, which the Lord and the Apostles attribute to Moses in more than twenty places, Delitzsch teaches that they are a *mixtum compositum* from all sorts of different workshops (p. 101).

A man who makes a novel out of the first chapter of Genesis must necessarily find the inerrancy of the Bible inconvenient (p. 106).

But an unknown forger had the impertinence to invent visions and to spread them among the people under the fraudulent name of Daniel . . . Certainly Mr. Kahnis has proved with this his disquisition that he believes in the Lord Himself as little as in the writings of Daniel. He—the Lord, after all—said to His Christians (Matt. 24:15): "When now you see the abomination of desolation of which it was spoken through the prophet Daniel". . . Here Christ not only attests the genuineness and truthfulness of the prophecies of Daniel, but also draws from this an important conclusion . . . I do not know whom Mr. Kahnis takes the Lord to be. But he who regards Him as the Son of God must regard Mr. Kahnis' disquisition as blasphemy. Yes, blasphemy. Let no one call this expression too strong! For when a pope seeks to strengthen his title of possession by means of the fraudulent Donation of Constantine, we heap contempt upon him, And the Son of the living God is supposed to have committed this same villainy; to have built His exhortation to the disciples on the product of a deceiver devoid of conscience (pp. 134-135).

134. C. S. Meyer, "Walther's Theology of the Word," *CTM*, vol. XLIII, no. 4 (April 1972), p. 262 .
135. A. L. Graebner, "Thesen ueber die Goettlichkeit der heiligen Schrift," Synodical Conference *Proceedings*, 1886, pp. 5 ff.
136. Quoted in Pieper, *op. cit.*, vol. I, p. 271.
137. F. Pieper, "Ein treffliches Bekenntnis Dr. Rupertis," *Lehre and Wehre*, vol. 37, no. 7 (July, 1891), pp. 193-197.
138. Hochstetter, *op. cit.*, p. 288.
139. Martin E. Marty, *Missouri in Perspective*, vol. 4, no. 3 (Dec. 20, 1976), p. 1.
140. Hochstetter, *op. cit.*, p. 445.
141. Krentz, *op. cit.*, pp. 8-10.
142. "Preface to the Old Testament" (1545), Dr. Martin Luther's *Vorreden zur deutschen Bibeluebersetzung* (St. Louis: Concordia, 1908), cc. 3-4.

143. St. Louis ed., IX, 1238.
144. Quoted in Pieper's, *Christian Dogmatics*, I. 275, n. 89.
145. Pieper, *Christian Dogmatics*, I, 158. Cf. F. E. Mayer, *The Story of Bad Boll* (St. Louis: Concordia, 1949), p. 16: "Dr. Elert maintained furthermore that the recent Luther studies, especially those of Karl Holl, have shown that Lutheran Confessions show a deviation from Luther. German Lutheran Scholars therefore are interested more in the study of Luther than of the Confessions."
146. Eugene Klug, *From Luther To Chemnitz* (Grand Rapids: Eerdmans, 1971), pp. 106-109.
147. Paul Althaus, *The Theology of Martin Luther*, tr Robert C. Schultz (Philadelphia: Fortress Press, 1966), pp. 50-52, quoted in J. W. Montgomery, ed., *God's Inerrant Word* (Minneapolis: Bethany, 1974), p. 92, n. 30.
148. Weimar edition, 48, 31, quoted in A. Skevington Wood, *Captive To The Word* (Exeter: Paternoster, 1969), p. 178.
149. That Barth had simply applied to the doctrine of the Word the basic Calvinistic axiom, *finitum non capax infiniti* (the finite has no capacity for the infinite), was recognised long ago by Wm. M. Oesch, *CTM*, vol. VI, no. 11 (Nov. 1935), p. 846.
150. Jaroslav Pelikan, *Luther The Expositor* (Companion Volume), *Luther's Works* (St. Louis: Concordia, 1959), pp. 48 ff.
151. *Australasian Theological Review*, vol. XXXII, no. 3 (September, 1961), p. 108. Having referred to a number of blunders in the book, Hamann concludes: "And, for that matter, where is the need of such a volume in an edition of *Luther's Works?*"
152. Jaroslav Pelikan, *Luther The Expositor,* pp. 86-87. Cf. his early work, *From Luther To Kierkegaard* (St. Louis: Concordia, 1950), pp. 17-18, and note 83 (p. 127) citing Pieper in refutation of "nineteenth century liberals" who "misinterpreted" Luther's thought.
153. F. Pieper, *op. cit.*, I, 291-292. See also M. Reu, *Luther and the Scriptures* reprinted in *The Springfielder* (August, 1960), pp. 24 ff.
154. T. Strieter, "Luther's View of Scripture," *Currents in Theology and Mission*, Dec. 1974, pp. 94-96. Strieter cites the bad mistranslation in *Luther's Works* (American Edition), 35, 239, which has Luther say that some of the Mosaic laws

in the Pentateuch "are to be regarded as foolish and useless." Luther said nothing of the kind. This is the same Preface to the Old Testament in which Luther had begged the reader not to despise the lowly matters he will encounter, but to regard them as "the very words, works, judgments, and narrations of the high divine majesty, might, and wisdom" (see note 142 above)! Luther's *"dass etliche Satzungen gleich naerrisch und vergeblich anzusehen sind"* means not that these laws "are to be regarded" as foolish, etc., but that they almost (*gleich*) seem that way, i.e. "to look at!"

155. Krentz, *op. cit.*, pp. 9-10.
156. Strieter, *loc. cit.*, pp. 91. 93-95.
157. J. F. Koestering, *Auswandering der saechsischen Lutheraner im Jahre 1838, ihre Niederlassung in Perry-Co., Mo., und damit zusammenhaengende interessante Nachrichten, nebst einem wahrheitsgetreuen Bericht von dem in den Gemeinden zu Altenburg und Frohna vorgefallenen sog. Chiliastenstreit in den Jahren 1856 und 1857* (St. Louis: A. Wiebusch and Son, 1866), pp. 173 ff.
158. See Pieper, *op. cit.*, vol. I, pp. 331-336.
159. H. Sasse, "Confession and Theology in the Missouri Synod," *Letters To Lutheran Pastors*, No. 20 (July, 1951).
160. *Speaking The Truth in Love* (Chicago: Willow Press, n.d.), p. 3.
161. Theo." Graebner, "The Cloak of the Cleric," *Concordia Historical Institute Quarterly (CHIQ)*, vol. XLIV, no. 1 [Feb. 1971], p. 6.
162. *Speaking The Truth In Love*, pp. 13-19.
163. F. Dean Lueking, *Mission in the Making* (St. Louis: Concordia, 1964) p. 258 .
164. *Ibid.*, pp. 270-276. See also Jack Treon Robinson, *The Spirit of Triumphalism in the Luthern Church-Missouri Synod*, pp. 126-151.
165. Robinson, *Spirit of Triumphalism*, pp. 203-206.
166. Martin H. Scharlemann, "Along the Horizon," *Concordia Journal*, Nov. 1976, p. 235.
167. *Speaking The Truth In Love*, p. 19.
168. Sasse, *Letter No. 20*, p. 28
169. *Speaking the Truth In Love*, Theses 5 and 8, pp. 7. 8.
170. *Australasian Theological Review*, vol. XXXII, no. 2 (June, 1961), pp. 35- 41.

171. Robinson, *Spirit of Triumphalism*, p. 229. 172. Tietjen, *op. cit.*, p. 158.
173. John H. Tietjen, *The Principles of Church Union Espoused in the Nineteenth Century Attempts To Unite the Lutheran Church in America* (Th. D. Thesis, Union Theological Seminary, 1959. University Microfilm) p. 260, n. 25. "the distinction between visible and invisible church employed by Lutheran Orthodoxy was a handy device for reconciling the unity of the universal church with its empirical divisions and for drugging any real concern to do something about the divisions."
l 74. Lueking, *op. cit.*, pp. 14, 16, 63-67.
175. *Ibid.*, pp. 305-306, Lueking's whole scheme of "evangelical confessionalism" vs. scholastic confessionalism" (pp. 12-23) is confused and arbitrary, lacking precise and cogent criteria. As a device for interpreting actual Missouri Synod developments it gives the impression of wishful thinking, not of a realistic model.
176. Malcolm Muggeridge, *Jesus Rediscovered* (London: Collins, Fontana Books, 1969), p. 38.
177. H. Sasse, *In Statu Confessionis,* I, 63.
178. *CTM*, vol. 18 (1947), pp. 39 ff. 301-302, 460-463, 534-537, 784-786, 815 ff., 899 ff.
179. *CTM*, vol. 19 (1948). p. 686.
180. *CTM* vol. 20 (1949), p. 625.
181. F. E. Mayer, *The Story of Bad Boll* (St. Louis: Concordia, 1949); M. H. Franzmann, *Bad Boll, 1949* (St. Louis: LCMS, 1950); Martin Hein, *An Evaluation of Bad Boll 1948 and 1949* (St. Louis: LCMS, n.d.).
182. In addition to material in note 181, cf. *CTM*, XX (1949), 119-124; 922-925.
183. Mayer, p. 34; Hein, p. 12.
184a. Quoted in letter of President F. Kreiss to Theo. Graebner, 2 August 1950, copy on file in Concordia Historical Institue, St. Louis (CHI).
184b. Yngve Brilioth, ed., *World Lutheranism of Today* (Stockholm: Svenska Kyrkans Diakonistyrelses Bokforlag, 1950), p. 115.
185. Letter of H. Sasse to Prof. Hans Kirsten, 10 September 1948, copy on file in CHI.
186. Letters of Theo. Graebner to Lic. Dr. Kressel, 28 Feb.,

1949 and to Bishop Meiser, 28 March 1949. In the letter to Kressel, Graebner, oddly enough, (1) makes a firm point of stating that he "in no way concur[s] in this (anti-EKiD] judgment of Sasse's", but (2) asks for clarification about certain points, including this question: "Is it true that by joining EKiD a territorial church has given up its independence (in matters of confession, of internal and external work, in synodical discipline)?" Copies of correspondence on file in CHI.

187. R. R. Caemmerer, Sr., "Recollections of 'A Statement.'" *CHIQ*, Vol. XLIII, no. 4 (Nov. 1970), p. 157.

188. Herbert Lindemann, "Personal Reflections on the Twenty-Fifth Anniversary of the Publication of 'A Statement,'" *CHIQ*, vol. XLIII, no. 4 (Nov. 1970), p. 165.

189. *Ibid.*, p. 166.

190. O. P. Kretzmann's letter to C. S. Meyer, August 5, 1970, in *CHIQ*, XLIII, 189.

191. FC, SD, XII, 40, Tappert, p. 636. 192. H. Lindemann, loc. cit., p. 166.

193. Report of the Commission on Constitutional Matters, *Book of Reports and Memorials* (LCMS, 1962), p. 230. Cf. W. G. Polack, *How The Missouri Synod Was Born* (Chicago: Walther League, 1947), p. 34: "Synod is not the Church."

194. *Die Verfassung der deutschen ev. -luth. Synode von Missouri, Ohio, und anderen Staaten* (St. Louis: Weber & Olshausen, 1846), p. 6.

195. *Ibid.*, pp. 11-12.

196. C.F.W. Walther, "Synodalrede" (Synodical Report), LCMS 1848 Convention Report, pp. 5-10.

197. F. Pieper, "Kirche und Kirchenregiment," LCMS 1896 Convention Report, pp. 27-46.

198. Tappert, p. 329.

199. See the unfortunate implication, despite some correctives, that "altar, pulpit, and synodical fellowship" is merely "man-made," compared to the real, Scriptural fellowship, in F. E. Mayer, *The New Testament Concept of Fellowship, CTM*, vol. XXIII, no. 9 (September 1952), pp. 632-644.

200. "Report of Mission Self-Study and Survey," LCMS *Convention Workbook*, 1965, p. 120. Yet on the very next page Kretzmann contradicts himself by stating the "principle that no ecumenical organisation is coextensive with the church but that it is no more than an association of socio-religious

institutions!"
201. Carl A. Gaertner, "The Lutheran World Federation," *CTM*, vol. XXXVIII, no. 1 (January, 1967), pp. 10-18.
202. President Fred Kreiss and Pastor Wilbert Kreiss, "Report To Our Church in France, Concerning the International Lutheran Theological Conference in Cambridge, July 9-11, 1968" (duplicated), p. 4. Copy on file in CHI.
203. Lutheran Church of Australia, 1966 Constituting Convention *Report*, p. 232.
204. The case against ALC fellowship was articulated especially by Prof. Robert D. Preus, *To Join Or Not To Join*. North Dakota District Convention Essay, 1968, and Dr. Waldo J. Werning, *Issues in Deciding the Lutheran Church-Missouri Synod American Lutheran Church Fellowship Matter*, Milwaukee, 1969.
205. Official fellowship with the ALC under its present theological leadership is simply untruthful, and is an offence to confessionally serious Lutheran churches throughout the world. As for LCUSA, Missouri undoubtedly has the obligation to engage in doctrinal discussions—provided they come to grips with real issues. Also, some strictly non-churchly machinery for joint approaches to government agencies may well be desirable—though not for the purpose of amplifying leftist political propaganda! However, the fiction that some sort of "consensus" about the "Gospel" or about "confessional subscription" underlies LCUSA must be clearly repudiated. Then the question needs to be faced whether LCUSA, despite a minor difference in wording in its "confessional paragraph," is not nevertheless church in the same sense as the LWF, i.e. being engaged in churchly tasks. If the term "purchase of service" is designed to cover up the necessary distinction between *churchly* functions (*sacra*) and mere externals, it even suggests simony. Finally, even if LCUSA were not unionistic *per se*, it must be remembered that in the *case of confession*, things in themselves indifferent must be rejected *if they are confessionally misleading*, FC X.
206. *Currents In Theology and Mission*, February, 1976.
207. *Currents In Theology and Mission*, October 1975, pp. 252-260.
208. M. L. Kretzmann, "What On Earth Does the Gospel Change?" *Lutheran World,* vol. XVI, no. 4 (1969), pp. 307-321.

209. Convention Workbook, 1965, p. 120.
210. *Faithful To Our Calling-Faithful To Our Lord*, An Affirmation in Two Parts By The Faculty [Majority] of Concordia Seminary (1973), vol. I, p. 32.
211. FC, SD, Rule and Norm 5, Tappert, p. 504.
212. *CTM*, XLII, 259. Italics in original.
213. *Dialog*, Autumn 1964, pp. 297 ff.
214. M. L. Kretzmann, "Lutherans and the Church of South India," *American Lutheran*, November and December, 1956. See the fair and sober analysis by Prof. H.P.A. Hamann, Sr., in the *Australasian Theological Review*, vol. XXIX, nos. 1-2 (March-June, 1958), pp. 18-42. Cf. also H. Sasse, *Church Union in South India: Some Considerations for Lutheran Theologians*, Adelaide, 1963; and E. M. Skibbe, *Protestant Agreement on the Lord's Supper* (Minneapolis: Augsburg, 1968), pp. 27-44.
215. *Australasian Theological Review*, XXIX, 32.
216. *The Lutheran Layman*, vol. 27, no. 4, April 1, 1957.
217. "India Seminary President Takes Issue With Dr. Sasse," *The Lutheran Layman*, vol. 27, no. 8, August 1, 1957, p. 7. See also no. 9, September 1 p. 5.
218. E. Clifford Nelson, ed., *The Lutherans in North America* (Philadelphia: Fortress, 1975), p. 535.
219. *Spectrum* (Concordia Seminary student publication), vol. 6, no. 1 (Sept. 7, 1973).
220. John Tietjen, "Theological Education in Ecumenical Perspective," *CTM*, vol. XLV. no. 1 (Jan. 1974), pp. 8-10.
221. *Missouri In Perspective*, May 10, 1976. p. 4-C.
222. *Reporter*, Oct. 18, 1976, p. 2.
223. *DCP-Trumpet, Christian News*, June 10, 1974.
224. LCMS 1965 (Detroit) *Proceedings*, p. 81.
225. LCMS 1965 *Convention Workbook*, p. 118.
226. Elwyn Ewald et. al., *Resource Book*, revised edition, May 1976, pp. 37-38.
227. *Faithful . . . I*, 9. 228. *Ibid.*, pp. 26-27.
229. H. P. Hamann, "The Church's Responsibility for the World: A Study in Law and Gospel," in H. P. Hamann, ed., *Theologia Crucis: Studies In Honour of Hermann Sasse* (Adelaide: Lutheran Publishing House 1975), p. 73. See also Robert D. Preus, "The Confessions and the Mission of the Church," *The Springfielder*, vol. XXXIX, no. 1 (June, 1975)

pp. 20-39.
230. Eric W. Gritsch and Robert W. Jenson, *Lutheranism* (Philadelphia: Fortress, 1976), p. 175.
231. See section II A 6 above.
232. E. Clifford Nelson, *Lutheranism in North America 1914-1970* (Minneapolis: Augsburg, 1972), p. 107. See also Tietjen, *Which Way To Lutheran Unity?* p. 127.
233. *Iowa Synod Lutheran* (LCA), February 6, 1976.
234. Tietjen, *Which Way*, p. 154.
235. D. P. Scaer, *The Lutheran World Federation Today* (St. Louis: Concordia, 1971), p. 38
236. *Lutheran World*, XIII, 186.
237. *Lutherischer Rundblick*, vol. 16, no. 1 (1968), p. 15.
238. *Lutheran Witness*, Dec. 12, 1961, p. 17; Tietjen, *Which Way*, p. 144. This is a theologically irresponsible basis for LCUSA, and ought to be repudiated. Note Franzmann's splendid formulation: "There seems to have been great variety in the organisational manifestations of unity in the New Testament church; but is there any evidence that there was anything like an organisational recognition of fractional obedience to the one Lord?" (*Essays on the Lutheran Confessions Basic To Lutheran Cooperation*, 1961, p. 22). If LCUSA is a mere association for discussion and cooperation in externals, it needs no previous doctrinal "consensus"; if it is more, it is churchly, hence unionistic, in the absence of consensus" in doctrine and in all its articles" (FC, SD X, 31).
239. *Who Can This Be?* (1967) Of Christ in Gethsemene it is said: "Likely he was even unaware of the resurrection that lay beyond the criminal's death" (p. 25). Or: "George S. Hendry affirms that Jesus' divinity is to be found in his compassion, not in his genealogy" (*Ibid.*)!
240. J. S. Setzer, "A Fresh Look At Jesus' Eschatology and Christology in Mark's Petrine Stratum." *Lutheran Quarterly*, vol. XXIV, no. 3 (August 1972).
241. J. H. Tietjen, "The Gospel and the Theological Task," *CTM*, vol. XL, nos. 6-7 (June, July, August, 1969), p. 114.
242. See A. C. Repp's effective analysis, "Scripture, Confessions and Doctrinal Statements," in *A Symposium of Essays and Addresses Given at the Counselors' Conference, Valparaiso, Ind.*, Sept. 7-14, 1960, pp. 100-112. The same collection includes an essay by A. O. Fuerbringer, John Tietjen's imme-

diate predecessor as president of Concordia Seminary, entitled: "Our Newest Frontier: Theology." To "conquer" this new frontier, "bold action" would be necessary, which might upset some people by giving them the "feeling that the boat is being rocked unnecessarily." The key to the problem is the assurance "that what is being said and done is in harmony with the confessional paragraph of our constitution . . . ." (p. 138).

243. *St. Louis Lutheran*, July 7, 1962.
244. *The Lutheran Standard*, quoted in *Crossroads*, a report issued in 1965 by the Parish Education Committee of the Evangelical Lutheran Church of Australia (p. 22).
245. *Lutheran Witness*, August 21, 1962, pp. 6, 7, 15.
246. Quoted in H. Sasse, "The Crisis of the Christian Ministry," *Lutheran Theological Journal* (Australia), vol. 2, no. 1 (May, 1968), p. 44.
247. H. P. A. Hamann, Sr., "The Heart of Confessionalism," *Australasian Theological Review*, vol. XXVII, no. 3 (September 1956), pp. 61 ff.
248. Tietjen, *Which Way*, p. 149.
249. M. Halverson and A. Cohen, eds., *A Handbook of Christian Theology* (London: Meridian, 1958), pp. 330-331.
250. K. Barth, *The Word of God and the Word of Man!* N.Y.: Harper, 1957), pp. 229-230.
251. Gritsch and Jenson, *Lutheranism*, pp. 173, 174.
252. Martin Luther, *The Bondage of the Will*, tr. by J. I. Packer (London: James Clarke & Co. Ltd.), pp. 66 ff.
253. Quoted in Harold Lindsell, "Dateline Bangkok," *Christianity Today*, March 30, 1973.
254. *Lutheran Theological Journal*, vol. 2, no. 2 (August-December 1968), p. 84.
255. "The Continuing Crisis," a supplement to *Forum Letter*, October, 1976.
256. See the trend of M. L. Kretzmann's argument: "Like the individual believer, the church is also at one and the same time justified and sinful," 1965 *Convention Workbook*, p. 119.
257. Longer Galatians Commentary, St. Louis ed., IX, 644-650.
258. St. Louis ed., XVII, 1343-1344.
259. L. Berkhof, *Systematic Theology* (Grand Rapids, Eerdmans, 1974), pp. 437, 473-476, 604, 606, 608. Since, according to Reformed theology, Christ died not for all men but only for the elect (pp. 394 ff.); no one can know from the Gos-

pel itself whether it is really meant for him (cf. p. 463). Hence the desperate need to "feel" God's working (p. 419). It seems misleading therefore to speak nevertheless of the sacraments as "objective channels" (p. 604).

260. Bultmann: "the evangelist while making free use of the tradition creates the figure of Jesus entirely from faith," quoted in Sten H. Stenson, *Sense and Nonsense in Religion* (Nashville: Abingdon, 1969), p. 153.
261. Smalcald Articles, III/VIII 3-13, Tappert, pp. 312-313.
262. H. Bettenson, ed., *Documents of the Christian Church* (Oxford University Press, 1963, 2nd ed.) pp. 281-282.
263. Smalcald Articles II/IV/9, Tappert, p. 300. See H. Sasse, "Church Government and Theology," *Lutheran Theological Journal, vol. 6, no. 2* [August 1972), pp. 37-44.
264. Lefferts A. Loetscher, *The Broadening Church* (Philadelphia: University of Pennsylvania Press, 1954), pp. 8, 59. It is noteworthy in this connection that two members of the Synodical Survey Commission, John C. Baur and Fred C. Rutz, submitted independent minority reports to the San Francisco (1959) Convention of the LC-MS, charging that the proposed reorganisation of Synod involved undue centralisation (*Reports and Memorials*, 1959, pp. 438-444)!
265. *Lutheran Cyclopedia*, pp. 193-194.
266. John Tietjen: "The issue of biblical authority has been manufactured and manipulated in the interest of power politics," *Christianity Today*, vol. XIX, no. 14 (April 11, 1975), p. 8.
267. Nelson (1975), p. 535.
268. Theses 4, 5, 11, *Truth in Love*, pp. 7-9.
269. *Christian Century*, January 11, 1961, italics added.
270. *Christianity Today*, January 29, 1965.
271. William M. Oesch, *Memorandum Inter Nos*, Part III (1960?). Quoted in *Crossroads* (Australia), p. 28.
272. *The Cresset*, April 1971, p. 27. Strietelmeier also notes that while he shares with his "fellow Liberals a feelings of resentment" over the attack on "what our party might justifiably consider its best gift to the church—the Seminary in its present form," he does "not share with (his] fellow Liberals . . . the feeling that there is anything evil or underhanded in the move against the Seminary. I expect the Conservatives to act as conservatives; indeed I would feel

that they had deceived the church if they did not."
273. Letter to author from Pastor Ray Mueller, S.T.M., of St. Louis, 2 September 1976.
274. Nelson. (1975), p. 528.
275. Concordia Seminary, St. Louis, *Faculty Journal, 1967-1968*, p. 114 (28 May, 1968).
276. Quoted in Tom Baker, *Watershed at the Rivergate* (Sturgis, Michigan, 1973), p. 62.
277. *Ibid.*, 58.
278. W. Thorkelson, *Lutherans in the USA* (Minneapolis: Augsburg, 1969), p. 26. Italics added.
279. *Missouri In Perspective*, Nov. 8, 1976, p. 8.
280. *American Lutheran*, vol. XLVII, no. 12 (Dec. 1964), pp. 316-317.
281. *St. Louis Post-Dispatch*, March 1, 1972.
282. *St. Louis Post-Dispatch*, June 8, 1972.
283. Report of W. C. Dissen, Secretary, Seminary Board of Control, at Griffith, Indiana, June 2, 1974.
284. J. G. Huber, "Theses on Ecumenical Truth and Heresy," *CTM*, vol. XL, no. 3 (May, 1969). pp. 298-299.
285. "A Place For Loyal Opposition" (Editorial), *CTM*, vol. LXIII, no. 11 (Dec. 1972), pp. 707-708.
286. Quoted in T. Baker, *op. cit.*, pp. 62, 63.,
287. Statement of President John H. Tietjen To the Seminary Community on March 6, 1972
288. *Faculty Journal, 1970-1971*, p. 39 (Nov. 17, 1970).
289. *Catalog* of Concordia Seminary, 1971/1972, pp. 10, 14, 17.
290. J. G. Huber, "Theses on Ecumenical Truth and Heresy," *CTM*, vol. XL, no. 3 (May, 1969), p. 299.
291. Arthur Cushman McGiffert, Jr., *No Ivory Tower: The Story of the Chicago Theological Seminary* (Chicago Theological Seminary, 1965), p. 262.
292. Wm. M. Oesch, "An Analysis of the Present Situation of Confessional Lutheranism in America and in the World." (1969 Bethany Reformation Lectures, no. II), *Lutheran Synod Quarterly*, vol. X, no. 2 (Winter 1969/1970), p. 25.
293. J. W. Behnken, *This I Recall* (St. Louis: Concordia, 1964), pp. 187 ff.
294. Western District, LC-MS, Proceedings, 1960, p. 91.
295. *Badger Lutheran*, August 4, 1960.
296. H. Otten, ed., *A Christian Handbook on Vital Issues* (New

Haven, Mo. Leader, 1973), pp. 729-731.
297. *Faculty Journal*, 1966-1967, p. 1 (Sept. 6, 1966).
298. *A Conference of the College of Presidents and the Seminary Faculties, Nov. 27-29, 1961*, pp. 15-49.
299. *Lutheran Witness*, Dec. 26, 1961, p. 16.
300. *Lutheran Witness*, April 30, 1963, p. 15.
301. Quoted in Baker, *op. cit.*, p. 46.
302. Quoted in *Crossroads* (Australia), pp. 41-42 .
303. LC-MS Public Relations Department news release, Jan. 24, 1974.
304. Theodore A. Aaberg, *A City Set On A Hill* (Mankato: Evangelical Lutheran Synod, 1968), esp. pp. 220-240.
305. *Dialog*, Winter, 1962. See also reference to Missouri's "important turn in the road," in Vajta and Weissgerber, eds., *The Church and the Confessions*, p. 82.
306. Evangelical Lutheran Church of Australia, Melbourne (1962) Convention *Report*, p. 37.
307. The LC-MS 1962 Convention Proceedings, as far as I have been able to ascertain, make no mention of the solemn communication sent by the Australian sister church, in convention assembled.
308. *Crossroads* was issued in 1965 by the Parish Education Committee of the Queensland District of the Evangelical Lutheran Church of Australia. The LC-MS 1965 Convention was misinformed by its floor-committee to the effect that "The Evangelical Lutheran Church of Australia, in convention assembled at Toowoomba in 1965, has rejected this report" (LC-MS 1965 *Proceedings*, p. 97). In point of fact the Australian convention took no action on *Crossroads*, but recognized, in a statement drafted jointly by the General President, Dr. H. Koehne, and the present writer, that the report was the responsibility of the Queensland District. Nor did the District repudiate the report. And all members of the responsible committee were re-elected. In a joint public statement, moreover, the District President, Pastor F. W. Noack, declared together with the committee: "the President, while not endorsing each individual judgment, fully backs the theology of *Crossroads*, because he is roundly opposed to every departure from the historic Scriptural faith of the Reformation of Dr. Martin Luther—such as Liberalism, Modernism, Neo-Orthodoxy, and Ecumenism, which evils are infiltrating

even the orthodox churches of our time."
309. W. M. Oesch, 1969 Reformation Lecture, p. 47.
310. Also concerned lay-leaders had arisen to plague the establishment with their inconvenient probings. See Marcus R. Braun, *A Layman's Concern About His Church* (An Address Before the Lutheran Laymen's League Zone Rally at St. John's Church, Clinton, Iowa, May 7, 1967); and Fred C. Rutz, *A Businessman Looks at His Church* (n.d.). Mr. Rutz's inquiries regarding Synod's financial operations received peculiarly evasive responses. As a member of Synod's Public Relations Board, of the Houston (1953) Convention's Finance Committee, and of the first Synodical Survey Commission, Mr. Rutz had been able to observe the financial structure at first hand.
311. *Christian News*, March 2, 1970. Note Richard Neuhaus' fascinating remark that it was not "senility" which caused Sasse to "put himself solidly on the side of Missouri's far right," but the failure of ELIM to make clear "that they are contending for a living theology, even for the faith, and not merely espousing tolerance" (*Forum Letter*, vol, 4, no. 4, April, 1975)!
312. *Affirm*, June, 1971.
313. K. Marquart, "The Swing of the Pendulum," *Occasional Papers* (*Affirm*), Spring, 1973, pp. 12-27.
314. *Faculty Journal*, 1969-1970, p. 75 (Systematics Dept., Feb. 11, 1970).
315. Bohlmann, Klann, Preus, Scharlemann, Wunderlich, "Data On Theological Differences Within The Faculty of Concordia Seminary, St. Louis," Jan. 18, 1971, p. 3.
316. *Ibid.*, p. 9.
317. *Missouri In Perspective*, Oct. 18, 1976, p. 5.
318. *Campus Commentary*, September, 1973.
319. Nelson. (1975), pp. 382-385; cf. Pieper, *Christian Dogmatics*, I. 181-182. 320. Nelson. (1975), p. 384.
321. Nelson. (19721, p. 12.
322. *Ibid.*, p. 72.
323. *Ibid.*, pp. 36-37, notes 71 and 87. 324. *Ibid.*, p. 37, n. 87.
325. Gerhard O. Forde, *The Law-Gospel Debate*, esp. pp. 3-11. See also G. Forde, "Law and Gospel as the Methodological Principle of Theology," *Theological Perspectives* (Decorah: Luther College Press, n.d.), pp. 50-69.

326. *CTM*, January 1939, p. 65.
327. Nelson. (1972), pp. 21-32; 95-108.
328. *Ibid.*, p. 107.
329. William Arndt, *Does The Bible Contradict Itself?* (St. Louis: Concordia, 1926); *Bible Difficulties*. (St. Louis: Concordia, 1932); See also *CTM*, vol. xx (1949), pp. 146-149; 382-383; 626-630; 783; 933-935.
330. Theo. Graebner, "The Cloak of the Cleric," *CHIQ*, XLIV (1971), 7. 331. Nelson. (1972), p. 163.
332. See the genuine appreciation expressed by the great conservative Reformed scholar Carl F. H. Henry in *Jesus of Nazareth: Saviour and Lord* (Grand Rapids: Erdmans, 1966) p. 5.
333. Gustaf Wingren, *Theology in Conflict* (Philadelphia: Muhlenberg, 1958), p. 125.
334. W. G. Kuemmel, *The New Testament: The History of the Investigation of Its Problems* (New York: Abingdon, 1972). p. 363.
335. *Ibid.*, p. 365 .
336. J. W. Montgomery, *Crisis in Lutheran Theology*, vol. I (Grand Rapids: Baker, 1967), p. 75.
337. See the delightful spoof in Robert McAfee Brown *The Collect'd Works of St. Hereticus* (Philadelphia: Westminster, 1964), pp. 97-99.
338. Arnold W. Hearn, "Fundamentalist Renascence," *Christian Century*, April 30, 1958.
339. Charles W. Kegley, "The New Crisis in American Lutheran Theology," *The Lutheran Quarterly*, vol. 1, no. 1 (Feb. 1949), pp. 31-45.
340. J. Sittler, *The Doctrine of the Word* (ULCA Board of Publications, 1948), pp. 11, 52, 68.
341. J. Sittler, "A Christology of Function," *The Lutheran Quarterly*, vol. VI, no. 2, May 1954.
342. Robert Paul Roth, "Heresy and the Lutheran Church." *The Lutheran Quarterly*, vol. VIII, no. 3 (August, 1956), pp. 245-252.
343. Nelson. (1972). p. 165.
344. *Christian Century*, vol. LXXII, no. 47, November 23, 1955, pp. 1355 ff.
345. *The Lutheran*, December, 1955, p. 18. See also *The Lutheran*, Nov. 16, 1955, p. 6.
346. *The Lutheran,* Feb. 1956, pp. 29-32. If this is the same

document Clifford Nelson describes as "unpublished," it was drafted by Theo. Tappert and Martin Heinecken (1972, p. 193, n. 9).
347. George Muedeking in *The Lutheran Outlook*, October 1950, p. 313. 348. Nelson. (1975), p. 505.
349. Nelson. (1972). p. 164.
350. H. Otten, editor, *A Christian Handbook on Vital Issues* (New Haven, Mo.: *Leader*, 1973), p. 71.
351. F. A. Schiotz, T*he Church's Confessional Stand Relative to the Scriptures* (ALC Office of Public Relations, n.d.), p. 7. Compare *The Bible: Book of Faith* (Minneapolis: Augsburg, 1964), p. 148: "The infallibility of the Scriptures is the infallibility of Jesus Christ and not the infallibility of the written text."
352. Jaroslav Pelikan, *The Riddle of Roman Catholicism* (New York: Abingdon, 1959), pp. 220, 229, 230.
353. C. S. Meyer, *Log Cabin To Luther Tower* (St. Louis: Concordia, 1965), p. 298.
354. R. R. Caemmerer, ed., "Essays on the Inspiration of Scripture," *CTM*, vol. XXV, no. 10 (Oct. 1954), p. 738.
355. Nelson. (1972), pp. 164-165. Italics added.
356. E. Schroeder, "Law-Gospel Reductionism in the History of the Lutheran Church-Missouri Synod," *CTM*, vol. XLIII, no. 4 (April 1972), pp. 232-247.
357. D. P. Scaer, "The Law-Gospel Debate in the Missouri Synod." *The Springfielder*, vol. XXXVI, no. 3 (December 1972), pp. 156-171.
358. Letter to J.A.O. Preus, 24 Feb., 1970, copy in Ft. Wayne Seminary Library, File 83. To the present writer Sasse wrote on 10 September 1967: "In the beginning of 1934 I offered, on behalf of the "Confessional Movement" in northern Germany to Elert the leadership of this movement. They were at that time prepared to follow him on the basis of the Augsburg Confession. He declined—so they offered the leadership to K. Barth. He [Elert] replied: Do you know where this will end? Are you prepared to sacrifice your professorship, your salary, etc. I could only answer: I do not know, but perhaps God would help me. He has given strength to your Fathers in Prussia (he came from the Prussian Free Church) to resist the King of Prussia. His reply was: They were wrong. They should have followed the commands of the

King and accepted the union. And this was the strongest of the Lutherans" (copy in Ft. Wayne Seminary Library).
359. H. Sasse, *In Statu Confessionis*, vol. II. p. 281.
360. *Walther League Messenger*, May 1959. Italics added.
361. Oxford University Press, 1961.
362a. Raymond Surburg, "The Historical Method in Biblical Interpretation," *CTM* vol. XXIII, no. 2 (Feb. 1952), pp. 81-104; "The Significance of Luther's Hermeneutics for the Protestant Reformation," *CTM*, vol. XXIV. no. 4 (April, 1953), pp. 241-261.
362b. See the extensive "Robert D. Preus: Bibliography" in THE SPRINGFIELDER, XXXVIII, pp. 95-98.
363. See for instance H. Hummel, "The Outside Limits of Lutheran Confessionalism in Contemporary Biblical Interpretation," *The Springfielder*, vol. XXXVI, no. 1, June, 1972; "Gospel and Bible," *Occasional Papers* (Affirm), Spring, 1973, pp. 28-30.
364. See for example Martin Scharlemann, "Some Sobering Reflections on the Use of the Historical-Critical Method." *Occasional Papers* (Affirm), Spring, 1973. 5-11.
365. *Zeitschrift fuer die neutestamentliche Wissenschaft*, LXIII U972), no. 1/2.
366. *Report of the Advisory Committee on Doctrine and Conciliation*, 1976 (henceforth referred to as ACDC Report), p. 83.
367. Paul G. Bretscher, *The Baptism of Jesus, Critically Considered*. CTCR Biblical Studies Series, no. 5, May 1973, p. 5.
368. ACDC Report, p. 76.
369. E. Krentz, *The Historical-Critical Method* (Philadelphia: Fortress, 1975) esp. pp. 1, 4, 13, 15, 16-30, 55.
370. Hans-Joachim Kraus, *Geschichte der historisch-kritischen Erforschung des Alten Testaments* (Neukirchener Verlag, 1969, 2nd ed.).
371. K. Marquart, "The Historical-Critical Method And Lutheran Presuppositions," *Lutheran Theological Journal*, vol. 8, no. 3 (Nov. 1974), pp. 106-124.
372. Krentz, *op. cit.*, p. 12, cf. pp. 13, 15.
373. *Ibid.*, p. 4, cf. p. 76.
374. Kraus, *op. cit.*, p. 254.
375. *Korrespondenzblatt* (Bavaria), 1969, pp. 128-130.
376. See G. Maier, *The End of the Historical-Critical Method* (St. Louis, Concordia, 1977). The German scholar Ferdinand

Hahn offers no solutions, but speaks darkly of "the end or at least a late phase of a process of dissolution which has been going on for centuries," *Zeitschrift fuer cie neutestamentliche Wissenschaft* (1972), no. 1/2. Krentz notes that there are problems (*op. cit.*, pp. 78-88), but is optimistic about historical criticism's "self-correction."

377. Peter Stuhlmacher quoted in Krentz, *op. cit.*, p. 85.
378. *Zeitschrift fuer die neutestamentliche Wissenschaft*, LXIII (1972), 20; cf. Krentz, *op. cit.*, p. 86.
379. H. Thielecke, *Between Heaven and Earth* (London: James Clarke, 1967), pp. 26, 75.
380. e.g. Troeltsch, Bultmann, Ebeling. Cf. Ernst and Marie-Louise Keller, *Miracles In Dispute* (Philadelphia: Fortress, 1969). For an incisive expose of the pseudoscientific, 19th century assumptions behind such critical dogmatism, see the mathematics professor, Hans Rohrbach's *Naturwissenschaft, Weltbild, Glaube* [Brockhaus, 1974, 8th ed.].
381. Stephen Neill, *The Interpretation of the New Testament, 1861-1961*, Oxford University Press, 1966.
382. ACDC Report, p. 72.
383. *Forum Letter*, May 1975. 384. *Dialog*, Spring, 1974.
385. *Faithful . . . I*, p. 41; ACDC Report, pp. 70, 84.
386. J. N. D. Anderson, OBE, *Christianity; The Witness of History* (London: Tyndale, 1969). p. 33.
387. Kraus, *op. cit.*, p. 112.
388. F. Hahn, "Probleme Historischer Kritik," *Zeitschrift fuer die neutestamentliche Wissenschaft*, vol. LXIII (1972), no. 1/2, p. 6.
389. Quoted in W. Kuenneth, *Die Grundlagenkrisis der Theologie Heute*; essay presented to the Council of the European Evangelical Alliance, London, 1968, p. 6.
390. *Ibid.*, p. 9.
391. Paul G. Bretscher, *After the Purifying* (River Forest: Lutheran Education Assn., 1975), pp. 86-87.
392. Paul G. Bretscher, "An Inquiry Into Article II," *CTM*, October, 1974, p. 41.
393. C. Hartlich and W. Sachs, *Der Ursprung des Mythosbegriffes in der modernen Bibelwissenschaft* (Tuebingen: Siebeck, 1952), p. 35.
394. N. Nagel, "Anglican Christology of the Upper Stream From *Lux Mundi* to *Essays Catholic and Critical*," *CTM*, vol.

XXVI, no. 6 (June, 1955), p. 404.
395. E. and M. L. Keller, *Miracles in Dispute*, pp. 176, 177, 215, 217, 224, 396. ACDC Report, p. 77.
397. Robert Scharlemann, "Shadow on the Tomb," *Dialog*, vol. 1, no. 2 (Spring, 1962), pp. 22-29.
398. W. Bouman, "History and Dogma in Christology," *CTM*, April, 1972, pp. 203-221.
399. P. Bretscher, *Baptism*, p. 8.
400. *Ibid.*, p. 5.
401. Sten H. Stenson, *Sense and Nonsense in Religion* (Nashville: Abingdon, 1969)' pp. 190, 232.
402. L. D. Jordahl, "Mo Synod: Dilemma or Trilemma?" *Dialog*, vol. 12, no. 2 (spring, 1973), p. 122.
403. *Faithful . . . I*, p. 40.
404. *Ibid.*, p. 3; cf. p. 21.
405. G. Gloege, *Mythologie und Luthertum* (Goettingen: Vandenhoeck and Ruprecht, 1963), pp. 41 ff., 171.
406. Robert Scharlemann, *loc. cit.*
407. Bretscher, *After the Purifying*, p. 94, n. 8. The same total misunderstanding is spelt out at greater length in Bretscher's 1974 essay, "A Statement and Confessional Lutheranism," distributed by *In Touch*, the monthly newsletter of the Lutheran Faculty Federation.
408. *Faithful . . . I*, p. 25.
409. *Ibid.*, p. 26 .
410. Paul G. Bretscher, "An Inquiry Into Article II,", p. 41.
411. W. R. Bouman, "History and Dogma In Christology", p. 211.
412. Krentz, *op. cit.*, p. 67.
413. Leonard R. Klein, "ELIM's Theological task: The promise and the peril," *Lutheran Forum*, May 1976, p. 18, Cf. *Reporter*, Oct. 4, 1976, p. 7.
414. *Reporter*, October 25, 1976, p. 7.
415. Eugene M. Skibbe, *Protestant Agreement on the Lord's Supper* (Minneapolis: Augsburg, 1968), p. 79.
416. *Marc Lienhard, Lutherisch-Reformierte Kirchengemeinschaft Heute*, 1972, p. 54.
417. FC, SD, VII, 42, Tappert, p. 576.
418. Krentz, *op. cit.*, p. 67.
419. Roy Harrisville, *His Hidden Grace* (Nashville, New York: Abingdon, 1965). pp. 52, 53.

420. *Ibid.*, p. 83.
421. ACDC Report, p. 40, passim, *'Faithful . . . I*, pp. 20, 21, 23, 25, 35.
422. F. Pieper, *Christian Dogmatics*, I, 137-138.
423. It is this important distinction between theology and apologetics which is behind the traditional Lutheran restriction of apologetics to a subsidiary, ancillary, negative role. J. W. Montgomery has regrettably attacked this position as not giving sufficient scope to apologetics; "Lutheranism and the Defence of the Christian Faith," *Lutheran Synod Quarterly*, vol. XI, no. 1 (Fall, 1970), pp. 16 ff.
424. J.N.D. Anderson, OBE, *Christianity: The Witness of History;* (London: Tyndale, 1969).
425. J. I. Packer, *"Fundamentalism" and the Word of God* (Grand Rapids: Eerdmans, 1958), p. 21.
426. Krentz, *op. cit.*, p. 67.
427. G. Bornkamm, quoted in Gloege, *op. cit.*, p. 183.
428. Quoted in Robert M. Grant, A Short History of The Interpretation of the Bible (New York: Macmillan, 1972), p. 163.
429. Semler, quoted in Gerhard Maier, Das Ende der historisch-kritischen Methode (Brockhaus, 1974), p. 9.
430. Krentz, *op. cit.*, pp. 62, 74 ff.
431. Paul G. Bretscher, After the Purifying, pp. 14-19; 86 ff; 97 ff.
432. *Faithful . . . I*, p. 36.
433. *Report of the Synodical President* (Blue Book), pp. 38-40.
434. Apology IV, 2, 5; FC, SD V, 1; Tappert, pp. 107, 108, 558.
435. Apology, XXVII, 60, Tappert, p. 279.
436. FC. SD, VII, 46, Tappert, p. 577.
437. Quoted in *Lutherischer Rundblick*, vol. 18, no. 4 (1970), p. 325.
438. *Faithful . . . I*, pp. 21, 37.
439. See Gerhard Forde's Argument in "Law and Gospel as the Methodological Principle of Theology," *Theological Perspectives* (Decorah: Luther College Press, n.d.), pp. 50-69. Although Forde says that the verbal inspiration approach is "exceedingly simple and readily understandable," he has not in fact understood it. He imagines that Pieper assumed inerrancy before even looking at the Bible. That is not what Pieper meant by his *a priori*, *Christian Dogmatics*, I, 238. He meant that Scripture in clear texts claims to be God's authoritative, indisputable Word, so that we approach its

study and especially its problems with the *a priori* of its own self-witness, not with our own *a prioris*! By the way, Forde's article is a perfect illustration of the utterly fuzzy and unworkable nature of his "Law/Gospel method."

440. Cf. R. Smith, "Cross Comments In Errancy," *In Touch*, April/May, 1975. Also, ACDC Report, p. 2: "we let the Bible itself define its inerrancy . . . we accept the Scriptures as they are."

441. ACDC Report, p. 4, cf. p. 75.

442. *Missouri In Perspective*, July 7, 1975, p. 5.

443. Krentz, *op. cit.*, pp. 30, 48.

444. Lawrence Kersten, *The Lutheran Ethic* (Wayne State University Press, 1970), p. 208.

445. David W. Melber, *Beliefs About Issues in Resolution 3-09 Of the New Orleans Convention of the Lutheran Church-Missouri Synod [A Sociological Study]*, p. 22. This 1975 synopsis of Melber's Master's Thesis at West Texas State University was distributed by ELIM at the Anaheim (1975) LC-MS Convention.

446. Frank Knopfelmacher, *Intellectuals and Politics* (Melbourne: Nelson, 1968), pp. 58-113.

447. Philip Hefner, "LCA Identity? or Please Pass The Onions and Garlic!" *Dialog*, vol. 13, no. 1 (Winter, 1974), pp. 7-10.

448. Note for instance W. R. Thompson, FRS, Introduction to Charles Darwin, *The Origin of Species* (Everyman's Library Centenary Edition, 1958), pp. vii-xxiv; Paul S. Moorhead, Martin M. Kaplan, eds., *Mathematical Challenges To the Neo-Darwinian Intervretation of Evolution* (Philadelphia: Wistar Institute Press, 1967), and for a thorough discussion of the implications of the mathematical argument see A. E. Wilder-Smith, *The Creation of Life: A Cybernetic Approach To Evolution* (Wheaton: Harold Shaw, 1974); Norman Macbeth, *Darwin Retried* (Boston: Gambit, 1971); important refutations of Jacques Monod's *Le Hasard et La Necessite* (1970) are Georges Salet, *Hasard et Certitude* (1973), and A. E. Wilder-Smith, *God: To Be Or Not To Be?* (Neuhausen-Stuttgart, Germany: TELOS-International, 1975). Wilder Smith quotes Walter Reitler, professor of theoretical physics in the University of Zurich, as follows: "Open minded science must come to the conclusion that new things have arisen in the world, that is, things which were not derived from pre-

vious things. Thus we are forced to speak of Creation. [The researcher] must at last free himself from the stupidity of materialism and positivism. To do this all the preconditions have been fulfilled today" (p.15).
449. Lefferts A. Loetscher, *op. cit.*, p. 10.
450. H. Sasse, "The Crisis of the Christian Ministry," *Lutheran Theological Journal*, vol. 2, no. 1 (May 1968), p. 44. *The Battle for the Bible* (Zondervan, 1976) by *Christianity Today* editor Harold Lindsell is a timely, no-nonsense treatment, and devotes a whole chapter to the Missouri Synod Controversy.
451. M. P. Strommen et al., *A Study of Generations* (Minneapolis: Augsburg, 1972), pp. 107-108, 110, 127, 288.
452. *Ibid.*, pp. 121, 123, 135, 136, 144, 146, 300.
453. *Missouri In Perspective*, Dec. 3, 1973.
454. *Missouri In Persepective*, vol. I, no. 4.
455. *The Lutheran Outlook*, October 1950, pp. 311-313.
456. James K. Fitzpatrick, *Jesus Christ Before He Became A Superstar* (New Rochelle, Arlington, 1976). The Missouri Synod controversy is briefly referred to in this discussion of secularisation, p. 88.
457. C. S. Lewis, *Undeceptions* (London: Geoffrey Bies, 1971), p. 68.
458. Malcolm Muggeridge, *Jesus Rediscovered* (London: Collins, Fontana, 1969), p. 33. The incredible depth of the secularist degradation was recently illustrated by the appearance of a series of alleged revelations from beyond the grave, from a deceased Chicago Lutheran theologian, A. D.Mattson. (Ruth Mattson Taylor, ed., *Witness From Beyond*, New York: Hawthorn, 1975). More than one Lutheran theologian could actually be found to endorse this sordid expedition into spiritism (pp. 9-12)!
459. H. Sasse, review of Nelson's *The Lutherans in North America* (1975), *Lutheran Theological Journal*, August 1976, p. 60.
460. C. S. Lewis, Introduction to *St. Athanasius on the Incarnation* (London: A. R. Mowbray, 1953), p. 4.

www.ingramcontent.com/pod-product-compliance
Lightning Source LLC
Chambersburg PA
CBHW050357120526
44590CB00015B/1721